enVision® Florida MATHEMATICS

Volume 2 Topics 8–16

Authors

Randall I. Charles
Professor Emeritus
Department of Mathematics
San Jose State University
San Jose, California

Jennifer Bay-Williams
Professor of Mathematics
Education
College of Education and Human
Development
University of Louisville
Louisville, Kentucky

Robert Q. Berry, III
Professor of Mathematics
Education
Department of Curriculum,
Instruction and Special Education
University of Virginia
Charlottesville, Virginia

Janet H. Caldwell
Professor Emerita
Department of Mathematics
Rowan University
Glassboro, New Jersey

Zachary Champagne
Assistant in Research
Florida Center for Research in
Science, Technology, Engineering,
and Mathematics (FCR-STEM)
Jacksonville, Florida

Juanita Copley
Professor Emerita
College of Education
University of Houston
Houston, Texas

Warren Crown
Professor Emeritus of Mathematics
Education
Graduate School of Education
Rutgers University
New Brunswick, New Jersey

Francis (Skip) Fennell
Professor Emeritus of
Education and Graduate and
Professional Studies
McDaniel College
Westminster, Maryland

Karen Karp
Professor of
Mathematics Education
School of Education
Johns Hopkins University
Baltimore, Maryland

Stuart J. Murphy
Visual Learning Specialist
Boston, Massachusetts

Jane F. Schielack
Professor Emerita
Department of Mathematics
Texas A&M University
College Station, Texas

Jennifer M. Suh
Associate Professor for
Mathematics Education
George Mason University
Fairfax, Virginia

Jonathan A. Wray
Mathematics Supervisor
Howard County Public Schools
Ellicott City, Maryland

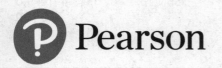
Pearson

Glenview, Illinois   Boston, Massachusetts
Chandler, Arizona   New York, New York

Mathematicians

Roger Howe
Professor of Mathematics
Yale University
New Haven, Connecticut

Gary Lippman
Professor of Mathematics and
Computer Science
California State University,
East Bay
Hayward, California

ELL Consultants

Janice R. Corona
Independent Education Consultant
Dallas, Texas

Jim Cummins
Professor
The University of Toronto
Toronto, Canada

Florida Reviewers

Robert Curran
Instructional Math Coach
Duval County Public Schools
Jacksonville, Florida

Megan Hanes
Math Coach
Marion County Public Schools
Ocala, Florida

Connie Jeppessen
Elementary Math Instructional Coach
Hernando County School District
Brooksville, Florida

Jacqueline LeJeune
Mathematics Academic Coach
Hillsborough County Public Schools
Tampa, Florida

Lesley Lynn
Academic Math Coach
Hillsborough County Public Schools
Tampa, Florida

Christina Pescatrice Mrozek
Assistant Principal
Orange County Public Schools
Orlando, Florida

Pam Root
Teacher
Felix A. Williams Elementary,
Martin County School District
Stuart, Florida

Ashley Russell
Elementary Math Teacher
Chets Creek Elementary
Jacksonville, Florida

Tiffany Thibault
Lead Teacher
Lake County Schools
Tavares, Florida

Shanna Uhe
Math Academic Coach
Hillsborough County Public Schools
Tampa, Florida

Copyright © 2020 by Pearson Education, Inc. All Rights Reserved. Printed in the United States of America. This publication is protected by copyright, and permission should be obtained from the publisher prior to any prohibited reproduction, storage in a retrieval system, or transmission in any form or by any means, electronic, mechanical, photocopying, recording, or otherwise. For information regarding permissions, request forms from the appropriate contacts within the Pearson Education Global Rights & Permissions Department. Please visit www.pearsoned.com/permissions/.

PEARSON, ALWAYS LEARNING, SCOTT FORESMAN, PEARSON SCOTT FORESMAN, and **enVision®** are exclusive trademarks owned by Pearson Education, Inc. or its affiliates in the U.S. and/or other countries.

Unless otherwise indicated herein, any third-party trademarks that may appear in this work are the property of their respective owners and any references to third-party trademarks, logos or other trade dress are for demonstrative or descriptive purposes only. Such references are not intended to imply any sponsorship, endorsement, authorization, or promotion of Pearson's products by the owners of such marks, or any relationship between the owner and Pearson Education, Inc. or its affiliates, authors, licensees or distributors.

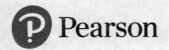

ISBN-13:   978-0-13-491079-6
ISBN-10:   0-13-491079-6

5   20

Digital Resources

You'll be using these digital resources throughout the year!

Go to PearsonRealize.com

 Interactive Student Edition
Access online or offline.

 Interactive Additional Practice Workbook
Access online or offline.

 Videos
Watch Math Practices Animations, Another Look Videos, and clips to support 3-Act Math.

 Math Tools
Explore math with digital tools.

A-Z **Glossary**
Read and listen in English and Spanish.

 Visual Learning
Interact with visual learning animations.

 Activity
Solve a problem and share your thinking.

 Practice Buddy
Do interactice practice online.

 Games
Play math games to help you learn.

 Assessment
Show what you've learned.

PEARSON realize™ Everything you need for math anytime, anywhere

Contents

Digital Resources at PearsonRealize.com

And remember your Interactive Student Edition is available at PearsonRealize.com!

This shows how to multiply two fractions.

TOPIC 8 Apply Understanding of Multiplication to Multiply Fractions

© Pearson Education, Inc. 5

This shows how to divide a whole number by a unit fraction using a model.

$3 \div \frac{1}{4} = 3 \times \frac{4}{1} = 12$

TOPIC 9 Apply Understanding of Division to Divide Fractions

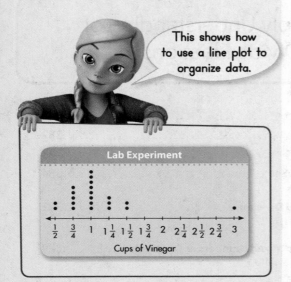

This shows how to use a line plot to organize data.

Lab Experiment

Cups of Vinegar

TOPIC 10 Represent and Interpret Data

© Pearson Education, Inc. 5

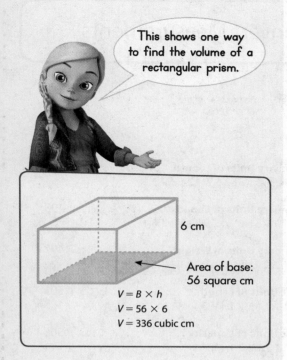

This shows one way to find the volume of a rectangular prism.

6 cm

Area of base: 56 square cm

$V = B \times h$
$V = 56 \times 6$
$V = 336$ cubic cm

TOPIC 11 Understand Volume Concepts

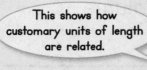

This shows how customary units of length are related.

1 foot (ft) = 12 inches (in.)
1 yard (yd) = 3 ft = 36 in.
1 mile (mi) = 1,760 yd = 5,280 ft

TOPIC 12 Convert Measurements

© Pearson Education, Inc. 5

This shows how to evaluate an expression using the order of operations.

$12 \div 4 + (9 - 2) \times (3 + 5)$

$12 \div 4 + \quad 7 \quad \times \quad 8$

$3 \quad + \quad 56$

59

TOPIC 13 Write and Interpret Numerical Expressions

This graph shows ordered pairs on a coordinate grid.

TOPIC 14 Graph Points on the Coordinate Plane

© Pearson Education, Inc. 5

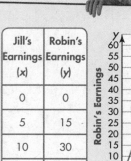

This shows how ordered pairs form a pattern on the coordinate grid.

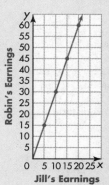

Jill's Earnings (x)	Robin's Earnings (y)
0	0
5	15
10	30
15	45
20	60

TOPIC 15 Algebra: Analyze Patterns and Relationships

These are different types of quadrilaterals.

TOPIC 16 Geometric Measurement: Classify Two-Dimensional Figures

Dear Families,

The standards on the following pages describe the math that students will learn this year.

MATHEMATICS FLORIDA STANDARDS (MAFS)

DOMAIN: Operations and Algebraic Thinking

MAFS.5.OA.1 Write and interpret numerical expressions.

MAFS.5.OA.1.1 Use parentheses, brackets, or braces in numerical expressions, and evaluate expressions with these symbols.

MAFS.5.OA.1.2 Write simple expressions that record calculations with numbers, and interpret numerical expressions without evaluating them. *For example, express the calculation "add 8 and 7, then multiply by 2" as $2 \times (8 + 7)$. Recognize that $3 \times (18932 + 921)$ is three times as large as $18932 + 921$, without having to calculate the indicated sum or product.*

MAFS.5.OA.2 Analyze patterns and relationships.

MAFS.5.OA.2.3 Generate two numerical patterns using two given rules. Identify apparent relationships between corresponding terms. Form ordered pairs consisting of corresponding terms from the two patterns, and graph the ordered pairs on a coordinate plane. *For example, given the rule "Add 3" and the starting number 0, and given the rule "Add 6" and the starting number 0, generate terms in the resulting sequences, and observe that the terms in one sequence are twice the corresponding terms in the other sequence. Explain informally why this is so.*

DOMAIN: Number and Operations in Base Ten

MAFS.5.NBT.1 Understand the place value system.

MAFS.5.NBT.1.1 Recognize that in a multi-digit number, a digit in one place represents 10 times as much as it represents in the place to its right and $\frac{1}{10}$ of what it represents in the place to its left.

MAFS.5.NBT.1.2 Explain patterns in the number of zeros of the product when multiplying a number by powers of 10, and explain patterns in the placement of the decimal point when a decimal is multiplied or divided by a power of 10. Use whole-number exponents to denote powers of 10.

MAFS.5.NBT.1.3 Read, write, and compare decimals to thousandths.

MAFS.5.NBT.1.3.a Read and write decimals to thousandths using base-ten numerals, number names, and expanded form, e.g., $347.392 = 3 \times 100 + 4 \times 10 + 7 \times 1 + 3 \times \left(\frac{1}{10}\right) + 9 \times \left(\frac{1}{100}\right) + 2 \times \left(\frac{1}{1000}\right)$.

MAFS.5.NBT.1.3.b Compare two decimals to thousandths based on meanings of the digits in each place, using $>$, $=$, and $<$ symbols to record the results of comparisons.

MAFS.5.NBT.1.4 Use place value understanding to round decimals to any place.

MAFS.5.NBT.2 Perform operations with multi-digit whole numbers and with decimals to hundredths.

MAFS.5.NBT.2.5 Fluently multiply multi-digit whole numbers using the standard algorithm.

MAFS.5.NBT.2.6 Find whole-number quotients of whole numbers with up to four-digit dividends and two-digit divisors, using strategies based on place value, the properties of operations, and/or the relationship between multiplication and division. Illustrate and explain the calculation by using equations, rectangular arrays, and/or area models.

MAFS.5.NBT.2.7 Add, subtract, multiply, and divide decimals to hundredths, using concrete models or drawings and strategies based on place value, properties of operations, and/or the relationship between addition and subtraction; relate the strategy to a written method and explain the reasoning used.

DOMAIN: Number and Operations – Fractions

MAFS.5.NF.1 Use equivalent fractions as a strategy to add and subtract fractions.

MAFS.5.NF.1.1 Add and subtract fractions with unlike denominators (including mixed numbers) by replacing given fractions with equivalent fractions in such a way as to produce an equivalent sum or difference of fractions with like denominators. *For example, $\frac{2}{3} + \frac{5}{4} = \frac{8}{12} + \frac{15}{12} = \frac{23}{12}$.* *(In general, $\frac{a}{b} + \frac{c}{d} = \frac{(ad + bc)}{bd}$.)*

MAFS.5.NF.1.2 Solve word problems involving addition and subtraction of fractions referring to the same whole, including cases of unlike denominators, e.g., by using visual fraction models or equations to represent the problem. Use benchmark fractions and number sense of fractions to estimate mentally and assess the reasonableness of answers. *For example, recognize an incorrect result $\frac{2}{5} + \frac{1}{2} = \frac{3}{7}$, by observing that $\frac{3}{7} < \frac{1}{2}$.*

MAFS.5.NF.2 Apply and extend previous understandings of multiplication and division to multiply and divide fractions.

MAFS.5.NF.2.3 Interpret a fraction as division of the numerator by the denominator $\left(\frac{a}{b} = a \div b\right)$. Solve word problems involving division of whole numbers leading to answers in the form of fractions or mixed numbers, e.g., by using visual fraction models or equations to represent the problem. *For example, interpret $\frac{3}{4}$ as the result of dividing 3 by 4, noting that $\frac{3}{4}$ multiplied by 4 equals 3, and that when 3 wholes are shared equally among 4 people each person has* a share of size $\frac{3}{4}$. *If 9 people want to share a 50-pound sack of rice equally by weight, how many pounds of rice should each person get? Between what two whole numbers does your answer lie?*

MAFS.5.NF.2.4 Apply and extend previous understandings of multiplication to multiply a fraction or whole number by a fraction.

MAFS.5.NF.2.4.a Interpret the product $\left(\frac{a}{b}\right) \times q$ as a parts of a partition of q into b equal parts; equivalently, as the result of a sequence of operations $a \times q \div b$. *For example, use a visual fraction model to show $\left(\frac{2}{3}\right) \times 4 = \frac{8}{3}$, and create a story context for this equation. Do the same with $\left(\frac{2}{3}\right) \times \left(\frac{4}{5}\right) = \frac{8}{15}$. (In general, $\left(\frac{a}{b}\right) \times \left(\frac{c}{d}\right) = \frac{ac}{bd}$.)*

MAFS.5.NF.2.4.b Find the area of a rectangle with fractional side lengths by tiling it with unit squares of the appropriate unit fraction side lengths, and show that the area is the same as would be found by multiplying the side lengths. Multiply fractional side lengths to find areas of rectangles, and represent fraction products as rectangular areas.

MAFS.5.NF.2.5 Interpret multiplication as scaling (resizing), by:

MAFS.5.NF.2.5.a Comparing the size of a product to the size of one factor on the basis of the size of the other factor, without performing the indicated multiplication.

MAFS.5.NF.2.5.b Explaining why multiplying a given number by a fraction greater than 1 results in a product greater than the given number (recognizing multiplication by whole numbers greater than 1 as a familiar case); explaining why multiplying a given number by a fraction less than 1 results in a product smaller than the given number; and relating the principle of fraction equivalence $\frac{a}{b} = \frac{(n \times a)}{(n \times b)}$ to the effect of multiplying $\frac{a}{b}$ by 1.

MAFS.5.NF.2.6 Solve real world problems involving multiplication of fractions and mixed numbers, e.g., by using visual fraction models or equations to represent the problem.

MAFS.5.NF.2.7 Apply and extend previous understandings of division to divide unit fractions by whole numbers and whole numbers by unit fractions.

MAFS.5.NF.2.7.a Interpret division of a unit fraction by a non-zero whole number, and compute such quotients. *For example, create a story context for $\left(\frac{1}{3}\right) \div 4$, and use a visual fraction model to show the quotient. Use the relationship between multiplication and division to explain that $\left(\frac{1}{3}\right) \div 4 = \frac{1}{12}$ because $\left(\frac{1}{12}\right) \times 4 = \frac{1}{3}$.*

© Pearson Education, Inc. 5

Florida Grade 5 Standards

MAFS.5.NF.2.7.b Interpret division of a whole number by a unit fraction, and compute such quotients. *For example, create a story context for $4 \div \frac{1}{5}$, and use a visual fraction model to show the quotient. Use the relationship between multiplication and division to explain that $4 \div \frac{1}{5} = 20$ because $20 \times \frac{1}{5} = 4$.*

MAFS.5.NF.2.7.c Solve real world problems involving division of unit fractions by non-zero whole numbers and division of whole numbers by unit fractions, e.g., by using visual fraction models and equations to represent the problem. *For example, how much chocolate will each person get if 3 people share $\frac{1}{2}$ lb of chocolate equally? How many $\frac{1}{3}$-cup servings are in 2 cups of raisins?*

DOMAIN: Measurement and Data

MAFS.5.MD.1 Convert like measurement units within a given measurement system.

MAFS.5.MD.1.1 Convert among different-sized standard measurement units (i.e., km, m, cm; kg, g; lb, oz.; l, ml; hr, min, sec) within a given measurement system (e.g., convert 5 cm to 0.05 m), and use these conversions in solving multi-step, real world problems.

MAFS.5.MD.2 Represent and interpret data.

MAFS.5.MD.2.2 Make a line plot to display a data set of measurements in fractions of a unit $\left(\frac{1}{2}, \frac{1}{4}, \frac{1}{8}\right)$. Use operations on fractions for this grade to solve problems involving information presented in line plots. *For example, given different measurements of liquid in identical beakers, find the amount of liquid each beaker would contain if the total amount in all the beakers were redistributed equally.*

MAFS.5.MD.3 Geometric measurement: understand concepts of volume and relate volume to multiplication and to addition.

MAFS.5.MD.3.3 Recognize volume as an attribute of solid figures and understand concepts of volume measurement.

MAFS.5.MD.3.3.a A cube with side length 1 unit, called a "unit cube," is said to have "one cubic unit" of volume, and can be used to measure volume.

MAFS.5.MD.3.3.b A solid figure which can be packed without gaps or overlaps using n unit cubes is said to have a volume of n cubic units.

MAFS.5.MD.3.4 Measure volumes by counting unit cubes, using cubic cm, cubic in, cubic ft, and improvised units.

MAFS.5.MD.3.5 Relate volume to the operations of multiplication and addition and solve real world and mathematical problems involving volume.

MAFS.5.MD.3.5.a Find the volume of a right rectangular prism with whole-number side lengths by packing it with unit cubes, and show that the volume is the same as would be found by multiplying the edge lengths, equivalently by multiplying the height by the area of the base. Represent threefold whole-number products as volumes, e.g., to represent the associative property of multiplication.

MAFS.5.MD.3.5.b Apply the formulas $V = \ell \times w \times h$ and $V = B \times h$ for rectangular prisms to find volumes of right rectangular prisms with whole-number edge lengths in the context of solving real world and mathematical problems.

MAFS.5.MD.3.5.c Recognize volume as additive. Find volumes of solid figures composed of two non-overlapping right rectangular prisms by adding the volumes of the non-overlapping parts, applying this technique to solve real world problems.

DOMAIN: Geometry

MAFS.5.G.1 Graph points on the coordinate plane to solve real-world and mathematical problems.

MAFS.5.G.1.1 Use a pair of perpendicular number lines, called axes, to define a coordinate system, with the intersection of the lines (the origin) arranged to coincide with the 0 on each line and a given point in the plane located by using an ordered pair of numbers, called its coordinates. Understand that the first number indicates how far to travel from the origin in the direction of one axis, and the second number indicates how far to travel in the direction of the second axis, with the convention that the names of the two axes and the coordinates correspond (e.g., x-axis and x-coordinate, y-axis and y-coordinate).

MAFS.5.G.1.2 Represent real world and mathematical problems by graphing points in the first quadrant of the coordinate plane, and interpret coordinate values of points in the context of the situation.

MAFS.5.G.2 Classify two-dimensional figures into categories based on their properties.

MAFS.5.G.2.3 Understand that attributes belonging to a category of two-dimensional figures also belong to all subcategories of that category. *For example, all rectangles have four right angles and squares are rectangles, so all squares have four right angles.*

MAFS.5.G.2.4 Classify and organize two-dimensional figures into Venn diagrams based on the attributes of the figures.

Florida Grade 5 Standards

MATHEMATICAL PRACTICES

MAFS.K12.MP.1.1 Make sense of problems and persevere in solving them.

MAFS.K12.MP.2.1 Reason abstractly and quantitatively.

MAFS.K12.MP.3.1 Construct viable arguments and critique the reasoning of others.

MAFS.K12.MP.4.1 Model with mathematics.

MAFS.K12.MP.5.1 Use appropriate tools strategically.

MAFS.K12.MP.6.1 Attend to precision.

MAFS.K12.MP.7.1 Look for and make use of structure.

MAFS.K12.MP.8.1 Look for and express regularity in repeated reasoning.

LANGUAGE ARTS FLORIDA STANDARDS (LAFS)

LAFS.5.SL.1 Comprehension and Collaboration

LAFS.5.SL.1.1 Engage effectively in a range of collaborative discussions (one-on-one, in groups, and teacher-led) with diverse partners on grade 5 topics and texts, building on others' ideas and expressing their own clearly.

  a. Come to discussions prepared, having read or studied required material; explicitly draw on that preparation and other information known about the topic to explore ideas under discussion.

  b. Follow agreed-upon rules for discussions and carry out assigned roles.

  c. Pose and respond to specific questions by making comments that contribute to the discussion and elaborate on the remarks of others.

  d. Review the key ideas expressed and draw conclusions in light of information and knowledge gained from the discussions.

LAFS.5.SL.1.2 Summarize a written text read aloud or information presented in diverse media and formats, including visually, quantitatively, and orally.

LAFS.5.SL.1.3 Summarize the points a speaker makes and explain how each claim is supported by reasons and evidence.

LAFS.5.W.1 Text Types and Purposes

LAFS.5.W.1.2 Write informative/explanatory texts to examine a topic and convey ideas and information clearly.

  a. Introduce a topic clearly, provide a general observation and focus, and group related information logically; include formatting (e.g., headings), illustrations, and multimedia when useful to aiding comprehension.

  b. Develop the topic with facts, definitions, concrete details, quotations, or other information and examples related to the topic.

  c. Link ideas within and across categories of information using words, phrases, and clauses (e.g., in contrast, especially).

  d. Use precise language and domain-specific vocabulary to inform about or explain the topic.

  e. Provide a concluding statement or section related to the information or explanation presented.

ENGLISH LANGUAGE DEVELOPMENT STANDARDS (ELDS)

ELD.K12.ELL.MA Language of Mathematics

ELD.K12.ELL.MA.1 English language learners communicate information, ideas and concepts necessary for academic success in the content area of Mathematics.

ELD.K12.ELL.SI Language of Social and Instructional Purposes

ELD.K12.ELL.SI.1 English language learners communicate for social and instructional purposes within the school setting.

© Pearson Education, Inc. 5

Math Practices and Problem Solving Handbook

A **Math Practices and Problem Solving Handbook** is available at PearsonRealize.com.

Math Practices

Problem Solving Guide
Problem Solving Recording Sheet
Bar Diagrams

TOPIC 8

Apply Understanding of Multiplication to Multiply Fractions

Essential Questions: What does it mean to multiply whole numbers and fractions? How can multiplication with whole numbers and fractions be shown using models and symbols?

Digital Resources

Interactive Student Edition · Activity · Visual Learning · Video · Practice

Assessment · Games · Tools · Glossary

MAFS.5.NF.2.4.a, 5.NF.2.4.b, 5.NF.2.5.a, 5.NF.2.5.b, 5.NF.2.6
MAFS.K12.MP.1.1, MP.2.1, MP.3.1, MP.4.1, MP.5.1, MP.6.1, MP.7.1, MP.8.1

Physical changes are reversible.

You can change a substance so that it looks and feels different, but it's still the same substance. The molecules haven't changed.

A substance can act differently because of a physical change. Here's a project about kitchen science.

⠿enVision® STEM Project: Kitchen Chemistry

Do Research Use the Internet or other sources to learn about physical changes to substances. Look for examples of physical changes that occur in the kitchen. When you condense, freeze, melt, vaporize, or whip air into a substance, you are making physical changes to that substance.

Journal: Write a Report Include what you found. Also in your report:

- Give examples of foods that are commonly condensed, frozen, melted, vaporized, or whipped.

- Write your favorite recipe that involves making physical changes to the food.

- Make up and solve multiplication problems with fractions and mixed numbers.

Name _____

Review What You Know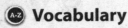

A-Z Vocabulary

Choose the best term from the box.
Write it on the blank.

• benchmark fractions	• mixed number
• equivalent fractions	• multiple
• factor	

1. To estimate the sum of two or more fractions, replace the addends with _____.

2. You can find _____ by multiplying both the numerator and the denominator of a fraction by the same nonzero number.

3. A _____ of a number is a product of the number and any nonzero whole number.

Multiply and Divide

Find each product or quotient.

4. 108×2

5. $270 \div 30$

6. 243×20

7. $288 \div 24$

8. 456×11

9. $432 \div 24$

Fraction Sums and Differences

Find each answer.

10. $\frac{5}{9} + \frac{8}{9}$

11. $2\frac{2}{3} + 5\frac{1}{2}$

12. $\frac{11}{12} - \frac{2}{3}$

13. $6\frac{7}{10} - 2\frac{3}{5}$

14. At the library, Herb spent $\frac{1}{6}$ hour looking for a book, $\frac{1}{4}$ hour reading, and $\frac{1}{2}$ hour doing research on the computer. How many hours did Herb spend at the library?

Common Denominators

15. Explain how you can find a common denominator for $\frac{3}{5}$ and $\frac{5}{8}$.

    © Pearson Education, Inc. 5

Name _____

PROJECT
8A

What story does your quilt tell?

Project: Design a Quilt

PROJECT
8B

Can you make art with just sticky notes?

Project: Create a Mosaic with Sticky Notes

PROJECT
8C

How much calcium does your body need?

Project: Analyze Menus for Calcium-Rich Foods

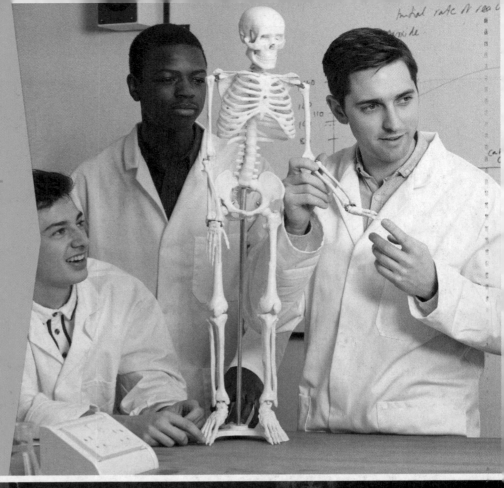

PROJECT
8D

Have you ever been in a cave?

Project: Create a Scale Model of a Cave

© Pearson Education, Inc. 5

Name _____

Activity

☆ Solve & Share

Sasha walked $\frac{1}{2}$ mile every day for 5 days. How far did she walk? Draw a picture or use any model to help you solve the problem.

I can ...
multiply a fraction by a whole number.

Model with Math
What are some different ways you can model multiplication problems?

MAFS.5.NF.2.4.a Interpret the product $\left(\frac{a}{b}\right) \times q$ as a parts of a partition of q into b equal parts; equivalently, as the result of a sequence of operations $a \times q \div b$. Also 5.NF.2.6 MAFS.K12.MP.3.1, MP.4.1, MP.7.1

Look Back! How does using a model help you multiply a fraction by a whole number?

Essential Question

What Are Some Ways to Multiply a Fraction by a Whole Number?

A

Joann wants to make 6 batches of fruit punch. How many cups of orange juice does she need?

I need to find $6 \times \frac{2}{3}$.

$\frac{2}{3}$ cup of orange juice for each batch

B One way to represent $6 \times \frac{2}{3}$ is to use repeated addition.

$6 \times \frac{2}{3} = \frac{2}{3} + \frac{2}{3} + \frac{2}{3} + \frac{2}{3} + \frac{2}{3} + \frac{2}{3}$

$\quad\quad\quad = \frac{6 \times 2}{3}$

$\quad\quad\quad = \frac{12}{3}$

So, $6 \times \frac{2}{3} = \frac{12}{3} = 4$.

C

You can think of $\frac{2}{3}$ as 2 times $\frac{1}{3}$.

$\frac{2}{3} = 2 \times \frac{1}{3}$

So, $6 \times \frac{2}{3} = 6 \times \left(2 \times \frac{1}{3}\right)$.

Use the Associative Property.

$6 \times \left(2 \times \frac{1}{3}\right) = (6 \times 2) \times \frac{1}{3}$

$\quad\quad\quad\quad\quad = 12 \times \frac{1}{3}$

$\quad\quad\quad\quad\quad = \frac{12}{3} = 4$

Joann needs 4 cups of orange juice to make 6 batches of punch.

Convince Me! **Use Structure** Find $10 \times \frac{3}{5}$. Use repeated addition to check your answer. Show all of your work.

© Pearson Education, Inc. 5

Practice Tools Assessment

☆ Guided Practice ☆

Do You Understand?

1. Explain why $8 \times \frac{3}{4}$ is the same as adding $\frac{3}{4} + \frac{3}{4} + \frac{3}{4} + \frac{3}{4} + \frac{3}{4} + \frac{3}{4} + \frac{3}{4} + \frac{3}{4}$.

2. Find $2 \times \frac{3}{5}$. Shade the model to help solve.

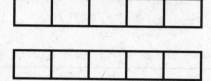

Do You Know How?

3. Find $3 \times \frac{2}{3}$ using repeated addition.

4. Find $6 \times \frac{3}{4}$ using the Associative Property.

☆ Independent Practice ☆

Leveled Practice In **5–7**, complete each equation to find the product.

5. $6 \times \frac{3}{4} = \frac{3}{4} + \frac{3}{4} + \frac{3}{4} + \frac{3}{4} + \frac{3}{4} + \frac{3}{4} = \frac{3 \times 6}{4} = \frac{18}{4} = \boxed{9/2}$

$8\overline{)48}$
48

6. $16 \times \frac{3}{8} = 16 \times \boxed{3} \times \frac{1}{8} = \frac{3 \times 1}{8} = \frac{48}{8} = \boxed{6}$

7. $500 \times \frac{2}{5} = \boxed{500} \times 2 \times \frac{2}{5} = \frac{\boxed{2} \times 1}{5} = \frac{1,000}{\boxed{5}} = \boxed{3 \times 500}$

In **8–15**, find each product. Use models to help, if necessary.

8. $35 \times \frac{2}{5}$
$35 \times \frac{2}{5} = \frac{70}{5} = 14$

9. $7 \times \frac{5}{12}$
$35 = 2\frac{11}{12}$

10. $9 \times \frac{2}{3} = \frac{18}{3} = 6$

11. $300 \times \frac{1}{2} = \frac{300}{2}$

12. $64 \times \frac{3}{8}$
$\frac{192}{8} = 24$

13. $900 \times \frac{2}{3}$
$\frac{1800}{3} = 600$

14. $84 \times \frac{1}{4}$
$\frac{84}{4} = 21$

15. $42 \times \frac{2}{7}$
$\frac{84}{7}$

Problem Solving

16. Higher Order Thinking Explain how you would find $36 \times \frac{3}{4}$ mentally.

108/4

17. Each lap around a track is $\frac{5}{6}$ kilometer. Samantha drove around the track 24 times. How far did Samantha drive?

120/6

18. Drake is making capes. He uses $\frac{1}{3}$ yard of fabric for each cape he makes. What is the total amount of fabric Drake needs to make 96 capes?

96/3

19. Bradley is making fruit salad. For each bowl of fruit salad, he needs $\frac{3}{4}$ cup of grapes. How many cups of grapes will he use if he makes 24 bowls of fruit salad?

72/4

20. Construct Arguments Do you think the difference $1.4 - 0.95$ is less than 1 or greater than 1? Explain.

Less than 1

21. Write a multiplication expression that shows 10^6.

$2 \times 10^3 = 10^6$

22. The table shows the number of miles each person ran this week. Who ran more miles by the end of the week? How many more?

	Monday	Wednesday	Saturday
Pat	2.75 mi	3 mi	2.5 mi
Toby	2 mi	2.25 mi	3.5 mi

Pat ran more miles

Assessment Practice

23. Select all equations that would be made true with the fraction $\frac{3}{8}$. **5.NF.2.4.a**

- ☑ $96 \times \boxed{} = 36$
- ☐ $38 \times \boxed{} = 14$
- ☑ $16 \times \boxed{} = 6$
- ☑ $56 \times \boxed{} = 21$

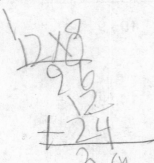

24. Select all equations that would be made true with the number 56. **5.NF.2.4.a**

- ☑ $\boxed{} \times \frac{1}{2} = 28$
- ☑ $\boxed{} \times \frac{2}{7} = 16$
- ☐ $\boxed{} \times \frac{8}{9} = 49$
- ☐ $\boxed{} \times \frac{1}{4} = 14$

© Pearson Education, Inc. 5

Name _____

Solve & Share

Brandon has 6 eggs. He needs $\frac{2}{3}$ of the eggs to make an omelet. How many eggs does he need?

Model with Math
Would a drawing help you picture the situation?

I can ...
multiply a whole number by a fraction.

MAFS.5.NF.2.4.a Interpret the product $\left(\frac{a}{b}\right) \times q$ as a parts of a partition of q into b equal parts; equivalently, as the result of a sequence of operations $a \times q \div b$. **Also 5.NF.2.6**
MAFS.K12.MP.3.1, MP.4.1

Look Back! Should your answer be less than or greater than 6? How do you know?

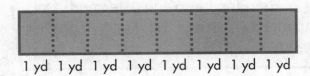

How Can You Multiply a Whole Number by a Fraction?

A

Claudia has 8 yards of fabric. She needs $\frac{3}{4}$ of the fabric to make a banner. How many yards of fabric does she need?

1 yd 1 yd 1 yd 1 yd 1 yd 1 yd 1 yd 1 yd

You can use models to represent the problem.

You need to find $\frac{3}{4}$ of 8.

B ## Step 1

Since you are finding $\frac{3}{4}$ of 8, divide the model into 4 equal parts.

$\frac{1}{4}$ of 8 $\frac{1}{4}$ of 8 $\frac{1}{4}$ of 8 $\frac{1}{4}$ of 8

$\frac{1}{4}$ of 8 $= \frac{1}{4} \times 8 = 2$

C ## Step 2

Since you are finding $\frac{3}{4}$ of 8, take 3 of those parts to make 6.

$\frac{3}{4} \times 8 = \left(3 \times \frac{1}{4}\right) \times 8 = 3 \times \left(\frac{1}{4} \times 8\right)$
$\qquad = 3 \times 2 = 6$

So, $\frac{3}{4} \times 8 = 6$.

Claudia needs 6 yards of fabric to make a banner.

Convince Me! **Model with Math**

Here is how Lydia found the product $\frac{4}{5} \times 10$.

$\frac{4}{5} \times 10 = 4 \times \frac{1}{5} \times 10$

$\qquad = 4 \times \frac{10}{5}$

$\qquad = 4 \times 2 = 8$

Use the model at the right to show that Lydia's answer is correct.

© Pearson Education, Inc. 5

Another Example

Find $\frac{3}{4} \times 2$.

Divide 2 into 4 equal parts.

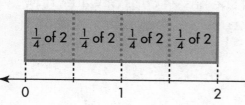

$$\frac{6}{4} = 1\frac{2}{4} = 1\frac{1}{2}$$

Think three-fourths of 2 wholes.

Each part is $\frac{1}{2}$. So 3 parts make $\frac{3}{2}$.

So, $\frac{3}{4} \times 2 = \frac{3}{2}$.

☆ Guided Practice*

Do You Understand?

1. Explain why the product of $4 \times \frac{2}{3}$ is the same as the product of $\frac{2}{3} \times 4$.

2. In the problem at the top of page 338, what multiplication equation could be used to find how many yards of fabric Claudia did not use?

Do You Know How?

In **3** and **4**, use the model to find each product.

3. $\frac{2}{3} \times 6$ 4

4. $\frac{3}{8} \times 4$ $\frac{12}{8} = 1\frac{4}{8}$

Independent Practice ☆

In **5–7**, find each product. Draw models to help.

5. $\frac{2}{3} \times 15$ $\frac{30}{3} = 10$

6. $\frac{11}{12} \times 6$ $\frac{66}{12} = 5\frac{6}{12}$

7. $\frac{5}{8} \times 16$ $\frac{80}{8} = 10$

Problem Solving

8. Construct Arguments Janice said that when you multiply a fraction less than 1 by a nonzero whole number, the product is always less than the whole number. Do you agree? Explain.

Yes

9. enVision® STEM A scientist wants to find out how the properties of water change when salt is added to it. For every cup of water she has, she replaces $\frac{1}{8}$ of it with salt. If she has 24 cups of water, how many cups will she replace with salt?

3

---

10. Shanna attends school for 1 week longer than $\frac{3}{4}$ of the year. How many weeks in a year does Shanna attend school?

13

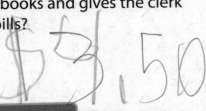

There are 52 weeks in a year.

11. Higher Order Thinking Gina has 48 stickers. $\frac{3}{8}$ of the stickers have pictures of flowers. $\frac{1}{8}$ of the stickers have pictures of plants. The rest of the stickers have pictures of people. How many stickers have pictures of people? Explain how you found your answer.

4 because 3+1 =4 then other 4

---

12. Two paperback books cost a total of $10. How much change will Stacy get if she buys two hardcover books and two paperback books and gives the clerk three $20 bills?

$3.50

Sale: Hardcover books, $18.25 each

---

13. Select each expression that has a product of 12. 〔5.NF.2.4.a〕

- ☑ $\frac{3}{4} \times 16$
- ☐ $\frac{5}{12} \times 12$
- ☑ $\frac{2}{5} \times 30$
- ☐ $\frac{2}{3} \times 15$

14. Select each equation that would be made true with the number 4. 〔5.NF.2.4.a〕

- ☑ $\frac{2}{3} \times \square = \frac{8}{3}$
- ☐ $\frac{5}{6} \times \square = 10$
- ☑ $\frac{1}{12} \times \square = \frac{1}{3}$
- ☑ $\frac{3}{8} \times \square = \frac{3}{2}$

© Pearson Education, Inc. 5

Name _____

Lesson 8-3
Multiply Fractions and Whole Numbers

Solve & Share

Julie has 10 yards of ribbon. She divides the ribbon into 3 equal pieces and uses 2 of the pieces on gifts. How much ribbon does she use? *Solve this problem any way you choose.*

10 yd

I can ...
multiply fractions and whole numbers.

MAFS.5.NF.2.4.a Interpret the product $\left(\frac{a}{b}\right) \times q$ as a parts of a partition of q into b equal parts; equivalently, as the result of a sequence of operations $a \times q \div b$.
MAFS.K12.MP.3.1, MP.4.1, MP.6.1

Model with Math You can use words, pictures, and equations to solve the problem. *Show your work in the space above!*

Look Back! Should the answer be less than or greater than 5? How do you know?

How Can You Multiply Fractions and Whole Numbers?

A

Hal spent $\frac{3}{4}$ hour reading each day for 7 days. How much total time did he spend reading?

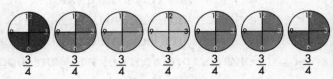

$\frac{3}{4}$ hours reading each day for 7 days

I need to find $7 \times \frac{3}{4}$.

B

Multiply to find the number of fourths.

$$7 \times \frac{3}{4} = 7 \times 3 \times \frac{1}{4}$$

$$= 21 \times \frac{1}{4}$$

$$= \frac{21}{4}$$

Rewrite as a mixed number.

$$\frac{21}{4} = 5\frac{1}{4}$$

Hal spent $5\frac{1}{4}$ hours reading.

To rename $\frac{21}{4}$, divide the numerator by the denominator.

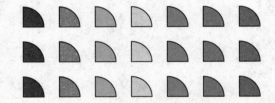

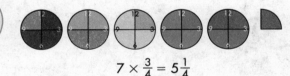

$$7 \times \frac{3}{4} = 5\frac{1}{4}$$

Convince Me! **Be Precise** What are the products $\frac{4}{9} \times 6$ and $6 \times \frac{4}{9}$?

© Pearson Education, Inc. 5

☆Guided Practice*

Do You Understand?

1. What is $\frac{3}{4}$ of a ribbon that is 7 feet long?

2. Explain how $\frac{3}{4} \times 7$, $7 \times \frac{3}{4}$, and $3 \times \frac{7}{4}$ are all related.

Do You Know How?

In **3–5**, find each product. Write the product as a mixed number.

3. $\frac{3}{8} \times 4 = \dfrac{\square \times \square}{\square} = \dfrac{\square}{\square} = \square\dfrac{\square}{\square} = \square\dfrac{\square}{\square}$

4. $8 \times \frac{5}{6} = \dfrac{\square \times \square}{\square} = \dfrac{\square}{\square} = \square\dfrac{\square}{\square} = \square\dfrac{\square}{\square}$

5. $5 \times \frac{4}{7} = \dfrac{\square \times \square}{\square} = \dfrac{\square}{\square} = \square\dfrac{\square}{\square}$

☆Independent Practice☆

Leveled Practice In **6–16**, find each product. Write the product as a mixed number.

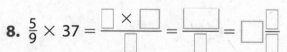
Remember: You can use division to rename a fraction as a mixed number.

6. $\frac{3}{4} \times 14 = \dfrac{3 \times 14}{4} = \dfrac{21}{2} = \square\dfrac{\square}{\square} = \square\dfrac{\square}{\square}$

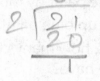

7. $600 \times \frac{2}{3} = \dfrac{\square \times \square}{\square} = \dfrac{\square}{\square} = \square$

8. $\frac{5}{9} \times 37 = \dfrac{\square \times \square}{\square} = \dfrac{\square}{\square} = \square\dfrac{\square}{\square}$

9. $\frac{4}{5} \times 500$

10. $5 \times \frac{2}{3}$

11. $17 \times \frac{6}{8}$

12. $\frac{9}{10} \times 25$

13. $\frac{7}{8} \times 320$

14. $28 \times \frac{7}{12}$

15. $\frac{2}{3} \times 1,287$

16. $900 \times \frac{2}{9}$

---

*For another example, see Set B on page 371.

Problem Solving

17. About 0.6 of the human body is made up of water. If a person has a mass of 75 kilograms, what is the mass of the water in this person's body?

18. Number Sense How can you use mental math to find $25 \times \frac{3}{10}$?

19. During a nature walk, Jill identified 20 species of animals and plants.

a Construct Arguments Jill said that $\frac{1}{3}$ of the species she identified were animals. Can this be correct? Explain.

b If $\frac{3}{5}$ of the species Jill identified were animals, how many plants did Jill identify?

20. A rectangular painting is 2 feet long and $\frac{5}{6}$ foot wide. What is the area of the painting?

21. Higher Order Thinking An art teacher makes a batch of purple paint by mixing $\frac{3}{4}$ cup red paint with $\frac{3}{4}$ cup blue paint. If she mixes 13 batches, how many cups of purple paint will she have?

22. enVision® STEM A water molecule is made up of 3 atoms. One third of the atoms are oxygen and the remaining atoms are hydrogen. If there are 114 water molecules, how many hydrogen atoms are there? Show your work.

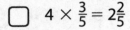 **Assessment Practice**

23. Select all that are true. 5.NF.2.4.a

- ☐ $4 \times \frac{3}{5} = 2\frac{2}{5}$
- ☐ $\frac{2}{9} \times 18 = \frac{1}{81}$
- ☐ $14 \times \frac{3}{7} = 6$
- ☐ $\frac{2}{3} \times 6 = \frac{1}{9}$

24. Select all that are true. 5.NF.2.4.a

- ☐ $\frac{3}{4} \times 2 = \frac{3}{8}$
- ☐ $\frac{11}{2} \times 4 = 22$
- ☐ $5 \times \frac{2}{3} = 3\frac{1}{3}$
- ☐ $8 \times \frac{3}{4} = \frac{3}{32}$

   © Pearson Education, Inc. 5

Name _____

☆ ☆
Solve & Share

The art teacher gave each student half of a sheet of paper. Then she asked the students to color one fourth of their pieces of paper. What part of the original sheet did the students color? **Solve this problem any way you choose.**

I can ...
use models to multiply two fractions.

MAFS.5.NF.2.4.a Interpret the product $\left(\frac{a}{b}\right) \times q$ as a parts of a partition of q into b equal parts; equivalently, as the result of a sequence of operations $a \times q \div b$.
MAFS.K12.MP.1.1, MP.2.1

You can draw a picture to represent the problem.

Look Back! **Reasoning** Should your answer be less than or greater than 1? How do you know?

Essential Question

How Can You Use a Model to Multiply Fractions?

A

There was $\frac{1}{4}$ of a pan of lasagna left. Tom ate $\frac{1}{3}$ of this amount. What fraction of a whole pan of lasagna did he eat?

Find $\frac{1}{3}$ of $\frac{1}{4}$ to solve the problem.

B ## One Way

Divide one whole into fourths.

Divide $\frac{1}{4}$ into 3 equal parts.

Divide the other $\frac{1}{4}$s into 3 equal parts.

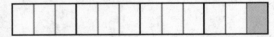

12 parts make one whole, so one part is $\frac{1}{12}$.

$$\frac{1}{3} \times \frac{1}{4} = \frac{1}{12}$$

C ## Another Way

Shade 1 of the 3 rows yellow to represent $\frac{1}{3}$.

Shade 1 of the 4 columns red to represent $\frac{1}{4}$.

The orange overlap shows the product.

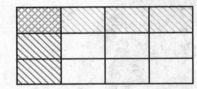

1 out of 12 parts are shaded orange.

$$\frac{1}{3} \times \frac{1}{4} = \frac{1 \times 1}{3 \times 4} = \frac{1}{12}$$

Tom ate $\frac{1}{12}$ of the pan of lasagna.

Convince Me! **Reasoning** Find $\frac{1}{4} \times \frac{1}{5}$ using the model. Explain your work.

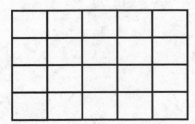

© Pearson Education, Inc. 5

Practice Tools Assessment

Another Example

Find $\frac{2}{3} \times \frac{3}{4}$ using a number line.

$\frac{1}{3}$ means 1 of 3 equal parts, so $\frac{1}{3}$ of $\frac{3}{4}$ is $\frac{1}{4}$.

$\frac{2}{3}$ means 2 of 3 equal parts, so $\frac{2}{3}$ of $\frac{3}{4}$ is 2 times $\frac{1}{4}$.

$\frac{2}{3} \times \frac{3}{4} = \frac{2}{4}$ or $\frac{1}{2}$

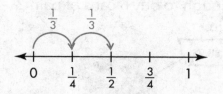

☆ Guided Practice *

Do You Understand?

1. Use the model in Box C on page 346 to find $\frac{2}{3} \times \frac{2}{4}$.

2. Create a story problem for $\frac{2}{3} \times \frac{2}{4}$.

Do You Know How?

3. Find $\frac{5}{6} \times \frac{1}{2}$. Shade the model to help solve.

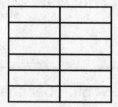

4. Find $\frac{3}{4}$ of $\frac{4}{9}$.

Independent Practice ☆

In **5–6**, find each product. Shade the model to help solve.

5. $\frac{1}{3} \times \frac{5}{6}$

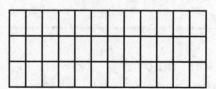

6. $\frac{2}{3} \times \frac{1}{12}$

In **7–14**, find each product. Use models to help.

7. $\frac{7}{8} \times \frac{1}{2}$ 8. $\frac{2}{5} \times \frac{1}{12}$ 9. $\frac{5}{7}$ of $\frac{7}{9}$ 10. $\frac{1}{2} \times \frac{3}{4}$

11. $\frac{1}{4} \times \frac{7}{8}$ 12. $\frac{5}{6}$ of $\frac{9}{10}$ 13. $\frac{1}{4} \times \frac{1}{8}$ 14. $\frac{1}{3}$ of $\frac{3}{7}$

*For another example, see Set C on page 372.   **Topic 8** | Lesson 8-4

Problem Solving

15. Make Sense and Persevere Will $50 be enough to buy 6 cans of paint? Explain.

$8.95

16. A scientist had $\frac{3}{4}$ of a bottle of a solution. She used $\frac{1}{6}$ of the solution in an experiment. How much of the bottle did she use?

17. Algebra What value of n makes the equation $\frac{2}{3} \times n = \frac{4}{9}$ true?

18. Write an expression that shows 10^4.

19. A plumber charges $45 for the first hour and $30 for each additional hour. How much does he charge if it takes him 4 hours to make a repair?

20. Higher Order Thinking If $\frac{7}{8}$ is multiplied by $\frac{4}{5}$, will the product be greater than either of the two factors? Explain.

21. In the voting for City Council Precinct 5, only $\frac{1}{2}$ of all eligible voters cast votes. What fraction of all eligible voters voted for Shelley? Morgan? Who received more votes?

DATA	Candidate	Fraction of Votes Received
	Shelley	$\frac{3}{10}$
	Morgan	$\frac{5}{8}$

Assessment Practice

22. Majid made the model to show multiplying a fraction by a fraction. Which multiplication equation does the model show? 🔵 5.NF.2.4.a

Ⓐ $\frac{3}{4} \times \frac{8}{9} = \frac{2}{3}$

Ⓑ $\frac{1}{3} \times \frac{1}{8} = \frac{1}{24}$

Ⓒ $\frac{3}{4} \times \frac{3}{9} = \frac{1}{4}$

Ⓓ $\frac{3}{9} \times \frac{8}{9} = \frac{8}{27}$

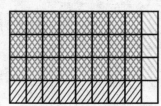

© Pearson Education, Inc. 5

Name _____

☆ ☆
Solve & Share

On Dan's eReader, $\frac{2}{3}$ of the books are fiction. Of the fiction books, $\frac{4}{5}$ are mysteries. What fraction of the books on Dan's eReader are mysteries? *Solve this problem any way you choose.*

Lesson 8-5
Multiply Two Fractions

I can ...
multiply two fractions.

MAFS.5.NF.2.4.a Interpret the product $\left(\frac{a}{b}\right) \times q$ as a parts of a partition of q into b equal parts; equivalently, as the result of a sequence of operations $a \times q \div b$.
MAFS.K12.MP.4.1, MP.6.1

You can model with math by writing a multiplication sentence to solve the problem.

Look Back! What fraction of the books are not mysteries? Explain.

How Can You Find the Product of Two Fractions?

A

Amelia takes pictures with her smartphone. Of the pictures, $\frac{5}{6}$ are of animals. What fraction of all her pictures are of dogs?

$\frac{3}{4}$ of her animal photos are of dogs.

You need to find $\frac{3}{4}$ of $\frac{5}{6}$ to answer the question.

B ## Step 1

Estimate $\frac{3}{4} \times \frac{5}{6}$.

Since both fractions are less than 1, the product will be less than 1.

C ## Step 2

Multiply the numerators. Then multiply the denominators.

$$\frac{3}{4} \times \frac{5}{6} = \frac{3 \times 5}{4 \times 6}$$
$$= \frac{15}{24}$$

Since $\frac{15}{24} < 1$, the answer is reasonable.

So, $\frac{15}{24}$ or $\frac{5}{8}$ of all Amelia's pictures have dogs in them.

$\frac{15}{24}$ and $\frac{5}{8}$ are equivalent fractions.

Convince Me! **Model with Math** $\frac{1}{10}$ of the animal pictures on Amelia's smartphone are of cats. Write and solve an equation to find what fraction of all her pictures have cats in them.

   © Pearson Education, Inc. 5

Name _____

☆ Guided Practice *

Do You Understand?

1. Is the product of $\frac{3}{6} \times \frac{5}{4}$ equal to the product of $\frac{3}{4} \times \frac{5}{6}$? Explain how you know.

2. How is adding $\frac{3}{9}$ and $\frac{6}{9}$ different from multiplying the two fractions? Explain.

Do You Know How?

In **3–10**, find each product.

3. $\frac{2}{3} \times \frac{1}{2}$ **4.** $\frac{5}{9}$ of $\frac{1}{9}$

5. $\frac{7}{10} \times \frac{3}{4}$ **6.** $\frac{1}{3} \times \frac{1}{4}$

7. $\frac{5}{6}$ of $\frac{3}{7}$ **8.** $\frac{3}{5} \times \frac{11}{12}$

9. $\frac{4}{10} \times \frac{2}{5}$ **10.** $\frac{3}{4} \times \frac{2}{9}$

☆ Independent Practice ☆

In **11–30**, find each product.

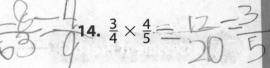

11. $\frac{9}{10} \times \frac{1}{2}$ $= \frac{9}{20}$ **12.** $\frac{5}{6} \times \frac{1}{3}$ $= \frac{5}{18}$ **13.** $\frac{4}{7}$ of $\frac{7}{9}$ $\frac{28}{63} = \frac{4}{9}$ **14.** $\frac{3}{4} \times \frac{4}{5}$ $= \frac{12}{20} = \frac{3}{5}$

15. $\frac{2}{3} \times \frac{7}{8}$ **16.** $\frac{5}{6}$ of $\frac{11}{12}$ **17.** $\frac{1}{3}$ of $\frac{3}{4}$ **18.** $\frac{6}{7} \times \frac{3}{8}$

19. $\frac{2}{5}$ of $\frac{5}{12}$ **20.** $\frac{2}{3} \times \frac{4}{5}$ **21.** $\frac{1}{2} \times \frac{1}{2}$ **22.** $\frac{1}{2}$ of $\frac{8}{9}$

23. $\left(\frac{1}{6} + \frac{1}{6}\right) \times \frac{3}{4}$ $= \frac{6}{4}$ **24.** $\left(\frac{3}{7} + \frac{2}{7}\right) \times \frac{2}{3}$ **25.** $\frac{1}{2} \times \left(\frac{1}{3} + \frac{1}{3}\right)$ $\frac{1}{3}$ **26.** $\left(\frac{9}{10} - \frac{3}{10}\right) \times \frac{1}{4}$

27. $\frac{2}{3} \times \left(\frac{3}{5} + \frac{1}{5}\right)$ **28.** $\left(\frac{8}{9} - \frac{1}{3}\right) \times \frac{3}{4}$ **29.** $\left(\frac{5}{12} + \frac{1}{6}\right) \times \frac{5}{6}$ **30.** $\frac{11}{12} \times \left(\frac{3}{4} - \frac{1}{2}\right)$

Problem Solving

31. Eduardo runs 6 laps around the track at Lincoln Park School. Then he runs $3\frac{1}{2}$ miles to get home. How far will he run in all? Show your work.

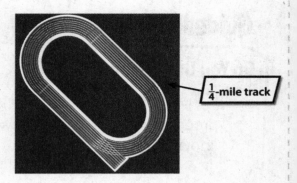

$\frac{1}{4}$-mile track

32. Be Precise To amend the U.S. Constitution, $\frac{3}{4}$ of the 50 states must approve the amendment. If 35 states approve an amendment, will the Constitution be amended?

33. Higher Order Thinking In Ms. Barclay's classroom, $\frac{2}{5}$ of the students play chess. Of the students who play chess, $\frac{5}{6}$ also play sudoku. If there are 30 students in her class, how many play chess and sudoku?

34. One sheet of stamps is shown at the right. Emma needs to buy 50 stamps to send out invitations for her graduation party. Will 2 sheets of stamps be enough? How do you know?

35. Choose all the expressions that have $\frac{3}{4}$ as a product. 🏴 5.NF.2.6.a

- [ ] $\frac{1}{2} \times \frac{1}{2}$
- [ ] $\frac{9}{10} \times \frac{5}{6}$
- [ ] $\frac{7}{8} \times \frac{6}{7}$
- [ ] $\frac{3}{4} \times \frac{3}{4}$
- [ ] $\frac{1}{4} \times \frac{1}{2}$

36. Choose all the multiplication sentences that have $\frac{1}{3}$ as the missing part. 🏴 5.NF.2.6.a

- [ ] $\frac{4}{5} \times \frac{5}{12} = \square$
- [ ] $\frac{1}{4} \times \square = \frac{1}{6}$
- [ ] $\frac{7}{8} \times \square = \frac{7}{24}$
- [ ] $\frac{5}{6} \times \frac{2}{5} = \square$
- [ ] $\frac{1}{6} \times \frac{2}{3} = \square$

© Pearson Education, Inc. 5

Name _____

Solve & Share

A rectangular poster is $\frac{1}{4}$ yard wide and $\frac{3}{4}$ yard tall. What is its area? *Solve this problem any way you choose.*

I can ...
find the area of a rectangle.

MAFS.5.NF.2.4.b Apply and extend previous understandings of multiplication to multiply a fraction or whole number by a fraction. Find the area of a rectangle with fractional side lengths by tiling it with unit squares of the appropriate unit fraction side lengths, and show that the area is the same as would be found by multiplying the side lengths. Multiply fractional side lengths to find areas of rectangles, and represent fraction products as rectangular areas. **MAFS.K12.MP.2.1, MP.3.1, MP.5.1**

You can use appropriate tools, like grid paper, to solve the problem.

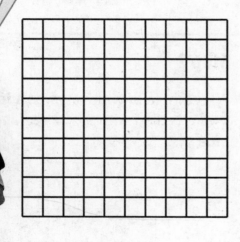

Look Back! Is the area of a poster that is $\frac{3}{4}$ yard wide and $\frac{1}{4}$ yard tall the same as the area of the poster above? Explain.

How Can You Find the Area of a Rectangle with Fractional Side Lengths?

A

Jenny has a rectangular garden. What is the area of her garden?

$\frac{5}{4}$ yards

$\frac{2}{3}$ yard

The area of a rectangle is found by multiplying the length by the width.

B # Step 1

$\frac{1}{4} \times \frac{1}{3} = \frac{1}{12}$ because 12 rectangles each $\frac{1}{4}$ wide and $\frac{1}{3}$ high fit in a unit square.

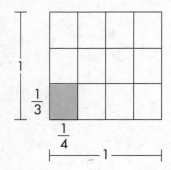

1

$\frac{1}{3}$

$\frac{1}{4}$

1

C # Step 2

A rectangle of width $\frac{5}{4}$ yards and height $\frac{2}{3}$ yard is tiled with 5×2 rectangles of area $\frac{1}{12}$.

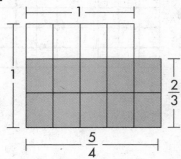

1

1

$\frac{2}{3}$

$\frac{5}{4}$

So, $\frac{5}{4} \times \frac{2}{3} = \frac{5 \times 2}{4 \times 3} = \frac{10}{12}$.

The area of Jenny's garden is $\frac{10}{12}$ square yard.

Convince Me! **Reasoning** Mason has a rectangular garden that is $\frac{2}{3}$ yard wide by $\frac{7}{4}$ yards long. What is the area of Mason's garden? Use a drawing to show your work.

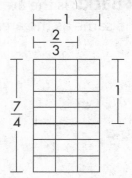

1

$\frac{2}{3}$

$\frac{7}{4}$

1

© Pearson Education, Inc. 5

Practice Tools Assessment

☆ Guided Practice*

Do You Understand?

1. If you do not remember the formula for finding the area of a rectangle, how can you find its area?

2. How could you define area?

Do You Know How?

3. Find the area of a rectangle with side lengths $\frac{2}{3}$ foot and $\frac{1}{2}$ foot.

4. Find the area of a square with side lengths of $\frac{5}{4}$ inches.

Independent Practice ☆

In **5–10**, find each area.

5.
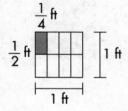

6.
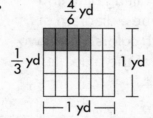

7.
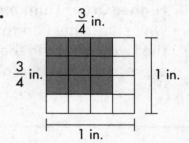

8.
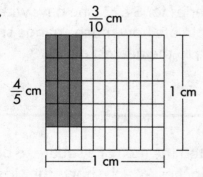

9.
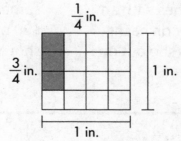

10.
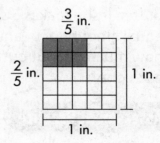

11. Find the area of a rectangle with side lengths $\frac{5}{3}$ feet and $\frac{3}{4}$ foot.

12. Find the area of a square with side lengths of $\frac{3}{8}$ inch.

13. Find the area of a rectangle with side lengths $\frac{7}{2}$ centimeters and $\frac{5}{4}$ centimeters.

*For another example, see Set E on page 372.

Problem Solving

14. Construct Arguments
Roy and Tom are working on a multiplication problem. Roy claims that $\frac{7}{4} \times \frac{3}{8} = \frac{21}{32}$. Tom claims that the correct answer is $\frac{21}{8}$. Who is correct? Explain your answer.

15. Emilio needs to know how much area to clear for his son's square sandbox. Each side of the sandbox is $\frac{3}{4}$ yard. Find the area that the sandbox will cover.

16. Margaret purchased a doormat measuring $\frac{1}{2}$ yard by $\frac{2}{3}$ yard for her back door step. If the step is $\frac{1}{4}$ square yard, will the mat fit? Explain.

17. Each person on a Ferris wheel pays $6.50 for a ticket. There are 72 passengers. How much money is collected from all the passengers?

18. Higher Order Thinking Kim is installing blue and white tile in her bathroom. She made a diagram of the layout showing the area of both colors. Write two expressions that describe the area of the blue tile.

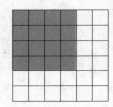

19. Wilhelmina has 8.3 ounces of peanut butter. If she makes 5 sandwiches with an equal amount of peanut butter on each, how much peanut butter does she put on each one?

20. Irene buys a talking doll for $10.66 and some batteries for $4.22. She pays with a $20 bill. Estimate how much change she should get, to the nearest dime.

21. Juno calculated the area of a square to be $\frac{4}{9}$ square yard. Which shows the side length of the square? **5.NF.2.4.b**

Ⓐ $\frac{2}{9}$ yard

Ⓑ $\frac{4}{9}$ yard

Ⓒ $\frac{2}{3}$ yard

Ⓓ $\frac{8}{9}$ yard

22. Bo calculated the area of a square to be $\frac{25}{4}$ square inches. Which shows the side length of the square? **5.NF.2.4.b**

Ⓐ $\frac{25}{2}$ inches

Ⓑ $\frac{25}{8}$ inches

Ⓒ $\frac{5}{2}$ inches

Ⓓ $\frac{5}{4}$ inches

© Pearson Education, Inc. 5

Name _____

Solve & Share

Look at the ingredients needed to make Josie's special pancakes. How much pancake mix and milk will you need if you want to double the recipe? To triple the recipe? *Solve this problem any way you choose.*

I can ...
multiply mixed numbers.

MAFS.5.NF.2.6 Solve real world problems involving multiplication of fractions and mixed numbers, e.g., by using visual fraction models or equations to represent the problem.
MAFS.K12.MP.1.1, MP.4.1, MP.8.1

Generalize
How can you use what you know about multiplying fractions to help you multiply mixed numbers?

Josie's Pancake Recipe

$2\frac{1}{4}$ cups pancake mix

1   egg

$1\frac{2}{3}$ cups milk

$\frac{3}{4}$ teaspoon vanilla

Look Back! What number sentence can you write using repeated addition to show how much pancake mix is needed if the recipe is tripled?

Essential Question

How Can You Find the Product of Mixed Numbers?

A

A clothing factory has machines that make jackets. The machines operate for $7\frac{1}{2}$ hours each day. How many jackets can Machine A make in one day?

DATA

Jackets Per Hour	
Machine A	Machine B
$2\frac{3}{4}$	$3\frac{1}{3}$

$7\frac{1}{2}$ times $2\frac{3}{4}$ is about 8 times 3. So, the answer should be about 24.

B ## One Way

You can use an area model to find the partial products. Then add to find the final product.

	7	$\frac{1}{2}$
2	$2 \times 7 = 14$	$2 \times \frac{1}{2} = 1$
$\frac{3}{4}$	$\frac{3}{4} \times 7 = \frac{21}{4} = 5\frac{1}{4}$	$\frac{3}{4} \times \frac{1}{2} = \frac{3}{8}$

$$14 + 1 + 5\frac{1}{4} + \frac{3}{8} =$$

$$14 + 1 + 5\frac{2}{8} + \frac{3}{8} = 20\frac{5}{8}$$

C ## Another Way

You can also use an equation to find the product. Rename the mixed numbers, then multiply.

$$7\frac{1}{2} \times 2\frac{3}{4} = \frac{15}{2} \times \frac{11}{4}$$
$$= \frac{165}{8}$$
$$= 20\frac{5}{8}$$

Machine A makes 20 jackets each day.

Since 20 is close to the estimate of 24, the answer is reasonable.

Convince Me! **Model with Math** How many jackets can Machine B make in one day? Write an equation to model your work.

☆ Guided Practice*

Do You Understand?

1. Explain how you would multiply $5 \times 2\frac{1}{2}$.

Do You Know How?

In **2** and **3**, estimate the product. Then complete the multiplication.

2. $2\frac{3}{4} \times 8 = \dfrac{\square}{4} \times \dfrac{8}{1} = \square$

3. $4\frac{1}{2} \times 1\frac{1}{4} = \dfrac{\square}{2} \times \dfrac{\square}{4} = \square$

☆ Independent Practice ☆

In **4–9**, estimate the product. Then complete the multiplication.

Compare your product against your estimate to check for reasonableness.

4. $3\frac{4}{5} \times 5 = \dfrac{\square}{5} \times \dfrac{5}{1} = \square$

5. $1\frac{3}{5} \times 2\frac{1}{4} = \dfrac{\square}{5} \times \dfrac{\square}{4} = \square$

6. $1\frac{1}{2} \times 3\frac{5}{6} = \dfrac{\square}{2} \times \dfrac{\square}{6} = \square$

7. $4\frac{2}{3} \times 4 = \dfrac{\square}{3} \times \dfrac{4}{1} = \square$

8. $3\frac{1}{7} \times 1\frac{1}{4} = \dfrac{\square}{7} \times \dfrac{\square}{4} = \square$

9. $1\frac{1}{3} \times 2\frac{1}{6} = \dfrac{\square}{3} \times \dfrac{\square}{6} = \square$

In **10–20**, estimate the product. Then find each product.

10. $2\frac{1}{6} \times 4\frac{1}{2}$

11. $\frac{3}{4} \times 8\frac{1}{2}$

12. $1\frac{1}{8} \times 3\frac{1}{3}$

13. $3\frac{1}{5} \times \frac{2}{3}$

14. $3\frac{1}{4} \times 6$

15. $5\frac{1}{3} \times 3$

16. $2\frac{3}{8} \times 4$

17. $4\frac{1}{8} \times 5\frac{1}{2}$

18. $\left(\frac{1}{6} + 2\frac{2}{3}\right) \times \left(1\frac{1}{4} - \frac{1}{2}\right)$

19. $\left(2\frac{4}{9} + \frac{1}{3}\right) \times \left(1\frac{1}{4} - \frac{1}{8}\right)$

20. $\left(1\frac{7}{8} + 2\frac{1}{2}\right) \times \left(1\frac{1}{5} - \frac{1}{10}\right)$

Problem Solving

In **21–23**, use the diagram at the right.

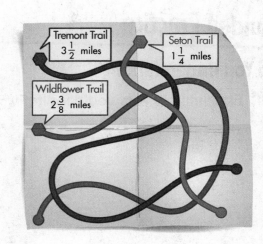

Tremont Trail $3\frac{1}{2}$ miles

Seton Trail $1\frac{1}{4}$ miles

Wildflower Trail $2\frac{3}{8}$ miles

21. Make Sense and Persevere
Bernie and Chloe hiked the Tremont Trail to the end and back. Then they hiked the Wildflower Trail to the end before stopping to eat lunch. How far did they hike before they ate lunch?

22. Higher Order Thinking In one day, Ricardo hiked $2\frac{2}{3}$ times as far as Bernie and Chloe hiked before they ate lunch. How far did he hike?

23. The city plans to extend the Wildflower Trail $2\frac{1}{2}$ times its current length in the next 5 years. How long will the Wildflower Trail be at the end of 5 years?

24. How can you use multiplication to find $3\frac{3}{5} + 3\frac{3}{5} + 3\frac{3}{5}$?

25. The world's smallest gecko is $\frac{3}{4}$ inch long. An adult male Western Banded Gecko is $7\frac{1}{3}$ times as long. How long is a Western Banded Gecko?

26. The Akashi-Kaikyo Bridge in Japan is about $1\frac{4}{9}$ times as long as the Golden Gate Bridge in San Francisco. The Golden Gate Bridge is about 9,000 feet long. About how long is the Akashi-Kaikyo Bridge?

27. Patty spent 3.5 times as much as Sandy on their shopping trip. If Sandy spent $20.50, how much did Patty spend?

Assessment Practice

28. Choose all that are true. 5.NF.2.6

- ☐ $4\frac{1}{12} \times 2\frac{3}{4} = 11\frac{11}{48}$
- ☐ $5\frac{1}{2} \times 5 = 25\frac{1}{2}$
- ☐ $1\frac{1}{2} \times 3\frac{1}{5} = 4\frac{1}{2}$
- ☐ $\frac{3}{4} \times 8\frac{1}{5} = 6\frac{3}{20}$
- ☐ $2\frac{1}{5} \times 6\frac{1}{4} = 13\frac{3}{4}$

29. Choose all that are true. 5.NF.2.6

- ☐ $15\frac{1}{4} = 5 \times 3\frac{1}{4}$
- ☐ $4\frac{1}{3} = 4\frac{1}{3} \times 1$
- ☐ $9\frac{3}{4} = 4\frac{1}{2} \times 2\frac{1}{6}$
- ☐ $3\frac{1}{3} = 6\frac{2}{3} \times \frac{1}{2}$
- ☐ $13\frac{3}{5} = 7\frac{1}{3} \times 2\frac{2}{5}$

© Pearson Education, Inc. 5

Name _____

Solve & Share

Without multiplying, circle the problem in each set with the greatest product and underline the problem with the least product. **Solve this problem any way you choose.**

I can ...
use multiplication to scale or resize something.

MAFS.5.NF.2.5.a Interpret multiplication as scaling (resizing), by comparing the size of a product to the size of one factor on the basis of the size of the other factor, without performing the indicated multiplication.
Also MAFS.5.NF.2.5.b.
MAFS.K12.MP.3.1, MP.6.1, MP.7.1

Set 1

a. $\frac{1}{2} \times 2$

b. $\frac{3}{3} \times 2$

c. $\frac{5}{4} \times 2$

Set 2

a. $3\frac{3}{4} \times 2\frac{1}{2}$

b. $\frac{3}{4} \times 2\frac{1}{2}$

c. $\frac{4}{4} \times 2\frac{1}{2}$

Set 3

a. $\frac{3}{4} \times \frac{6}{6}$

b. $\frac{3}{4} \times 1\frac{5}{6}$

c. $\frac{3}{4} \times \frac{5}{6}$

How can you use what you know about multiplying fractions to help you find the problem with the greatest product?

Look Back! Construct Arguments How is $\frac{3}{3} \times 2$ like 1×2?

Essential Question

How Can You Use Number Sense to Evaluate the Size of a Product?

A

Sue knitted scarves that are 4 feet long for herself and her friends Joe and Alan. After a month, they compared the lengths of their scarves. Some scarves had stretched and some had shrunk. The results are shown in the chart. How had the lengths of Joe's and Alan's scarves changed?

Think of multiplication as scaling or resizing.

DATA

Sue	4
Joe	$1\frac{1}{2} \times 4$
Alan	$\frac{3}{4} \times 4$

B Alan's scarf

Alan's scarf shrank.

$$\frac{3}{4} \times 4 < 4$$

Multiplying a number by a fraction less than 1 results in a product less than the given number.

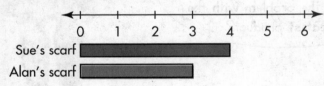

Sue's scarf
Alan's scarf

C Joe's scarf

Joe's scarf stretched.

$$1\frac{1}{2} \times 4 > 4$$

Multiplying a number by a fraction greater than 1 results in a product greater than the starting number.

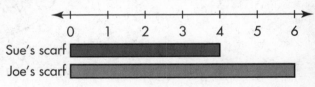

Sue's scarf
Joe's scarf

Convince Me! **Use Structure** Sue knitted a scarf for her friend June that was also 4 feet long. After a month, the length of June's scarf could be represented by the expression $\frac{3}{3} \times 4$. How did the length of June's scarf change? Explain.

© Pearson Education, Inc. 5

Name _____

 Guided Practice *

Do You Understand?

1. Why does multiplying a number by $3\frac{1}{2}$ increase its value?

2. Which of the following are less than 8?

   $8 \times \frac{9}{10}$

   $8 \times \frac{7}{6}$

   $\frac{3}{5} \times 8$

Do You Know How?

In **3–5**, without multiplying decide which symbol belongs in the box: $<, >,$ or $=$.

3. $3\frac{1}{2} \times 2\frac{2}{3}$ ☐ $2\frac{2}{3}$

4. $\frac{4}{5} \times 2\frac{2}{3}$ ☐ $2\frac{2}{3}$

5. $4\frac{3}{5}$ ☐ $4\frac{3}{5} \times \frac{4}{4}$

Independent Practice

In **6–17**, without multiplying, decide which symbol belongs in the box: $<, >,$ or $=$.

6. $2\frac{1}{2} \times 1\frac{2}{3}$ ☐ $1\frac{2}{3}$

7. $\frac{3}{5} \times 4\frac{4}{5}$ ☐ $4\frac{4}{5}$

8. $1\frac{2}{7}$ ☐ $1\frac{2}{7} \times \frac{5}{5}$

9. $\frac{1}{3} \times 2\frac{2}{5}$ ☐ $2\frac{2}{5}$

10. $3\frac{3}{5}$ ☐ $3\frac{3}{5} \times \frac{2}{2}$

11. $4\frac{1}{3} \times 2\frac{2}{7}$ ☐ $2\frac{2}{7}$

12. $2\frac{1}{5} \times \frac{1}{10}$ ☐ $2\frac{1}{5}$

13. $\frac{1}{2} \times 1\frac{2}{5}$ ☐ $1\frac{2}{5}$

14. $4\frac{3}{4} \times 3\frac{1}{4}$ ☐ $4\frac{3}{4}$

15. $1\frac{3}{4}$ ☐ $1\frac{1}{12} \times 1\frac{3}{4}$

16. $5\frac{1}{3} \times \frac{5}{6}$ ☐ $5\frac{1}{3}$

17. $\frac{5}{5} \times 4\frac{2}{3}$ ☐ $4\frac{2}{3}$

In **18** and **19**, without multiplying, order the following products from least to greatest.

18. $2 \times \frac{3}{5}$ $2\frac{1}{4} \times \frac{3}{5}$ $\frac{3}{4} \times \frac{3}{5}$ $\frac{5}{5} \times \frac{3}{5}$

19. $\frac{1}{5} \times \frac{2}{3}$ $4\frac{1}{2} \times \frac{2}{3}$ $\frac{1}{3} \times \frac{2}{3}$ $4 \times \frac{2}{3}$

In **20** and **21**, without multiplying, order the following products from greatest to least.

20. $3 \times \frac{3}{4}$ $\frac{2}{3} \times \frac{3}{4}$ $1\frac{1}{4} \times \frac{3}{4}$ $\frac{4}{4} \times \frac{3}{4}$

21. $\frac{3}{3} \times \frac{1}{3}$ $4 \times \frac{1}{3}$ $2\frac{2}{3} \times \frac{1}{3}$ $2\frac{1}{3} \times \frac{1}{3}$

*For another example, see Set G on page 374.   **Topic 8** | Lesson 8-8   363

Problem Solving

22. Who ran farther by the end of the week? How much farther? Use the table below that shows the distances in miles.

DATA		Monday	Tuesday	Wednesday	Thursday	Friday
	Holly	$1\frac{1}{2}$	$\frac{1}{2}$	$2\frac{1}{4}$	$\frac{3}{4}$	$1\frac{1}{2}$
	Yu	$1\frac{3}{4}$	$1\frac{1}{2}$	$2\frac{3}{4}$	$1\frac{1}{4}$	$\frac{1}{2}$

23. Be Precise Ethan took a quiz with 15 questions. If he answered $\frac{3}{5}$ of the questions correctly, how many did he get wrong?

24. At a taffy pull, George stretched the taffy to 3 feet. Jose stretched it $1\frac{1}{3}$ times as far as George. Maria stretched it $\frac{2}{3}$ as far as George. Sally stretched it $\frac{6}{6}$ as far. Who stretched it the farthest? the least?

25. Higher Order Thinking Without multiplying, decide which symbol belongs in the box: $<$, $>$, or $=$. Explain how you decided.

$$4\frac{3}{4} \times 3\frac{1}{4} \square 4\frac{1}{2}$$

26. Write two decimals with a product close to 6.3.

$$\_\_.\_\_ \times \_\_.\_\_ \approx 6.3$$

> $\approx$ is a symbol that means *is approximately equal to.*

Assessment Practice

27. Write each expression in the correct answer space to show products less than $4\frac{1}{2}$ and those greater than $4\frac{1}{2}$. 5.NF.2.5.a

Less than $4\frac{1}{2}$	Greater than $4\frac{1}{2}$

$4 \times 4\frac{1}{2}$ $1\frac{1}{12} \times 4\frac{1}{2}$ $4\frac{1}{2} \times \frac{3}{4}$ $\frac{4}{5} \times 4\frac{1}{2}$

28. Write each expression in the correct answer space to show products less than $1\frac{3}{4}$ and those greater than $1\frac{3}{4}$. 5.NF.2.5.a

Less than $1\frac{3}{4}$	Greater than $1\frac{3}{4}$

$1\frac{3}{4} \times 1\frac{3}{4}$ $\frac{9}{10} \times 1\frac{3}{4}$ $1\frac{3}{4} \times \frac{1}{2}$ $5\frac{1}{6} \times 1\frac{3}{4}$

© Pearson Education, Inc. 5

Name _____

☆ ⭐ ☆
Solve & Share

A rectangular dog park was built with the dimensions shown. The fencing that completely surrounds the park cost $12 a yard. Each square yard of grass sod that covers the entire park cost $8. What was the total cost for the fencing and the sod? *Solve this problem any way you choose.*

I can ...
make sense of problems and keep working if I get stuck.

🐦 **MAFS.K12.MP.1.1** Make sense and persevere. Also, MP.3.1, MP.4.1
MAFS.5.NF.2.6 Solve real world problems involving multiplication of fractions and mixed numbers, e.g., by using visual fraction models or equations to represent the problem.

$8\frac{1}{4}$ yd

$25\frac{1}{2}$ yd

Thinking Habits

Be a good thinker!
These questions can help you.

• What do I need to find?

• What do I know?

• What's my plan for solving the problem?

• What else can I try if I get stuck?

• How can I check that my solution makes sense?

Look Back! **Make Sense and Persevere** Before solving the problem, how do you know that the area of the dog park must be greater than 200 square yards?

How Can You Make Sense of Problems and Persevere in Solving Them?

A

Gwen is planning to tile the entire floor of the family room and kitchen. Tile costs $12 per square foot. What is the total cost of tiling the family room and kitchen floors?

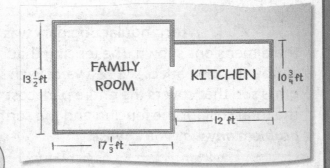

FAMILY ROOM   KITCHEN

$13\frac{1}{2}$ ft $10\frac{3}{4}$ ft

12 ft

$17\frac{1}{3}$ ft

You can make sense of the problem by answering these questions. What do you know? What are you asked to find?

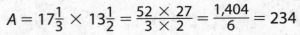

Here's my thinking...

B **How can I make sense of and solve the problem?**

I can

- identify the quantities given.

- understand how the quantities are related.

- choose and implement an appropriate strategy.

- check to be sure my work and answer make sense.

C Find the area of the family room.

$$A = 17\frac{1}{3} \times 13\frac{1}{2} = \frac{52 \times 27}{3 \times 2} = \frac{1,404}{6} = 234$$

The area of the family room is 234 square feet.

Find the area of the kitchen.

$$A = 12 \times 10\frac{3}{4} = \frac{12 \times 43}{1 \times 4} = \frac{516}{4} = 129$$

The area of the kitchen is 129 square feet.

Add to find the total area. $234 + 129 = 363$

Calculate the total cost. $363 \times 12 = 4,356$

The total cost is $4,356.

Convince Me! **Make Sense and Persevere** How much more does it cost to tile the family room floor than the kitchen floor? Show your work.

© Pearson Education, Inc. 5

Practice   Tools   Assessment

☆ Guided Practice*

Make Sense and Persevere

A website has a daily trivia contest. On Mondays, Wednesdays, and Fridays, you have $1\frac{1}{2}$ hours to submit an answer. On Tuesdays and Thursdays, you have $1\frac{1}{4}$ hours. On Saturdays and Sundays, you have only $\frac{3}{4}$ of an hour. How many hours each week do you have to submit an answer?

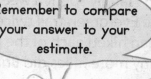
Remember to compare your answer to your estimate.

1. Estimate the total hours each week you have to submit an answer. Write an equation to show your work.

2. Write an equation using multiplication and a variable to represent the problem. Then solve the equation and answer the question.

Independent Practice ☆

Make Sense and Persevere

Isabel is buying framing to go around the perimeter of one of her paintings. Each inch of framing costs $0.40. What is the total cost of the framing for the painting?

$6\frac{1}{4}$ in.

$10\frac{1}{4}$ in.

3. What is the first step you need to do? What is the answer to the first step? Write an equation to show your work.

4. What is the next step to solve the problem? What is the answer to the problem? Write an equation to show your work.

5. How can you check that your answer makes sense?

Problem Solving

Performance Task

Hiking Trails

The Farina family spent a week at the state park. Christine hiked the Evergreen trail twice and the Yellow River trail once. Brian hiked each of the three longest trails once. How many more miles did Brian hike than Christine?

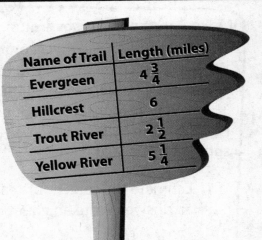

Name of Trail	Length (miles)
Evergreen	$4\frac{3}{4}$
Hillcrest	6
Trout River	$2\frac{1}{2}$
Yellow River	$5\frac{1}{4}$

6. Make Sense and Persevere What do you know? What are you asked to find? What information do you not need? 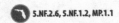 5.NF.2.6, 5.NF.1.2, MP.1.1

7. Make Sense and Persevere What information do you need to find before you can answer the final question? 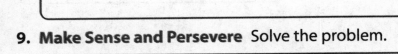 5.NF.2.6, 5.NF.1.2, MP.1.1

Read the problem carefully so you can identify what you know and what you are asked to find.

8. Model with Math Write equations to represent the information in Exercise 7. 5.NF.2.6, 5.NF.1.2, MP.4.1

9. Make Sense and Persevere Solve the problem. 5.NF.2.6, 5.NF.1.2, MP.1.1

10. Construct Arguments Explain why your answer makes sense. MP.3.1

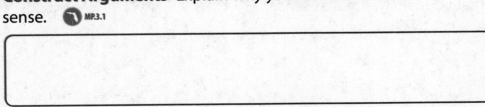

© Pearson Education, Inc. 5

Name _____

Point & Tally

Work with a partner. Get paper and a pencil. Each partner chooses light blue or dark blue.

At the same time, Partner 1 and Partner 2 each point to one of their black numbers. Both partners find the product of the two numbers.

The partner who chose the color where the product appears gets a tally mark. Work until one partner has seven tally marks.

I can ...
multiply multi-digit whole numbers.

MAFS.5.NBT.2.5

Partner 1					Partner 2
11	16,016	2,600	16,275	2,343	**100**
93	42,600	1,925	8,200	4,550	**175**
26	50,512	42,036	9,300	17,466	**213**
82	37,064	5,538	14,350	19,809	**452**
200	35,000	90,400	11,752	20,000	**616**
	4,972	123,200	57,288	6,776	

Tally Marks for Partner 1

Tally Marks for Partner 2

A-Z
Glossary

Word List

- area model
- Associative Property of Multiplication
- benchmark fractions
- Commutative Property of Multiplication
- mixed number
- round

Understand Vocabulary

Choose the best term from the box. Write it on the blank.

1. To estimate the product of two mixed numbers, _____ each factor to the nearest whole number.

2. Using _____ can help make it easier to estimate computations.

3. The product of two fractions can be represented by a(n) _____ .

4. Another way to write the fraction $\frac{19}{5}$ is as a _____ , $3\frac{4}{5}$.

True or False

Estimate each product to decide if the comparison is true or false. Write T for true or F for false.

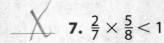

_____ **5.** $6\frac{3}{5} \times 5\frac{7}{8} < 42$

_____ **6.** $8\frac{2}{9} \times 9\frac{1}{4} > 90$

_____ **7.** $\frac{2}{7} \times \frac{5}{8} < 1$

_____ **8.** $5\frac{1}{10} \times 3 > 15$

Use Vocabulary in Writing

9. Suppose you know the answer to $\frac{4}{5} \times \left(20 \times 1\frac{7}{8}\right)$. Explain how the Commutative and Associative Properties of Multiplication can make the computation easier. Then find the answer.

© Pearson Education, Inc. 5

Name _____

Set A pages 333–336 _____

Find $4 \times \frac{2}{3}$ using a number line.

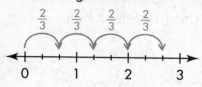

Each jump is $\frac{2}{3}$.

$1 \times \frac{2}{3} = \frac{2}{3}$

$2 \times \frac{2}{3} = \frac{4}{3} = 1\frac{1}{3}$

$3 \times \frac{2}{3} = \frac{6}{3} = 2$

$4 \times \frac{2}{3} = \frac{8}{3} = 2\frac{2}{3}$

So, $4 \times \frac{2}{3} = 2\frac{2}{3}$.

This makes sense because $\frac{2}{3}$ is less than 1, so $4 \times \frac{2}{3}$ should be less than 4.

Remember to multiply the numerator of the fraction by the whole number.

Find each product. Use number lines, fraction strips, or drawings to help you.

1. $4 \times \frac{3}{4}$ **2.** $7 \times \frac{1}{4}$

3. $8 \times \frac{5}{6}$ **4.** $10 \times \frac{1}{2}$

5. $9 \times \frac{1}{3}$ **6.** $9 \times \frac{2}{3}$

7. $3 \times \frac{7}{8}$ **8.** $7 \times \frac{3}{8}$

9. $5 \times \frac{5}{6}$ **10.** $12 \times \frac{2}{3}$

11. $15 \times \frac{4}{5}$ **12.** $2 \times \frac{9}{10}$

Set B pages 337–340, 341–344 _____

Mary's clock uses $\frac{3}{4}$ of the batteries in the package. How many batteries does the clock need?

8 batteries in each package

Find $\frac{3}{4}$ of 8.

$\frac{1}{4}$ of 8 is 2.

$\frac{3}{4}$ is three times as much as $\frac{1}{4}$.

So, $\frac{3}{4}$ of 8 is three times as much as 2.

$\frac{3}{4}$ of 8 is 6.

Mary's clock needs 6 batteries.

Remember that the word *of* often means to multiply.

Find each product.

1. $4 \times \frac{1}{2}$ **2.** $\frac{3}{4}$ of 16

3. $24 \times \frac{1}{8}$ **4.** $\frac{4}{7}$ of 28

5. $\frac{4}{5} \times 37$ **6.** $\frac{7}{8} \times 219$

7. Marco weighs 80 pounds. His bones make up about $\frac{1}{5}$ of his body weight. How much do his bones weigh?

8. Monica bought 12 gallons of paint. She used $\frac{2}{3}$ of the paint to paint her house. How many gallons of paint did she use?

9. A soccer coach gives each player $\frac{1}{2}$ liter of water at halftime. If there are 11 players, how many liters does he need?

Set C | pages 345–348

Find $\frac{2}{3} \times \frac{5}{6}$.

A drawing can show fraction multiplication. Start with a rectangle that has 3 rows and 6 columns. There are 18 sections in all.

For $\frac{2}{3}$, shade 2 rows.

For $\frac{5}{6}$, shade 5 columns.

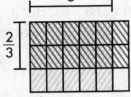

Count the sections in the overlap.

10 of the 18 squares are in the overlap area. So, $\frac{5}{6} \times \frac{2}{3} = \frac{10}{18}$ or $\frac{5}{9}$.

Remember to use each denominator to make the grid.

Find each product. Use models to help.

1. $\frac{2}{3} \times \frac{3}{8}$ 2. $\frac{1}{4} \times \frac{3}{5}$

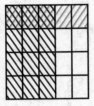

3. $\frac{1}{6} \times \frac{1}{8}$ 4. $\frac{4}{7} \times \frac{4}{7}$

Set D | pages 349–352

Find $\frac{4}{5} \times \frac{3}{4}$.

Multiply the numerators to find the numerator of the product. Multiply the denominators to find the denominator of the product.

$\frac{4}{5} \times \frac{3}{4} = \frac{4 \times 3}{5 \times 4} = \frac{12}{20}$ or $\frac{3}{5}$

Remember to multiply the numerators together and the denominators together.

1. $\frac{6}{7} \times \frac{1}{2}$ 2. $\frac{3}{8} \times \frac{8}{3}$

3. $\frac{2}{3} \times \frac{1}{3}$ 4. $\frac{7}{8} \times \frac{3}{2}$

Set E | pages 353–356

Find the area of a rectangle with length $\frac{3}{2}$ and width $\frac{1}{3}$.

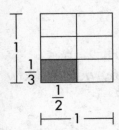
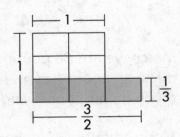

The rectangle of length $\frac{3}{2}$ and width $\frac{1}{3}$ is tiled with 3 rectangles of area $\frac{1}{2 \times 3}$.

So, the area of the rectangle is $\frac{3}{6}$ or $\frac{1}{2}$ square unit.

Remember that a unit square can be used to help find areas of rectangles.

Find the area of a rectangle with the given dimensions.

1. Length: $\frac{8}{5}$ units
   Width: $\frac{3}{4}$ unit

2. Length: $\frac{4}{3}$ units
   Width: $\frac{7}{10}$ unit

3. Gabriel has a square canvas that measures $\frac{5}{4}$ feet on each side. What is the area of Gabriel's canvas?

© Pearson Education, Inc. 5

Name _____

Set F pages 357–360 _____

Find $3\frac{1}{2} \times 2\frac{7}{8}$.

Estimate: $3\frac{1}{2} \times 2\frac{7}{8}$ is about $4 \times 3 = 12$.

Rename fractions, then multiply.

$\frac{7}{2} \times \frac{23}{8} = \frac{161}{16} = 10\frac{1}{16}$

The product $10\frac{1}{16}$ is close to the estimate, 12.

An area model can also represent the product of mixed numbers.

A rectangular field of crops is $4\frac{2}{3}$ miles by $2\frac{3}{4}$ miles. Calculate $4\frac{2}{3} \times 2\frac{3}{4}$ to find the area.

Estimate: $4\frac{2}{3} \times 2\frac{3}{4}$ is about $5 \times 3 = 15$.

Use an area model to find the partial products.

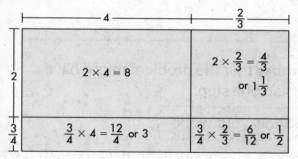

Add the partial products.

$8 + 1\frac{1}{3} + 3 + \frac{1}{2} =$

$8 + 1\frac{2}{6} + 3 + \frac{3}{6} =$

$8 + 3 + 1\frac{2}{6} + \frac{3}{6} = 12\frac{5}{6}$

So, $4\frac{2}{3} \times 2\frac{3}{4} = 12\frac{5}{6}$.

The area of the field is $12\frac{5}{6}$ square miles. The product is close to the estimate of 15, so the answer is reasonable.

Remember to compare your answer with your estimate.

Estimate. Then find each product.

1. $2\frac{1}{3} \times 4\frac{1}{5}$

2. $4\frac{1}{2} \times 6\frac{2}{3}$

3. $3\frac{3}{5} \times 2\frac{5}{7}$

4. $14\frac{2}{7} \times 4\frac{3}{10}$

Use the grid. Write the missing labels and find the product.

5. $6\frac{2}{3} \times 3\frac{3}{5}$

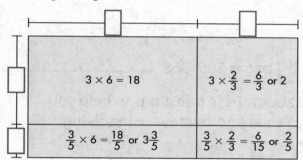

6. $2\frac{5}{12} \times 3\frac{1}{3}$

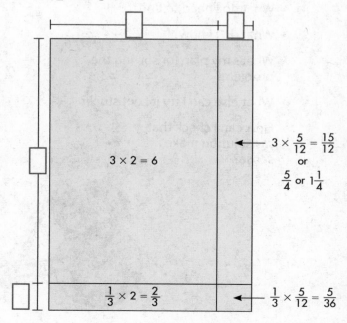

Multiplication can be thought of as scaling, or resizing, a fraction.

Will the product of $4\frac{1}{2} \times \frac{3}{4}$ be greater than or less than $4\frac{1}{2}$? How can you tell without multiplying?

Since $\frac{3}{4} < 1$, $4\frac{1}{2} \times \frac{3}{4} < 4\frac{1}{2} \times 1$.

So, $4\frac{1}{2} \times \frac{3}{4}$ will be less than $4\frac{1}{2}$.

Will the product of $4\frac{1}{2} \times 2\frac{1}{3}$ be greater than or less than $4\frac{1}{2}$? How can you tell without multiplying?

Since $2\frac{1}{3} > 1$, $4\frac{1}{2} \times 2\frac{1}{3} > 4\frac{1}{2} \times 1$.

So, $4\frac{1}{2} \times 2\frac{1}{3}$ will be greater than $4\frac{1}{2}$.

Remember that a fraction is equal to 1 if the numerator and denominator are the same.

Without multiplying, decide which symbol belongs in the box: $<$, $>$, or $=$.

1. $2\frac{1}{10} \times \frac{3}{5} \ \square\ 2\frac{1}{10}$ 2. $\frac{3}{4} \times \frac{5}{5} \ \square\ \frac{3}{4}$

3. $7\frac{1}{2} \times 1\frac{1}{6} \ \square\ 7\frac{1}{2}$ 4. $\frac{8}{3} \times \frac{9}{10} \ \square\ \frac{8}{3}$

Order each set of numbers from least to greatest.

5. $3\frac{1}{5}$, $3\frac{1}{5} \times \frac{9}{10}$, $3\frac{1}{5} \times 1\frac{1}{2}$

6. $\frac{2}{3} \times \frac{3}{4}$, $\frac{2}{3} \times \frac{5}{4}$, $\frac{2}{3}$

7. $2\frac{1}{3} \times \frac{5}{5}$, $2\frac{1}{3} \times \frac{6}{5}$, $2\frac{1}{3} \times \frac{1}{5}$

Think about these questions to help you **make sense and persevere** in solving them.

Thinking Habits

- What do I need to find?
- What do I know?
- What's my plan for solving the problem?
- What else can I try if I get stuck?
- How can I check that my solution makes sense?

Remember that the problem might have more than one step.

Solve. Show your work.

1. John has $1\frac{1}{2}$ hours of homework each day from Monday through Thursday and $2\frac{3}{4}$ hours over the weekend. How much homework does John have in a week?

2. Elle is buying new flooring for her kitchen and laundry room. She knows that the area of the kitchen is 132 square feet. The laundry room is $8\frac{1}{3}$ feet by $6\frac{3}{4}$ feet. What is the total area of the two rooms?

Name _____

1. Which rectangle has the greater area, a rectangle with length $\frac{1}{12}$ foot and width $\frac{3}{4}$ foot or a rectangle with length $\frac{1}{16}$ foot and width $\frac{4}{5}$ foot?

2. Alberto runs $3\frac{1}{4}$ miles each day.

n total miles

$3\frac{1}{4}$	$3\frac{1}{4}$	$3\frac{1}{4}$	$3\frac{1}{4}$	$3\frac{1}{4}$	$3\frac{1}{4}$	$3\frac{1}{4}$

A. Write an equation using the variable *n* to model how far he runs in 7 days.

B. How far does he run in 7 days?

C. Explain how to estimate how far he would run in 11 days.

3. Is the following equation true? Explain.

$$\frac{5}{6} \times \frac{8}{4} = \frac{5}{3}$$

4. Complete the equation. Show your work.

$$16 \times \frac{5}{8} = ?$$

5. Select all the expressions that are equal to $\frac{4}{7} \times 6$.

- [ ] $4 \div 6 \times 7 = \frac{14}{3}$
- [ ] $\frac{6}{7} \times 4 = \frac{24}{7}$
- [ ] $6 \div 4 \times 7 = 10\frac{1}{2}$
- [ ] $4 \times 6 \div 7 = 3\frac{3}{7}$
- [ ] $7 \div 4 \times 6 = \frac{21}{2}$

6. Tracy took a test that had 24 questions. She got $\frac{5}{6}$ of the questions correct. How many questions did she answer correctly? Write an equation to model your work.

7. Jenna ran $2\frac{7}{8}$ kilometers each day for a week. How far did she run in all? Give an estimate, then find the actual amount. Show your work.

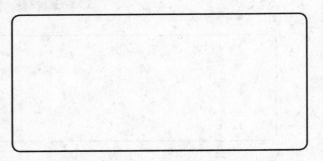

8. Eduardo has a recipe that uses $\frac{2}{3}$ cup of flour for each batch. If he makes 4 batches, how many cups of flour will he need? How many cups of flour will he need in total if he makes 3 more batches? Write your answers as mixed numbers. Use the number line to help.

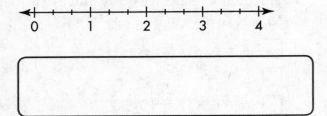

9. Complete the equation. Explain how you got your answer.

$\frac{6}{7} \times \frac{2}{5} = ?$

10. Ted and his friends are rolling out clay for art class. Ted rolled out his clay until it was 2 feet long. Noah rolled out his clay $\frac{3}{5}$ as long as Ted's clay. Jeannine rolled out her clay until it was $1\frac{1}{2}$ times as long as Ted's clay. Miles rolled out his clay $\frac{5}{5}$ as long as Ted's clay.

A. Without completing the multiplication, whose clay is longer than Ted's clay? How can you tell?

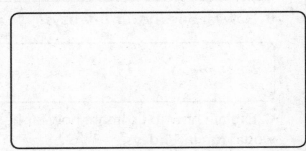

B. Without completing the multiplication, whose clay is shorter than Ted's clay? How can you tell?

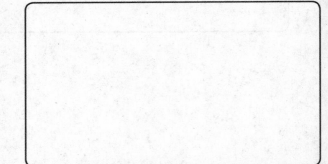

C. Whose clay is the same length as Ted's clay? How can you tell?

© Pearson Education, Inc. 5

Name _____

11. Find the product of $\frac{7}{8} \times \frac{9}{10}$. Then write another product with the same answer.

12. Which of the following is equal to $\frac{4}{7} \times \frac{11}{15}$?

Ⓐ $\frac{4 \times 7}{11 \times 15} = \frac{28}{165}$

Ⓑ $\frac{4 \times 15}{7 \times 11} = \frac{60}{77}$

Ⓒ $\frac{4 \times 11}{7 \times 15} = \frac{44}{105}$

Ⓓ $\frac{7 \times 15}{4 \times 11} = \frac{105}{44}$

13. Members of a landscaping company built a retaining wall. They used brick to make the top $\frac{2}{3}$ of the wall.

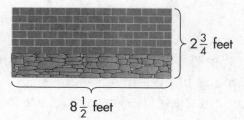

$2\frac{3}{4}$ feet

$8\frac{1}{2}$ feet

A. What is the height of the brick portion of the wall? Write an equation to model your work.

B. Estimate the area of the whole retaining wall.

C. What is the area of the whole retaining wall? Write an equation to show your work. Compare your answer to your estimate to see if your answer is reasonable.

14. Tyler's family rented 15 DVDs last month.

A. Of the 15 DVDs, $\frac{1}{5}$ were documentaries. How many of the movies were documentaries? Use the model to help you.

B. Of the 15 DVDs, $\frac{3}{5}$ were comedies. How many movies were comedies? Use the model to help you.

C. What relationship do you notice between the number of comedies and the number of documentaries?

15. Kristen and Niko buy a canvas for their art studio.

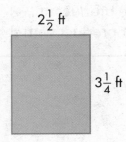

A. Estimate the area of their canvas. Write an equation to model your work.

B. Find the actual area of their canvas. Write your answer as a mixed number.

C. Compare your answer to your estimate to see if your answer is reasonable.

   © Pearson Education, Inc. 5

Name _____

What's for Dinner?

Branden and Ashley are making the casserole in the **Tuna Casserole Recipe** card.

1. Branden is trying to decide how much tuna casserole to make.

Part A

How many cups of tuna does Branden need to make 3 times the recipe? Draw a model to show how to solve. 🔊 5.NF.2.5

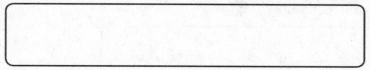

> **Tuna Casserole Recipe**
>
> $2\frac{3}{4}$ cups cooked macaroni
>
> $\frac{3}{4}$ cup canned tuna
>
> $1\frac{1}{3}$ cups condensed cream of mushroom soup
>
> 2 cups shredded cheddar cheese
>
> $1\frac{1}{2}$ cups fried onion rings
>
> Preheat oven

Part B

How many cups of shredded cheddar cheese does Branden need to make $\frac{2}{3}$ of the recipe? Draw a model to show your work. 🔊 5.NF.2.5

Part C

How many cups of fried onion rings does Branden need to make $2\frac{1}{2}$ times the recipe? Show how to use a model and partial products to multiply. 🔊 5.NF.2.5

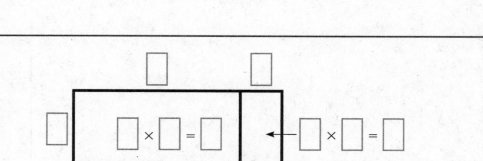

Part D

How many cups of cooked macaroni does Branden need to make $2\frac{1}{2}$ times the recipe? Show how to rename fractions, then multiply. 5.NF.2.5

2. Ashley's casserole dish is shown in the **Ashley's Dish** drawing.

Ashley's Dish

$\frac{5}{6}$ ft long

$\frac{3}{4}$ ft wide

Part A

What is the area of the bottom of Ashley's dish? Complete the model to show your work. 5.NF.2.4

Part B

Branden's casserole dish is $1\frac{1}{2}$ times as wide and $1\frac{4}{5}$ times as long as Ashley's dish. Is Branden's dish longer or shorter than Ashley's dish? Explain your reasoning. 5.NF.2.4

Part C

What is the area of the bottom of Branden's dish? Show your work. 5.NF.2.4

Apply Understanding of Division to Divide Fractions

Essential Questions: How are fractions related to division? How can you divide with whole numbers and unit fractions?

Digital Resources

Interactive Student Edition   Activity   Visual Learning   Video   Practice

Assessment   Games   Tools   Glossary

The thermal energy of an object depends on its temperature and on how many particles it contains.

A cup of hot cocoa has more thermal energy than a cup of cold milk.

MAFS.5.NF.2.3, 5.NF.2.7.a, 5.NF.2.7.b, 5.NF.2.7.c
MAFS.K12.MP.1.1, MP.2.1, MP.3.1, MP.4.1, MP.5.1, MP.6.1, MP.7.1, MP.8.1

I can chill with that! Five marshmallows roasting on a stick have more thermal energy than just one! Here's a project about thermal energy.

enVision STEM Project: Thermal Energy

Do Research Use the Internet or other sources to learn about thermal energy. Make a list of 3 ways you use thermal energy in your home and at school. Which use is most important to you? Why?

Journal: Write a Report Include what you found. Also in your report:

- Ask each member of your household 3 ways they use thermal energy. Organize your data in a table.

- Draw conclusions from your data. How does your household use thermal energy?

- Make up and solve problems with fraction division.

Name _____

Review What You Know

A-Z Vocabulary

Choose the best term from the list at the right.
Write it on the blank.

- common factor
- equivalent fractions
- estimate
- like denominators
- mixed number
- quotient

1. To find an approximate answer or solution is to _____.

2. The fractions $\frac{3}{4}$ and $\frac{17}{4}$ are fractions with _____.

3. The fractions that name the same amount are _____.

4. The answer to a division problem is the _____.

5. A number that has a whole-number part and a fraction part is called a _____.

Meaning of Fractions

Each rectangle represents one whole. Write the shaded part of each rectangle as a fraction.

6.

7.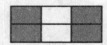

Fraction Computation

Find each sum, difference, or product.

8. $\frac{2}{5} + \frac{1}{4}$

9. $\frac{5}{6} - \frac{1}{4}$

10. $2\frac{5}{8} + 7\frac{1}{4}$

11. $14 - 3\frac{5}{8}$

12. $3\frac{2}{3} + 4\frac{1}{2}$

13. $\frac{3}{8} \times 2$

14. $\frac{1}{4} \times \frac{3}{5}$

15. $8 \times \frac{9}{10}$

16. $3\frac{1}{2} \times 2\frac{3}{5}$

© Pearson Education, Inc. 5

Name _____

PROJECT 9A

Will your prototype make you rich and famous?

Project: Build a Fraction-Division Prototype

PROJECT 9B

Why do so many math problems use pizza?

Project: Write a Skit About Pizza

PROJECT 9C

Would you like to improve your memory?

Project: Create a Mnemonic Device

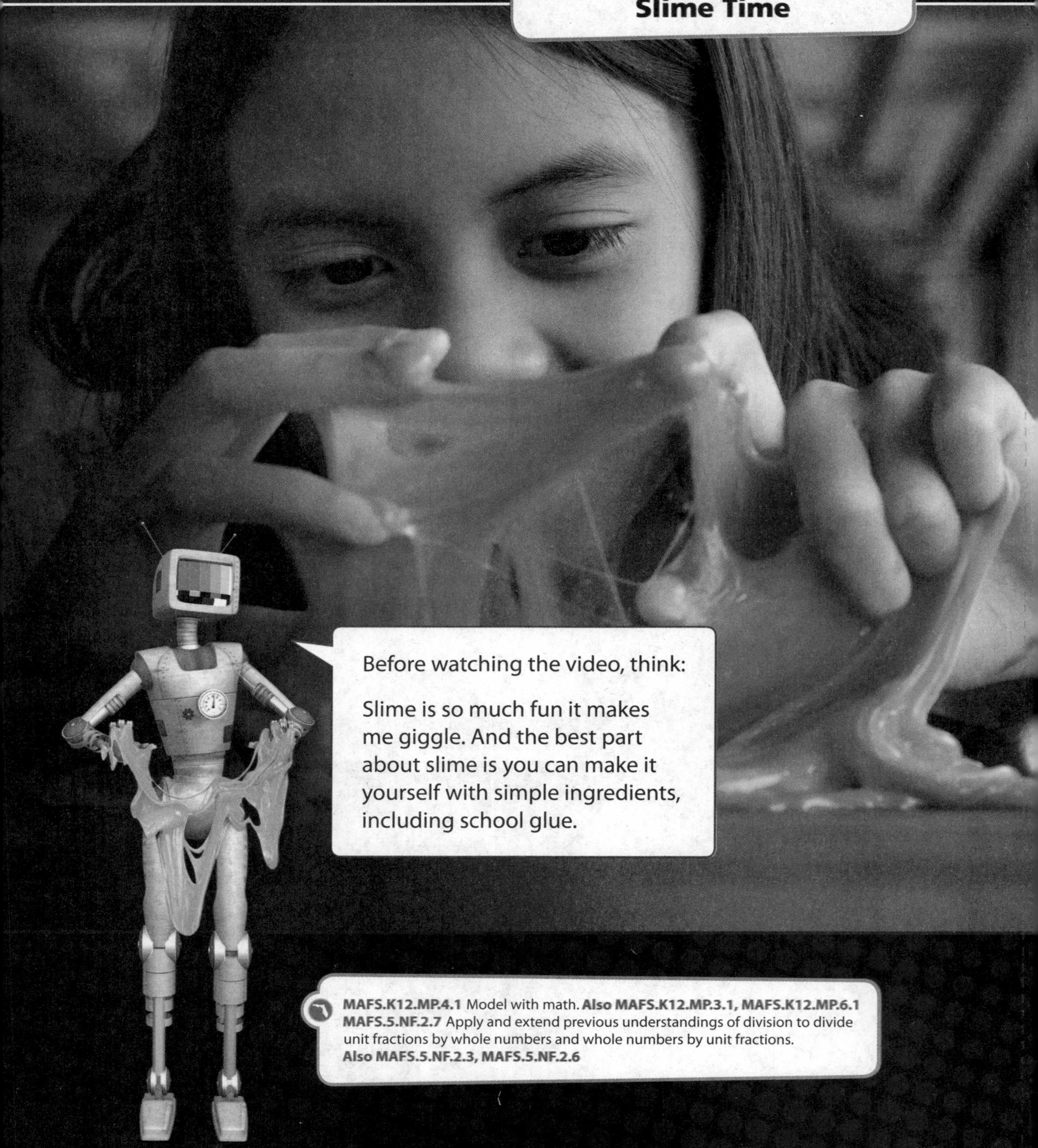

Before watching the video, think:

Slime is so much fun it makes me giggle. And the best part about slime is you can make it yourself with simple ingredients, including school glue.

MAFS.K12.MP.4.1 Model with math. **Also MAFS.K12.MP.3.1, MAFS.K12.MP.6.1**
MAFS.5.NF.2.7 Apply and extend previous understandings of division to divide unit fractions by whole numbers and whole numbers by unit fractions.
Also MAFS.5.NF.2.3, MAFS.5.NF.2.6

© Pearson Education, Inc. 5

Name _____

☆ **Solve & Share**

Four people want waffles for breakfast. There are 6 waffles left. How can 6 waffles be shared equally among 4 people? How much does each person get? Draw a picture and write a division expression to model the problem.

I can ...

understand how fractions are related to division.

MAFS.5.NF.2.3 Interpret a fraction as division of the numerator by the denominator $\left(\frac{a}{b} = a \div b\right)$. Solve word problems involving division of whole numbers leading to answers in the form of fractions or mixed numbers, e.g., by using visual fraction models or equations to represent the problem.
MAFS.K12.MP.1.1, MP.2.1, MP.3.1

You can use a circle to represent each whole waffle.

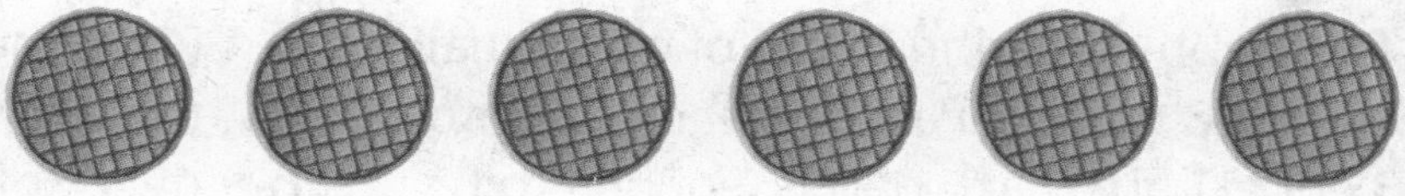

Look Back! **Construct Arguments** One of the waffles was burnt. Explain how they can share 5 waffles equally.

How Are Fractions Related to Division?

A

Tom, Joe, and Sam each made a clay pot in his favorite color. They were given a total of two rolls of clay. If they shared the clay equally, how much clay did each friend use?

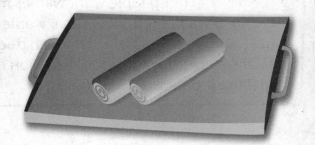

Divide 2 by 3 to find what fraction of the clay each person used.

B ## One Way

Think about sharing 2 rolls of clay equally among 3 people. Partition each roll into 3 equal parts. Each part is $\frac{1}{3}$ of one roll.

 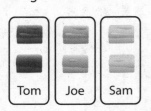

Tom | Joe | Sam

Each person colored one part from each roll of clay for a total of 2 parts.

So, $2 \div 3 = 2 \times \frac{1}{3} = \frac{2}{3}$. Each friend used $\frac{2}{3}$ of a roll of clay.

C ## Another Way

Place the rolls end-to-end and divide the 2 rolls among 3 people. Each person gets $\frac{1}{3}$ of 2 wholes. You can see this with shading on a number line.

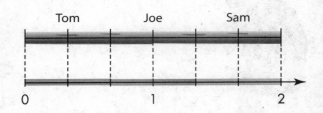

So, $2 \div 3 = \frac{2}{3}$. Each friend used $\frac{2}{3}$ of a roll of clay.

Convince Me! **Reasoning** Amelia is sharing 4 slices of cheese with 5 friends. How much cheese will each person get? Explain how you decided.

Name_____

☆ Guided Practice ☆

Do You Understand?

1. Explain how to write $\frac{3}{10}$ as a division expression.

2. Explain how to write $2 \div 5$ as a fraction.

3. Use the number line below to show $3 \div 4$.

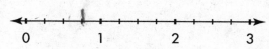

0   1   2   3

Do You Know How?

In **4** and **5**, write a division expression for each fraction.

4. $\frac{1}{9}$

5. $\frac{7}{8}$

In **6** and **7**, tell what fraction each person gets when they share equally.

6. Five friends share 8 apples.

$\frac{8}{5}$

7. Two friends share 1 bagel.

$\frac{1}{2}$

☆ Independent Practice ☆

In **8–12**, write a division expression for each fraction.

8. $\frac{6}{7}$ 9. $\frac{1}{4}$ 10. $\frac{6}{11}$ 11. $\frac{4}{9}$ 12. $\frac{8}{15}$

$6 \div 7$ $4 \div 4$ $6 \div 11$ $4 \div 9$ $8 \div 15$

In **13–17**, write each division expression as a fraction.

13. $9 \div 11$ 14. $1 \div 10$ 15. $7 \div 13$ 16. $11 \div 17$ 17. $25 \div 75$

$9/11$ $1/10$ $7/13$ $11/17$ $25/75$

In **18–21**, tell what fraction each person gets when they share equally.

18. 8 students share 6 breakfast bars.

$8/6$

19. 6 soccer players share 5 oranges.

20. 10 friends share 7 dollars.

21. 8 friends share 8 muffins.

Problem Solving

22. Four friends are baking bread. They equally share 3 sticks of butter. Write an equation to find the fraction of a stick of butter that each friend uses.

$$\frac{3}{4} \qquad 3 \div 4 \qquad 4\overline{)3}$$

3 sticks of butter

23. A group of friends went to the movies. They shared 2 bags of popcorn equally. If each person got $\frac{2}{3}$ of a bag of popcorn, how many people were in the group?

24. Higher Order Thinking Missy says that $\frac{5}{6}$ equals $6 \div 5$. Is she correct? Why or why not?

25. Make Sense and Persevere
The table shows the food and drinks Tabitha bought for herself and 4 friends for her party. How much did Tabitha spend for each person? Show your work.

DATA	Item	Number Bought	Cost Each
	Sandwiches	5	$2.89
	French Fries	5	$1.99
	Pitcher of Juice	2	$4.95

Assessment Practice

26. Which equation is made true with the number 5? 🌴 5.NF.2.3

Ⓐ $2 \div \square = \frac{2}{5}$

Ⓑ $4 \div 20 = \square$

Ⓒ $\square \div 5 = \frac{3}{5}$

Ⓓ $\square \div 6 = \frac{6}{5}$

27. Which equation is made true with the number 3? 🌴 5.NF.2.3

Ⓐ $\square \div 3 = \frac{1}{3}$

Ⓑ $2 \div \square = \frac{3}{2}$

Ⓒ $\square \div 8 = \frac{3}{8}$

Ⓓ $3 \div 9 = \square$

 © Pearson Education, Inc. 5

Name _____

⭐ **Solve & Share**

Jonah has an 8-pound bag of potting soil. He divides it evenly among 5 flowerpots. How much soil is in each pot? Show your answer as a fraction or mixed number. *Solve this problem any way you choose.*

I can ...
show quotients as fractions and mixed numbers.

MAFS.5.NF.2.3 Interpret a fraction as division of the numerator by the denominator $\left(\frac{a}{b} = a \div b\right)$. Solve word problems involving division of whole numbers leading to answers in the form of fractions or mixed numbers, e.g., by using visual fraction models or equations to represent the problem.
MAFS.K12.MP.3.1, MP.6.1

You can write an equation or draw a picture to help find the answer.

Potting Soil
8 lbs

Look Back! **Be Precise** Suppose one of the pots breaks, so Jonah has to divide the soil evenly among 4 pots. How much soil is in each pot then?

How Can You Show a Quotient Using a Fraction or Mixed Number?

A

Three friends are going hiking. They bought a tub of trail mix to share equally. How much will each friend get?

You can divide to share 4 pounds among 3 people: 4 ÷ 3.

B Divide each pound into 3 equal parts.
Each part is $1 \div 3$ or $\frac{1}{3}$.

Each friend gets 1 pound plus $\frac{1}{3}$ of a pound, or $1 + \frac{1}{3} = 1\frac{1}{3}$ pounds of trail mix in all.

So, $4 \div 3 = \frac{4}{3} = 1\frac{1}{3}$.

Convince Me! **Construct Arguments** Kate shares a 64-ounce bottle of apple cider with 5 friends. Each person's serving will be the same number of ounces. Between what two whole number of ounces will each person's serving be? Explain using division.

© Pearson Education, Inc. 5

☆ Guided Practice *

Do You Understand?

1. How can you write $\frac{10}{3}$ as a division expression and as a mixed number?

2. Suppose 3 friends want to share 16 posters equally. For this situation, why does the quotient 5 R1 make more sense than the quotient $5\frac{1}{3}$?

Do You Know How?

3. Find $11 \div 10$ and $10 \div 11$. Write each quotient as a fraction or mixed number.

In **4** and **5**, tell how much each person gets when they share equally.

4. 2 friends share 3 apples.

5. 3 students share 5 breakfast bars.

☆ Independent Practice ☆

In **6–13**, find each quotient. Write each answer as either a fraction or mixed number.

6. $11 \div 6$

7. $1 \div 5$

8. $18 \div 4$

9. $5 \div 9$

10. $9 \div 8$

11. $23 \div 10$

12. $12 \div 17$

13. $28 \div 20$

In **14–17**, tell how much each person gets when they share equally.

14. 2 girls share 7 yards of ribbon.

15. 4 friends share 7 bagels.

16. 4 cousins share 3 pies.

17. 8 soccer players share 12 oranges.

Problem Solving

18. Daniella made gift bows from 8 yards of ribbon. The bows are all the same size. If she made 16 bows, how much ribbon did she use for each one? Give the answer as a fraction or mixed number.

19. Be Precise Tammi has 4 pounds of gala apples and $3\frac{1}{2}$ pounds of red delicious apples. If she uses $1\frac{3}{4}$ pounds of gala apples in a recipe, how many pounds of apples does she have left?

20. Casey bought a 100-pound bag of dog food. He gave his dogs the same amount of dog food each week. The dog food lasted 8 weeks. How much dog food did Casey give his dogs each week? Give the answer as a fraction or mixed number.

21. Higher Order Thinking Write a word problem that can be solved by dividing 6 by 5.

22. The amount of fabric needed for an adult and a baby scarecrow costume is shown at the right. The amount of fabric for an adult scarecrow costume is how many times the amount of fabric for a baby scarecrow costume? Give the answer as a fraction or mixed number.

Baby: 2 yards   Adult: 7 yards

23. Jamal had 37 feet of decorative tape to share with 5 friends and himself. How much tape does each person get? 5.NF.2.3

- Ⓐ $\frac{6}{37}$ feet
- Ⓑ $6\frac{1}{6}$ feet
- Ⓒ $6\frac{5}{6}$ feet
- Ⓓ $6\frac{1}{37}$ feet

24. Lindsay divides 40 by 9. Between what two whole numbers is her answer? 5.NF.2.3

- Ⓐ 2 and 3
- Ⓑ 3 and 4
- Ⓒ 4 and 5
- Ⓓ 5 and 6

   © Pearson Education, Inc. 5

Name _____

Solve & Share

A sandwich shop prepares large wraps and cuts them into fourths. Each fourth is one serving. William buys 5 whole wraps for a party. How many servings in all does he get? *Solve this problem any way you choose.*

I can ...
connect dividing by a fraction to multiplication.

MAFS.5.NF.2.7.b Interpret division of a whole number by a unit fraction, and compute such quotients. **Also 5.NF.2.7.c MAFS.K12.MP.4.1, MP.7.1**

How could fraction strips, bar diagrams, or other models help you visualize the problem?

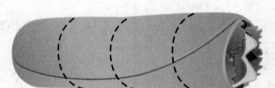

Look Back! **Model with Math** Write an equation that represents the problem about the wraps.

Essential Question

How Is Dividing by a Fraction Related to Multiplication?

A

If a bottle of liquid plant food contains 3 cups, how many plants will you be able to feed? Explain why your answer makes sense.

Plant Food
Use 1/8 cup per plant.

Use $\frac{1}{8}$ cup per plant.

You need to find how many eighths are in 3 cups.
$3 \div \frac{1}{8} = ?$

B How many $\frac{1}{8}$s are in 3?

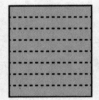 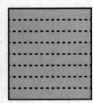 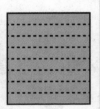

Use a model and multiplication to solve.

Since there are 8 eighths in each whole, there are $3 \times 8 = 24$ eighths in 3 wholes.

So, $3 \div \frac{1}{8} = 24$.

The plant food can feed 24 plants.

C Does the answer make sense?
Do 24 eighths equal 3?

Use multiplication to check.

$24 \times \frac{1}{8} = \frac{24}{8} = 3$

Yes, 24 eighths equals 3, so the answer makes sense.

The inverse relationship between multiplication and division applies to fraction computation, too!

The division equation $3 \div \frac{1}{8} = 24$ is true because the multiplication equation $24 \times \frac{1}{8} = 3$ is true.

Convince Me! Use Structure Use the same numbers in the multiplication equation $15 \times \frac{1}{3} = 5$ to write a division equation. Draw a diagram to show that your division equation makes sense.

© Pearson Education, Inc. 5

Name _____

☆ Guided Practice *

Do You Understand?

1. Explain how to use multiplication to find $4 \div \frac{1}{5}$.

2. Show how to use multiplication to check your answer to Exercise 1.

Do You Know How?

3. Find $3 \div \frac{1}{10}$.

4. Draw a model to find $2 \div \frac{1}{6}$.

5. Use a multiplication equation to check your answer to Exercise 4.

Independent Practice ☆

In **6–9**, use the model to find each quotient. Use multiplication to check your answer.

6. $3 \div \frac{1}{4}$

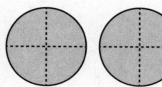

7. $2 \div \frac{1}{12}$

8. $4 \div \frac{1}{9}$

9. $3 \div \frac{1}{6}$

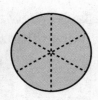

In **10–12**, draw a model to find each quotient. Use multiplication to check your answer.

10. $5 \div \frac{1}{6}$

11. $4 \div \frac{1}{8}$

12. $3 \div \frac{1}{3}$

Problem Solving

13. Model with Math Write and solve a division equation to find the number of $\frac{1}{3}$-pound hamburger patties that can be made from 4 pounds of ground beef.

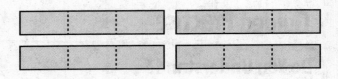

---

14. Write and solve a word problem for the expression $8 \div \frac{1}{2}$.

15. Use the numbers in the multiplication equation $28 \times \frac{1}{7} = 4$ to write a division equation involving division by a fraction.

---

16. Number Sense Sally and Timothy have two different answers for $1{,}785 \div 35$. Without dividing, how can you tell whose answer is wrong?

Sally: $1{,}785 \div 35 = 51$
Timothy: $1{,}785 \div 35 = 501$

17. Higher Order Thinking A restaurant charges $3.50 for a slice of pie that is one sixth of a pie and $3.00 for a slice that is one eighth of a pie. One day they baked 5 pies, all the same size. If they sell all the slices, would they make more money by slicing each pie into sixths or eighths? How much more? Explain.

---

18. Javier drew a model to determine how many fifths are in 6 wholes.

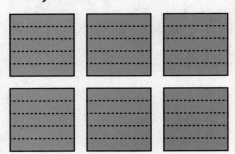

Part A

Describe Javier's work by writing a division equation that includes a fraction. 🐢 5.NF.2.7.b

Part B

Check your answer by using the numbers in your division equation to write a multiplication equation. 🐢 5.NF.2.7.b

   © Pearson Education, Inc. 5

Name _____

Activity

Solve & Share

One ball of dough can be stretched into a circle to make a pizza. After the pizza is cooked, it is cut into 8 equal slices. How many slices of pizza can you make with 3 balls of dough? *Solve this problem any way you choose.*

I can ...
divide a whole number by a unit fraction.

MAFS.5.NF.2.7.b Interpret division of a whole number by a unit fraction, and compute such quotients. Also 5.NF.2.7.c
MAFS.K12.MP.1.1, MP.5.1, MP.7.1

You can use appropriate tools to help find the answer. *Show your work!*

Look Back! Into how many slices of pizza will each ball of dough be divided? What fraction of a whole pizza does 1 slice represent?

How Can You Divide by a Unit Fraction?

A

Joyce is making sushi rolls. She needs $\frac{1}{4}$ cup of rice for each sushi roll. How many sushi rolls can she make if she has 3 cups of rice?

1 cup   1 cup   1 cup

$\frac{1}{4}$ is a unit fraction. A unit fraction is a fraction that describes one part of the whole. So, it has a numerator of 1.

B One Way

Use an area model to find how many $\frac{1}{4}$s are in 3.

There are four $\frac{1}{4}$s in 1 whole cup. So, there are twelve $\frac{1}{4}$s in three whole cups. So, Joyce can make 12 sushi rolls.

You can use multiplication to check your answer.
$3 \times 4 = 12$

C Another Way

Use a number line to find how many $\frac{1}{4}$s are in 3.

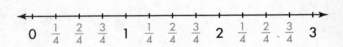

0 $\frac{1}{4}$ $\frac{2}{4}$ $\frac{3}{4}$ 1 $\frac{1}{4}$ $\frac{2}{4}$ $\frac{3}{4}$ 2 $\frac{1}{4}$ $\frac{2}{4}$ $\frac{3}{4}$ 3

You can see that there are four $\frac{1}{4}$s in between each whole number.

There are four $\frac{1}{4}$s in 1 whole, eight $\frac{1}{4}$s in 2 wholes, and twelve $\frac{1}{4}$s in 3 wholes.

So, $3 \div \frac{1}{4} = 12$.

Joyce can make 12 sushi rolls.

Convince Me! **Use Structure** Use the diagram below to find $4 \div \frac{1}{3}$.

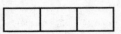 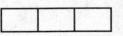 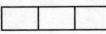 

$4 \div \frac{1}{3} = $ ____

© Pearson Education, Inc. 5

Name _____

Do You Understand?

1. In the example at the top of page 398, if Joyce had 4 cups of rice, how many rolls could she make?

2. In the example at the top of page 398, how does the number line help to show that $3 \div \frac{1}{4}$ is equal to 3×4?

Do You Know How?

In **3** and **4**, use the picture below to find each quotient.

3. How many $\frac{1}{3}$s are in 3?

$3 \div \frac{1}{3} = \underline{9}$

4. How many $\frac{1}{3}$s are in 6?

$6 \div \frac{1}{3} = \underline{18}$

Independent Practice

Leveled Practice In **5** and **6**, use the picture to find each quotient.

5. How many $\frac{1}{6}$s are in 1?

$1 \div \frac{1}{6} = \underline{\hphantom{xx}}$

6. How many $\frac{1}{6}$s are in 5?

$5 \div \frac{1}{6} = \underline{\hphantom{xx}}$

In **7–14**, draw a picture or use a number line to find each quotient. Then use multiplication to check your answer.

7. $4 \div \frac{1}{2}$

$4 \times 2 = 8$

8. $2 \div \frac{1}{8}$

9. $2 \div \frac{1}{3}$

10. $6 \div \frac{1}{4}$

11. $8 \div \frac{1}{3}$

12. $3 \div \frac{1}{10}$

13. $9 \div \frac{1}{8}$

14. $15 \div \frac{1}{5}$

15. Dan has 4 cartons of juice. He pours $\frac{1}{8}$ carton for each person on a camping trip. How many people can he serve? Draw a picture to help you answer the question.

16. **Higher Order Thinking** Write a word problem that can be solved by dividing 10 by $\frac{1}{3}$. Then answer the problem.

17. **Number Sense** The Nile River is the longest river in the world. It is 4,160 miles long. You want to spend three weeks traveling the entire length of the river, traveling about the same number of miles each day. Estimate the number of miles you should travel each day.

18. **Make Sense and Persevere**
Maria used one bag of flour. She baked two loaves of bread. Then she used the remaining flour to make 48 muffins. How much flour was in the bag when Maria began?

DATA	Recipe	Amount of Flour Needed
	Bread	$2\frac{1}{4}$ cups per loaf
	Muffins	$3\frac{1}{4}$ cups per 24 muffins
	Pizza	$1\frac{1}{2}$ cups per pie

Assessment Practice

19. Deron is making light switch plates from pieces of wood. He starts with a board that is 18 feet long. How many light switch plates can he make? 5.NF.2.7.b

   Ⓐ 9 light switch plates

   Ⓑ 24 light switch plates

   Ⓒ 27 light switch plates

   Ⓓ 54 light switch plates

DATA	Wood Projects	
	Item	**Length Needed for Each**
	Cabinet Shelf	$\frac{3}{4}$ foot
	Light Switch Plate	$\frac{1}{3}$ foot
	Shingle	$\frac{2}{3}$ foot

© Pearson Education, Inc. 5

Solve & Share

Yesterday, the cooking club made a pan of lasagna. They left half of the lasagna for 4 members of the photography club to share equally. What fraction of the pan of lasagna did each photography club member get? *Solve this problem any way you choose.*

I can ...
divide a unit fraction by a non-zero whole number.

MAFS.5.NF.2.7.a Interpret division of a unit fraction by a non-zero whole number, and compute such quotients. **Also 5.NF.2.7.c** MAFS.K12.MP.2.1, MP.3.1, MP.5.1

You can use appropriate tools to show how to divide what is left. *Show your work!*

Look Back! What equation can you write to model this problem?

Essential Question

How Can You Model Dividing a Unit Fraction by a Whole Number?

A

Half of a pan of cornbread is left over. Ann, Beth, and Chuck are sharing the leftovers equally. What fraction of the original cornbread does each person get?

You can make a drawing to show $\frac{1}{2}$ of the cornbread.

B ## One Way

On an area model, divide $\frac{1}{2}$ into 3 equal parts.

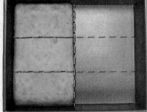

$$\frac{1}{2} \div 3$$

Each part contains $\frac{1}{6}$ of the whole.

$$\frac{1}{2} \div 3 = \frac{1}{6}$$

Each person gets $\frac{1}{6}$ of the cornbread.

C ## Another Way

Use a number line. Shade $\frac{1}{2}$ on the number line. Partition $\frac{1}{2}$ into 3 equal parts.

$$\frac{1}{2} \div 3 \qquad \begin{array}{ccccccc} 0 & \frac{1}{6} & \frac{2}{6} & \frac{1}{2} & \frac{4}{6} & \frac{5}{6} & 1 \end{array}$$

Each part is $\frac{1}{6}$.

$$\frac{1}{2} \div 3 = \frac{1}{6}$$

Each person gets $\frac{1}{6}$ of the cornbread.

Convince Me! **Reasoning** In the example above, how is dividing by 3 the same as multiplying by $\frac{1}{3}$?

© Pearson Education, Inc. 5

Name _____

☆ Guided Practice *

Do You Understand?

1. In the example at the top of page 402, suppose that 4 people were sharing half of the cornbread equally. What fraction of the original cornbread would each person get? Draw a picture or use objects to help.

2. When you divide a unit fraction by a non-zero whole number greater than 1, will the quotient be greater than or less than the unit fraction?

Do You Know How?

In **3–6**, find each quotient. Use the picture or objects to help.

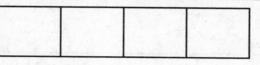

3. $\frac{1}{4} \div 2$ 4. $\frac{1}{4} \div 4$

5. $\frac{1}{2} \div 2$ 6. $\frac{1}{2} \div 4$

☆ Independent Practice ☆

Leveled Practice In **7** and **8**, find each quotient. Use a picture or objects to help.

7. $\frac{1}{2} \div 5$

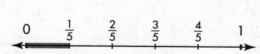

8. $\frac{1}{5} \div 2$

0    $\frac{1}{5}$ $\frac{2}{5}$ $\frac{3}{5}$ $\frac{4}{5}$ 1

Partitioning pictures or objects can help when dividing fractions by a whole number.

In **9–14**, find each quotient.

9. $\frac{1}{2} \div 7 = 1/14$ 10. $\frac{1}{4} \div 3 = 1/12$ 11. $\frac{1}{6} \div 2 = 1/12$

12. $\frac{1}{3} \div 4 = 1/12$ 13. $\frac{1}{4} \div 5 \; 1/20$ 14. $\frac{1}{5} \div 3 = 1/15$

*For another example, see Set C on page 419.

Problem Solving

15. Vin, Corrie, Alexa, and Joe equally shared one fourth of a submarine sandwich. What fraction of the original sandwich did each friend get? Use the number line to help you find the answer.

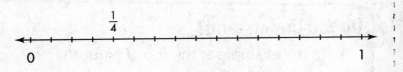

16. Sue has $\frac{1}{2}$ gallon of milk to share evenly among four people. How much milk, in gallons, should she give each person?

17. Critique Reasoning Taryn says that $\frac{1}{4}$ of a cereal bar is larger than $\frac{1}{3}$ of the cereal bar. Is she correct? Explain.

18. Algebra On Saturday, Amir ran $1\frac{3}{4}$ miles, and Janie ran $2\frac{1}{2}$ miles. Who ran farther? How much farther? Write an equation to find d, the difference of the two distances.

19. Higher Order Thinking Five friends equally shared half of one large pizza and $\frac{1}{4}$ of another large pizza. What fraction of each pizza did each friend get? How do the two amounts compare to each other?

Assessment Practice

20. Jamie cut a rope into thirds. He used two of the pieces to make a swing. He used equal lengths of the leftover rope on four picture frames. What fraction of the original rope did he use for each picture frame? 5.NF.2.7.a

Ⓐ $\frac{1}{4}$

Ⓑ $\frac{1}{12}$

Ⓒ $\frac{1}{16}$

Ⓓ $\frac{3}{4}$

21. One half of an apple pie is left for 5 family members to share equally. What fraction of the original pie will each member get? 5.NF.2.7.a

Ⓐ $\frac{1}{10}$

Ⓑ $\frac{1}{7}$

Ⓒ $\frac{1}{3}$

Ⓓ $\frac{2}{5}$

© Pearson Education, Inc. 5

Name _____

☆ **Solve & Share**

The Brown family is planting $\frac{1}{3}$ of their garden with flowers, $\frac{1}{3}$ with berries, and $\frac{1}{3}$ with vegetables. The vegetable section has equal parts of carrots, onions, peppers, and tomatoes. What fraction of the garden is planted with carrots? *Solve this problem any way you choose.*

Activity

MAFS.5.NF.2.7.a Interpret division of a unit fraction by a non-zero whole number, and compute such quotients. **Also 5.NF.2.7.b, 5.NF.2.7.c**
MAFS.K12.MP.1.1, MP.2.1, MP.4.1

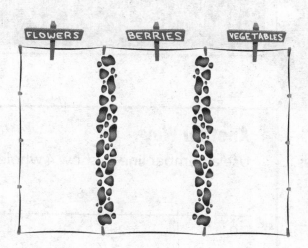

How can you show an equal share of each vegetable?

Look Back! **Model with Math** Write an equation that models this problem. Explain your reasoning.

Essential Question

How Can You Divide with Unit Fractions and Whole Numbers?

A

A utility company is planning to install wind turbines on 4 square miles of land. Each turbine requires $\frac{1}{6}$ square mile of land. How many turbines can be installed?

Model the problem with a picture or an equation to help you.

B ## One Way

Use an area model to show 4 square miles. Divide each square mile into 6 equal parts to represent $\frac{1}{6}$ square mile.

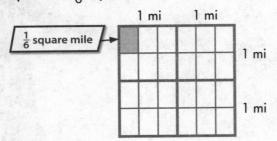

$\frac{1}{6}$ square mile

1 mi   1 mi

1 mi

1 mi

There are 24 parts.
So, 24 wind turbines will fit on the land.

C ## Another Way

Use a number line to show 4 wholes.

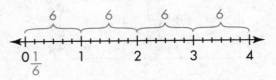

There are 6 $\frac{1}{6}$s in each whole.

So, there are 24 $\frac{1}{6}$s in 4 wholes.

$4 \div \frac{1}{6} = 24$

24 wind turbines will fit on the land.

Convince Me! **Reasoning** Use an area model to find $2 \div \frac{1}{4}$. Then use multiplication to check your answer.

© Pearson Education, Inc. 5

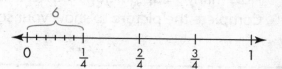

Another Example

Use a number line to find $\frac{1}{4} \div 6$.

If you partition $\frac{1}{4}$ into 6 equal segments, how long is each segment?

$\frac{1}{4} \div 6 = \frac{1}{24}$

Check your answer using multiplication: $\frac{1}{24} \times 6 = \frac{1}{4}$.

☆ Guided Practice *

Do You Understand?

1. When you divide a whole number by a fraction less than 1, will the quotient be greater than or less than the whole number?

2. 4 square miles of land is separated into sections that each have an area of $\frac{1}{2}$ square mile. How many sections are there?

$4 \div \frac{1}{2}$

Do You Know How?

In **3–6**, find each quotient.

3. $2 \div \frac{1}{4}$ 4. $3 \div \frac{1}{4}$

5. $\frac{1}{6} \div 2$ 6. $2 \div \frac{1}{3}$

Draw a number line or use a model to help you find the answers!

Independent Practice ☆

Leveled Practice In **7–10**, find each quotient. Use a model or number line to help.

7. $5 \div \frac{1}{2}$

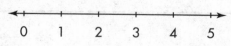

8. $\frac{1}{2} \div 5$

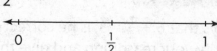

9. $6 \div \frac{1}{3}$

10. $\frac{1}{3} \div 6$

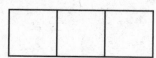

Problem Solving

11. Keiko divided 5 cups of milk into $\frac{1}{4}$-cup portions. How many $\frac{1}{4}$-cup portions did Keiko have? Complete the picture to show your solution.

12. Algebra Ms. Allen has $\frac{1}{8}$ of a pan of brownies left to divide between 2 children. Draw a picture to find what fraction, f, of the original pan of brownies each child gets. Write an equation for f that models the solution.

13. Make Sense and Persevere A regular polygon has a perimeter of 2 feet. If each side measures $\frac{1}{3}$ foot, what is the name of the polygon?

A regular polygon has equal side lengths and equal angle measures.

14. Higher Order Thinking Mr. Brent uses $\frac{1}{4}$ cup of blue paint and $\frac{1}{4}$ cup of yellow paint to make each batch of green paint. How many batches of green paint can he make with the amount of paint he has left? Explain how you found your answer.

DATA	Paint Color	Amount Left
	Blue	3 cups
	Red	2 cups
	Yellow	4 cups

15. Jordan says that $6 \div \frac{1}{2} = 3$. Is he correct? If not, justify your reasoning and give the correct quotient. 🔹 5.NF.2.7.a

Name _____

Solve & Share

Organizers of an architectural tour need to set up information tables every $\frac{1}{8}$ mile along the 6-mile tour, beginning $\frac{1}{8}$ mile from the start of the tour. Each table needs 2 signs. How many signs do the organizers need? **Solve this problem any way you choose.**

I can ...
solve division problems involving unit fractions.

MAFS.5.NF.2.7.c Solve real world problems involving division of unit fractions by non-zero whole numbers and division of whole numbers by unit fractions, e.g., by using visual fraction models and equations to represent the problem. Also 5.NF.2.7.b
MAFS.K12.MP.1.1, MP.2.1

0   1   2   3   4   5   6

Make Sense and Persevere What steps do you need to do to solve this problem? *Show your work!*

Look Back! How does the number line help you solve this problem?

How Can You Solve Division Problems with Unit Fractions?

A

John plans to buy sheets of plywood like the ones shown to make boxes with lids. Each box is a cube that has $\frac{1}{3}$-foot edges. How many sheets of plywood does John need in order to make 5 boxes with lids?

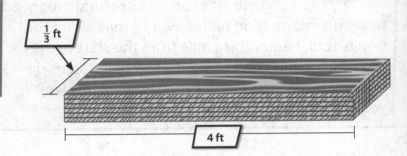

$\frac{1}{3}$ ft

4 ft

Remember, a cube has 6 identical faces.

B **What do you know?**

Six pieces of plywood are needed for each of the 5 boxes.

Boxes are $\frac{1}{3}$-foot cubes.

Each sheet of plywood is $\frac{1}{3}$ foot wide and 4 feet long.

What are you asked to find?

The number of sheets of plywood John needs to buy

C **Write an equation to help answer each question.**

1. How many pieces of plywood are needed for 5 boxes with lids?

   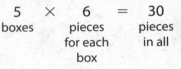

5	×	6	=	30
boxes		pieces for each box		pieces in all

2. How many pieces can be cut from 1 sheet of plywood?

   $4 \div \frac{1}{3} = 12$

   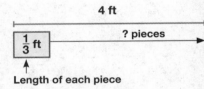

   4 ft

   $\frac{1}{3}$ ft   ? pieces

   Length of each piece

3. How many sheets of plywood does John need for 5 boxes with lids?

   $30 \div 12 = 2\ R6$

   John needs 3 sheets of plywood.

Convince Me! **Reasoning** Write a real-world problem that can be solved by first adding 24 and 36 and then dividing by $\frac{1}{4}$. Find the solution to your problem and explain your answer.

Name_____

☆ Guided Practice*

Do You Understand?

1. In the example on page 410, why were additional questions answered to help solve the problem?

2. What equations were used to solve the example on page 410?

Do You Know How?

3. Tamara needs tiles to make a border for her bathroom wall. The border will be 9 feet long and $\frac{1}{3}$ foot wide. Each tile measures $\frac{1}{3}$ foot by $\frac{1}{3}$ foot. Each box of tiles contains 6 tiles. How many boxes of tiles does Tamara need? Write two equations that can be used to solve the problem.

☆ Independent Practice ☆

Write the equations needed to solve each problem. Then solve.

4. Robert wants to use all the ingredients listed in the table at the right to make trail mix. How many $\frac{1}{2}$-pound packages can he make?

Equations: _____

Answer: _____

DATA	Ingredient	Weight (in pounds)
	Dried Apples	$2\frac{1}{2}$
	Pecans	4
	Raisins	$1\frac{1}{2}$

5. Rachel used $\frac{2}{3}$ of a package of cornbread mix. She will use equal parts of the leftover mix to make 2 batches of cornbread. What fraction of the original package will she use for each batch?

Equations: _____

Answer: _____

Problem Solving

6. **Make Sense and Persevere** Sandra is making vegetable soup. If she makes 12 cups of soup, how many cups of onions does she need? Use the data table on the right. Write the equations needed to solve the problem. Then solve.

Vegetable	Amount Needed for 3 Cups of Soup
Carrots	$\frac{1}{3}$ cup
Onions	$\frac{1}{8}$ cup
Peas	$\frac{1}{4}$ cup

7. Emily needs to buy fabric to make curtain panels for her windows. Each panel will be 4 feet long and $\frac{1}{2}$ foot wide. Each piece of fabric that she can buy is 4 feet long and 2 feet wide. How many panels can she make from 1 piece of fabric?

8. **Algebra** Barry buys a package of pasta for $2.39 and a jar of tomato sauce for $3.09. He uses a $0.75 coupon and a $0.50 coupon. What is the total cost of Barry's purchase? Write an expression to show your work.

9. **Higher Order Thinking** Mr. Moss had 4 gallons of paint. He painted 8 doors. How many benches can he paint with the paint that is left? Show your work.

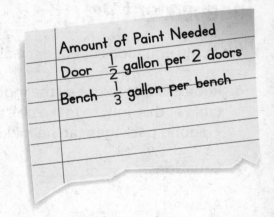

Amount of Paint Needed
Door $\frac{1}{2}$ gallon per 2 doors
Bench $\frac{1}{3}$ gallon per bench

Assessment Practice

10. Sophia uses $\frac{1}{2}$ pound of white flour to make one loaf of bread and $\frac{1}{4}$ pound of cake flour to make one cake. Which shows how many cakes and loaves of bread Sophia can make with the amount of flour that she has? 5.NF.2.7.c

Flour in Pantry	
Kind of Flour	Amount
Cake	3 pounds
White	2 pounds
Whole Wheat	4 pounds

Ⓐ 12 cakes, 4 loaves of bread

Ⓑ 6 cakes, 8 loaves of bread

Ⓒ 8 cakes, 6 loaves of bread

Ⓓ 4 cakes, 12 loaves of bread

© Pearson Education, Inc. 5

Name _____

Solve & Share

What do you notice about the calculations below? Make a generalization about what you notice. Complete the remaining examples.

Sue's Equations	Randy's Equations
$4 \div \frac{1}{3} = 12$ $\longrightarrow$	$\frac{1}{3} \div 4 = \frac{1}{12}$
$8 \div \frac{1}{10} = 80$ $\longrightarrow$	$\frac{1}{10} \div 8 = \frac{1}{80}$
$5 \div \frac{1}{4} = 20$ $\longrightarrow$	$\frac{1}{4} \div 5 = \frac{1}{20}$
$12 \div \frac{1}{2} = $ ____ $\longrightarrow$	$\frac{1}{2} \div 12 = $ ____
$6 \div \frac{1}{100} = $ ____ $\longrightarrow$	$\frac{1}{100} \div 6 = $ ____

I can ...

notice repetition in calculations and describe a general method for dividing whole numbers and unit fractions.

MAFS.K12.MP.8.1 Repeated reasoning. **Also MP.2.1, MP.4.1**
MAFS.5.NF.2.7.a Interpret division of a unit fraction by a non-zero whole number, and compute such quotients.

Thinking Habits

Be a good thinker! These questions can help you.

- Are any calculations repeated?

- Can I generalize from examples?

- What shortcuts do I notice?

Look Back! **Generalize** Test your general method by writing another pair of equations like Sue's and Randy's equations.

Essential Question

How Do You Use Repeated Reasoning When Dividing Whole Numbers and Unit Fractions?

Visual Learning Bridge

A

Ali partitioned a 4-foot board into $\frac{1}{2}$-foot pieces. She counted 8 pieces.

Then she partitioned a $\frac{1}{2}$-foot board into 4 equal pieces. Each piece was $\frac{1}{8}$ of a foot.

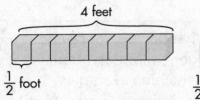

4 feet

$\frac{1}{2}$ foot

4

$\frac{1}{2}$ foot

Study the equations below. What generalizations can you make? Explain.

$$4 \div \frac{1}{2} = 8 \qquad \frac{1}{2} \div 4 = \frac{1}{8}$$

$$4 \times 2 = 8 \qquad \frac{1}{2} \times \frac{1}{4} = \frac{1}{8}$$

What do I need to do?

I need to understand the equations and make generalizations about them.

B

How can I make a generalization from repeated reasoning?

I can

- look for things that repeat in a problem.

- test whether my generalization works for other numbers.

C

I see that

$$4 \div \frac{1}{2} = 4 \times 2 \text{ and } \frac{1}{2} \div 4 = \frac{1}{2} \times \frac{1}{4}.$$

Here's my thinking...

Check if the same relationship applies to other numbers.

$$10 \div \frac{1}{3} = 30 \text{ and } 10 \times 3 = 30$$

$$\frac{1}{3} \div 10 = \frac{1}{30} \text{ and } \frac{1}{3} \times \frac{1}{10} = \frac{1}{30}$$

Dividing a whole number by a unit fraction is the same as multiplying a whole number by the denominator of the unit fraction.

Dividing a unit fraction by a whole number other than zero is the same as multiplying the unit fraction by a unit fraction with the whole number as the denominator.

Convince Me! **Generalize** Marcus made the following generalization: $12 \div \frac{1}{5} = \frac{1}{12} \times \frac{1}{5}$. Is he correct? Explain.

© Pearson Education, Inc. 5

☆ Guided Practice*

Generalize

Nathan has two 8-foot boards. He cuts one board into $\frac{1}{4}$-foot pieces. He cuts the other board into $\frac{1}{2}$-foot pieces.

1. Write and solve a division equation to find how many $\frac{1}{4}$-ft pieces can be cut from an 8-foot board. Explain your reasoning.

> Repeated reasoning can help you find a general method for solving problems that are the same type.

2. Find how many $\frac{1}{2}$-ft pieces can be cut from the 8-foot board. Can you repeat the method you used in Exercise 1 to solve this problem? Explain.

☆ Independent Practice ☆

Generalize

A landscaper's truck is filled with $\frac{1}{2}$ ton of gravel. The gravel is shared equally among 3 projects.

> Remember, the method for dividing a whole number by a unit fraction is different from the method for dividing a unit fraction by a whole number.

3. Write and solve a division equation to find how much gravel each project will get. Explain your reasoning.

4. Suppose another truck is filled with $\frac{1}{2}$ ton of gravel. Find how much gravel each project will get if the $\frac{1}{2}$ ton of gravel is shared equally among 8 projects. Can you repeat the method you used in Exercise 3 to solve this problem? Explain.

Problem Solving

Pet Food

Karl has a cat and a dog. He buys one bag of cat food and one bag of dog food. How many $\frac{1}{4}$-lb servings of cat food can he get from one bag? How many $\frac{1}{2}$-lb servings of dog food can he get from one bag?

DATA	Pet Food	Bag Size
	Fish	5 lb
	Cat	12 lb
	Dog	20 lb

5. Reasoning Karl thinks that he will be able to get more servings of dog food than cat food because the bag of dog food weighs more than the bag of cat food. Do you agree with his reasoning? Explain. 5.NF.2.7.a, MP.2.1

6. Model with Math Write a division and a multiplication equation that Karl could use to find the number of servings of cat food in one bag. 5.NF.2.7.a, MP.4.1

When you use repeated reasoning, you notice repetition in calculations.

7. Generalize What generalization can you make that relates the division equation to the multiplication equation you wrote in Exercise 6? 5.NF.2.7.a, MP.8.1

8. Generalize Find how many servings of dog food are in one bag. Can you repeat the method you used in Exercise 6 to solve this problem? Explain. 5.NF.2.7.a, MP.8.1

© Pearson Education, Inc. 5

Name _____

Follow the Path

Solve each problem. Follow problems with an answer of 3,456 to shade a path from **START** to **FINISH**. You can only move up, down, right, or left.

I can ...
multiply multi-digit whole numbers.

 MAFS.5.NBT.2.5

Start				
576 × 6	101 × 34	350 × 16	436 × 16	127 × 28
96 × 36	462 × 13	64 × 54	48 × 72	144 × 24
108 × 32	192 × 18	288 × 12	82 × 42	216 × 16
303 × 12	317 × 48	456 × 11	2,586 × 12	128 × 27
66 × 51	286 × 40	360 × 36	230 × 56	384 × 9
				Finish

TOPIC 9 | Vocabulary Review

A-Z
Glossary

Word List
- dividend
- divisor
- factor
- inverse operations
- product
- quotient
- unit fraction

Understand Vocabulary

Write *always*, *sometimes*, or *never*.

1. A whole number divided by a fraction less than 1 is a mixed number. _____

2. The answer to a division problem is greater than the dividend. _____

3. A fraction less than 1 divided by a whole number is a whole number. _____

4. Dividing by $\frac{1}{2}$ means you are finding how many halves are in the dividend.

   _____

5. The dividend is the greatest number in a division problem. _____

6. A whole number can be written as a fraction with 1 as the denominator. _____

Draw a line from each number in Column A to the correct answer in Column B.

Column A

Column B

7. $\frac{1}{3} \div 6$ 12

8. $3 \div \frac{1}{2}$ 2

9. $2 \div \frac{1}{6}$ 6

10. $\frac{1}{6} \div 2$ $\frac{1}{18}$

                        $\frac{1}{12}$

Use Vocabulary in Writing

11. Explain how to use what you know about whole number division to check your work when you divide with fractions. Use at least three terms from the Word List in your explanation.

     © Pearson Education, Inc. 5

Set A pages 385–388, 389–392

You can represent the fraction $\frac{3}{4}$ as division.

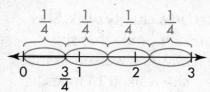

Think: $\frac{1}{4}$ of 3 wholes.

So, $\frac{3}{4} = 3 \div 4$.

Remember that any fraction can be represented as division of the numerator by the denominator.

Reteaching

> Write a division expression for each fraction.

1. $\frac{7}{9}$ 2. $\frac{11}{17}$ 3. $\frac{10}{3}$

7÷9   √÷17   10÷3

> Write each expression as a fraction or mixed number.

4. $7 \div 12$ 5. $13 \div 20$

7/12   13/20

6. $9 \div 5$ 7. $17 \div 7$

9/5 $2\frac{3}{7}$

Set B pages 393–396, 397–400

A 4-foot board is cut into pieces that are $\frac{1}{2}$ foot in length. How many pieces are there?

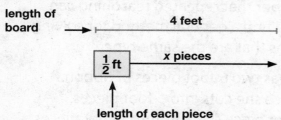

$4 \div \frac{1}{2} = 4 \times 2 = 8$

There are 8 pieces.

Remember that you can use multiplication to check your answer.

1. A 12-foot-long playground is marked off into $\frac{1}{5}$-foot-long sections for a game. How many sections are there?

60/5

2. A 4-pound package of peanuts is divided into $\frac{1}{4}$-pound packages. How many $\frac{1}{4}$-pound packages are there?

16

Set C pages 401–404, 405–408

Find $\frac{1}{2} \div 4$.

Use a number line. Partition $\frac{1}{2}$ into 4 equal parts.

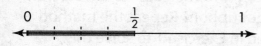

Each part is $\frac{1}{8}$.

So, $\frac{1}{2} \div 4 = \frac{1}{8}$.

Remember that you can use objects or a number line to help you divide.

1. $\frac{1}{3} \div 2$ 2. $\frac{1}{7} \div 7$

2/6   7/49

3. $\frac{1}{2} \div 8$ 4. $\frac{1}{8} \div 2$

1/16   2/16

5. $7 \div \frac{1}{2}$ 6. $25 \div \frac{1}{6}$

14   1/50

Set D pages 409–412

Helen has $97 in quarters and half dollars combined. She has $13 in quarters. How many half dollars does she have?

How much does Helen have in half dollars?

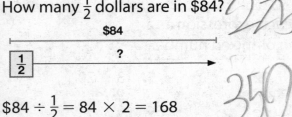

$97 − $13 = $84

How many $\frac{1}{2}$ dollars are in $84?

$84 ÷ \frac{1}{2}$ = 84 × 2 = 168

Helen has 168 half dollars.

Set E pages 413–416

Think about these questions to help you use **repeated reasoning** when solving division problems.

Thinking Habits

- Are any calculations repeated?

- Can I generalize from examples?

- What shortcuts do I notice?

Remember to read the problem carefully and make sure that you answer the right question and that your answer makes sense.

1. Ana participated in a charity walk. She raised $0.25 for each $\frac{1}{2}$ mile that she walked. The first day, Ana walked 11 miles. The second day, she walked 14 miles. How much money did Ana raise?

$350

2. Mr. Holms used $\frac{4}{5}$ of a carton of orange juice. He used equal amounts of the leftover juice for 2 servings. What fraction of the whole carton of juice did he use for each serving?

$\frac{1}{5}$

Remember that repeated reasoning can help you find a general method for solving problems that are the same type.

Teresa has two 6-foot pieces of ribbon. One piece she cuts into $\frac{1}{4}$-foot pieces. The other piece she cuts into $\frac{1}{2}$-foot pieces.

1. How many $\frac{1}{4}$-foot pieces can she cut from one piece of ribbon? Explain.

24

2. How many $\frac{1}{2}$-foot pieces can be cut from the 6-foot ribbon? Repeat the method you used in Exercise 1 to solve this problem.

© Pearson Education, Inc. 5

1. If the diameter of a tree trunk is growing $\frac{1}{4}$ inch each year, how many years will it take for the diameter to grow 8 inches? Explain how you found your answer.

2. Select all the equations that the number 4 will make true.

- [ ] $1 \div 4 = ?$
- [ ] $5 \div ? = \frac{4}{5}$
- [x] $? \div 7 = \frac{4}{7}$
- [x] $2 \div ? = \frac{1}{2}$
- [ ] $4 \div ? = 16$

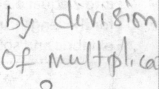
by division.
Of multiplication
$\frac{2}{4} =$

3. Mrs. Webster wants to divide 6 pints of water into $\frac{1}{3}$-pint servings. How many servings are possible? Explain how you found your answer.

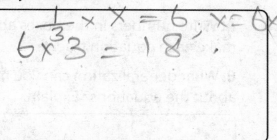
$\frac{1}{3} \times X = 6$, $x = 6 \times 3$
$6 \times 3 = 18$.

4. How many $\frac{1}{8}$s are in 25? What multiplication equation can you use to check your answer?

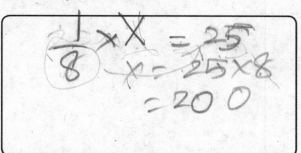
$\frac{1}{8} \times X = 25$
$x = 25 \times 8$
$= 200$

5. Raven is making pillows. She needs $\frac{1}{5}$ yard of fabric for each pillow. If she has 6 yards of fabric, how many pillows can she make? Use the number line. Choose the equation that represents the problem.

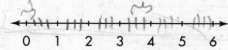

Ⓐ $\frac{1}{5} \div 6 = \frac{1}{30}$ Ⓒ $6 + 5 = 11$

Ⓑ $6 + \frac{1}{5} = \frac{7}{5}$ Ⓓ $6 \div \frac{1}{5} = 30$

6. A farmer owns 24 acres of land. He plans to use 6 acres for an entrance into the farm and partition the remaining land into $\frac{1}{3}$-acre lots. How many $\frac{1}{3}$-acre lots will he have?

$18 = X \times \frac{1}{3} = 18 \times 3$

Ⓐ 6 lots   Ⓒ 54 lots

Ⓑ 18 lots   Ⓓ 72 lots

$18 \times 3 = 54$

7. One half of a cantaloupe was shared equally among 3 people. What fraction of the whole cantaloupe did each person get? Explain how you found your answer.

1/6

8. Cecil and three friends ran a 15-mile relay race. Each friend ran an equal distance. Use an equation to find the distance each friend ran.

9. Match each expression to its quotient.

	$\frac{3}{4}$	12	$\frac{1}{12}$	$1\frac{1}{3}$
$4 \div 3$	☐	☐	☐	☑
$4 \div \frac{1}{3}$	☐	☑	☐	☐
$3 \div 4$	☑	☐	☐	☐
$\frac{1}{3} \div 4$	☐	☐	☑	☐

10. A. Select all the expressions that are equal to $\frac{1}{6}$.

☐ $6 \div 1$ ☑ $1 \div 6$

☑ $3 \div 18$ ☑ $\frac{1}{3} \div 2$

☐ $2 \div \frac{1}{3}$

B. How can you check your answer?

11. Josie has a rug with an area of 18 square feet that is 6 feet long and 3 feet wide. She will put the rug on a floor that is covered in $\frac{1}{3}$-square-foot tiles. How many tiles will the rug cover? What equation can you use to check your answer?

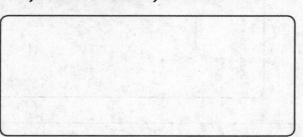

12. Ellen says that $1\frac{2}{5}$ equals $5 \div 7$. Is she correct? Explain.

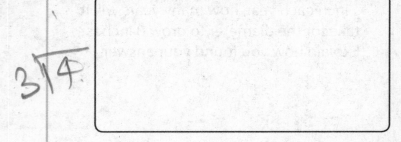

13. Corey has a piece of fabric that is $\frac{1}{4}$ yard long. He cuts the length of the fabric into 2 equal pieces. Write an expression for the length, in yards, of each piece of fabric and solve.

14. Look at the equations below.

$8 \div \frac{1}{3} = \square$ $2 \div \frac{1}{9} = \square$

$8 \times 3 = \square$ $2 \times 9 = \square$

A. Write numbers in the boxes above to make each equation true.

B. What generalization can you make about the equations? Explain.

© Pearson Education, Inc. 5

Making Cloth Dolls

Julie and Erin are making cloth dolls for the craft fair. The figure below shows some of the materials they need for each doll.

1. The **Julie and Erin's Supplies** table shows the amounts they have of some of the materials they need.

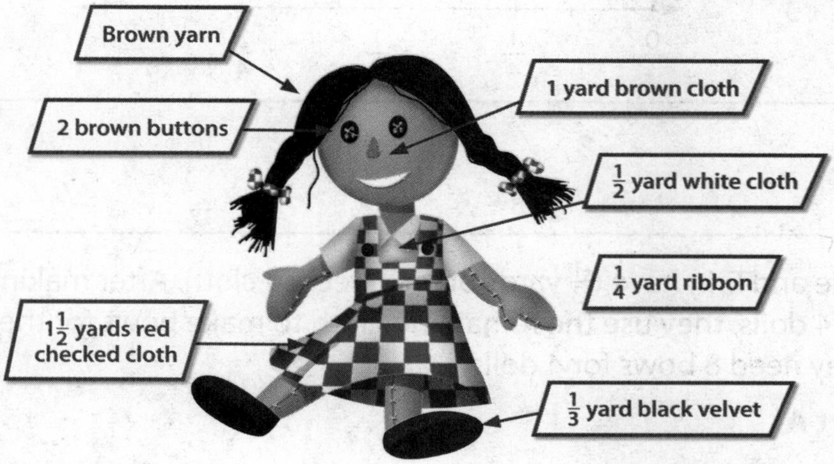

Brown yarn

2 brown buttons

1 yard brown cloth

$\frac{1}{2}$ yard white cloth

$\frac{1}{4}$ yard ribbon

$1\frac{1}{2}$ yards red checked cloth

$\frac{1}{3}$ yard black velvet

Part A

If Julie and Erin use the brown yarn they have to make 4 dolls, how much yarn can they use for each doll? Show your work. 🐊 5.NF.2.3

Part B

How many dolls can Julie and Erin make with the amount of black velvet they have? Complete the model to represent the problem. 🐊 5.NF.2.7.b

$\dfrac{2 \times 3}{1}$

Julie and Erin's Supplies	
Supply	**Amount**
Buttons	9
Brown yarn	10 yd
Black velvet	4 yd
White cloth	5 yd

Part C

How many dolls can Julie and Erin make with the amount of white cloth they have? Write an equation to represent the problem. Use multiplication to check your answer. 🐊 5.NF.2.7.b

Part D

The ribbon used for each doll is divided into 3 equal pieces. What is the length in yards of each piece? Complete the number line to solve.

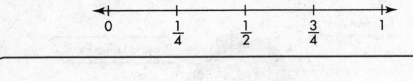

2. Julie and Erin have $6\frac{1}{3}$ yards of red checked cloth. After making dresses for 4 dolls, they use the remaining cloth to make bows for the dolls' hair. They need 8 bows for 4 dolls.

Part A

How much cloth do Julie and Erin have for each bow? Explain. 5.NF.2.3

Part B

Julie wrote the equations shown. What is the pattern in her equations? Explain how to use the pattern to find the quotient you found in Part A. 5.NF.2.7.a, MP.8.1

Julie's Equations

$$\frac{1}{2} \div 3 = \frac{1}{2} \times \frac{1}{3} = \frac{1}{6}$$

$$\frac{1}{3} \div 3 = \frac{1}{3} \times \frac{1}{3} = \frac{1}{9}$$

$$\frac{1}{2} \div 4 = \frac{1}{2} \times \frac{1}{4} = \frac{1}{8}$$

$$\frac{1}{3} \div 4 = \frac{1}{3} \times \frac{1}{4} = \frac{1}{12}$$

© Pearson Education, Inc. 5

Represent and Interpret Data

Essential Question: How can line plots be used to represent data and answer questions?

Digital Resources

Interactive Student Edition · Activity · Visual Learning · Video · Practice

Assessment · Games · Tools · Glossary

Wildfires help nature by burning away dead plant material.

Lightning can cause wildfires. But did you know human activities cause 9 out of 10 wildfires?

MAFS.5.MD.2.2, 5.NBT.1.4, 5.NF.1.2, 5.NF.2.6

MAFS.K12.MP.1.1, MP.2.1, MP.3.1, MP.4.1, MP.6.1, MP.8.1

I'm shocked! It's time for some trailblazing research! Here's a project about wildfires.

enVision STEM Project: Wildfires

Do Research Use the Internet and other sources to learn more about wildfires. Investigate how wildfires affect ecosystems. Explore the costs and benefits of wildfires. List five living things in an ecosystem. Research how long each one takes to recover from a wildfire.

Journal: Write a Report Include what you found. Also in your report:

- Make a pamphlet to show how wildfires affect ecosystems.

- Suggest ways to prevent wildfires.

- Make a line plot to show your data.

- Make up and solve problems using line plots.

Name _____

Review What You Know

Vocabulary

Choose the best term from the Word List.
Write it on the blank.

- bar graph
- compare
- frequency table
- overestimate
- underestimate

1. A display that shows how many
times an event occurs is a(n) _____.

2. A display that uses bars to show data is a(n) _____.

3. Rounding each factor in a multiplication to a greater number gives a(n)
_____ of the actual product.

4. You can use the length of the bars in a bar graph to _____
two similar data sets.

Fraction Computation

Find each answer.

5. $2\frac{1}{2} + 5\frac{1}{3}$

6. $13\frac{3}{10} - 8\frac{1}{5}$

7. $8\frac{1}{3} + 7\frac{11}{12}$

8. $15 - 5\frac{2}{9}$

9. $7\frac{5}{8} + 13\frac{11}{20}$

10. $15\frac{4}{5} + 1\frac{2}{3}$

11. $\frac{7}{8} \times 4$

12. $5 \times 1\frac{2}{3}$

13. $2\frac{1}{8} \times \frac{2}{3}$

Bar Graphs

Use the bar graph to answer the questions.

14. Which animal has about 34 teeth?

15. About how many more teeth does a dog
have than a hyena?

16. About how many more teeth does a hyena
have than a walrus?

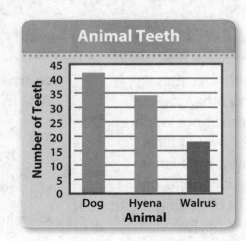

© Pearson Education, Inc. 5

Name_____

PROJECT 10A

How big is Big Data?

Project: Make Line Plots for Data

PROJECT 10B

What was the first U.S. penny?

Project: Design a Coin

Why are sequoia trees so big?

Project: Measure Trees

How are plant leaves different?

Project: Make a Leafy Line Plot

© Pearson Education, Inc. 5

Name _____

☆ ★ ☆
Solve & Share

Several students were asked how many blocks they walk from home to school each day. The results are shown in the line plot below. Miguel walks the shortest distance. Jila walks the longest distance. How much farther than Miguel does Jila walk?

I can ...
read a line plot.

MAFS.5.MD.2.2 Make a line plot to display a data set of measurements in fractions of a unit $\left(\frac{1}{2}, \frac{1}{4}, \frac{1}{8}\right)$. Use operations on fractions for this grade to solve problems involving information presented in line plots. **Also 5.NF.1.2** MAFS.K12.MP.1.1, MP.2.1

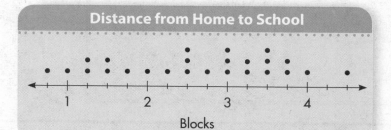

Distance from Home to School

Blocks

Make Sense and Persevere
How can you find the shortest distance walked?

Look Back! What can you tell about the distance most of the students in the group walk to school each day?

Essential Question

How Can You Analyze Data Displayed in a Line Plot?

A

A line plot, or dot plot, shows data along a number line. Each dot or X represents one value in the data set.

In science class, Abby and her classmates performed an experiment in which they used different amounts of vinegar. The table below shows how much vinegar each person used. What amount was most often used in the experiment?

A line plot shows how often each value occurs.

DATA

Cups of Vinegar						
$\frac{1}{2}$	1	1	$1\frac{1}{2}$	$\frac{3}{4}$	1	$\frac{3}{4}$
$1\frac{1}{4}$	$\frac{3}{4}$	$\frac{1}{2}$	2	1	$\frac{3}{4}$	$1\frac{1}{2}$
1	1	$1\frac{1}{4}$	$\frac{3}{4}$	1	$1\frac{1}{4}$	1

B Read the line plot.

A line plot can be used to organize the amount of vinegar each person used.

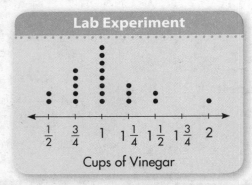

Lab Experiment

Cups of Vinegar

$\frac{1}{2}$ $\frac{3}{4}$ 1 $1\frac{1}{4}$ $1\frac{1}{2}$ $1\frac{3}{4}$ 2

C Analyze the data.

Use the data to answer your original question. What amount was most often used in the experiment?

Most of the data points are at 1, so 1 cup of vinegar was most often used in the experiment.

Convince Me! **Reasoning** How does the line plot show what the largest amount of vinegar used was?

  © Pearson Education, Inc. 5

Guided Practice*

Do You Understand?

1. Why does data need to be ordered from least to greatest before creating a line plot?

2. In the line plot on the previous page, do any values occur the same number of times? Explain.

3. Describe any patterns in the line plot on the previous page.

Do You Know How?

In **4** and **5**, use the data set to answer the questions.

4. Students ran for 10 minutes. They ran the following distances, in miles:

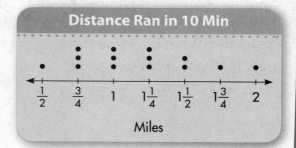

$\frac{3}{4}$, $\frac{1}{2}$, $1\frac{3}{4}$, $1\frac{1}{4}$, $\frac{3}{4}$, 1

$1\frac{1}{2}$, $1\frac{1}{4}$, 2, $1\frac{1}{2}$, 1, $1\frac{1}{4}$, $\frac{3}{4}$, 1

How many distances are recorded?

5. Use the line plot that shows the data.

Distance Ran in 10 Min

Miles

Which distances occurred most often?

Independent Practice

In **6–8**, use the line plot to answer the questions.

6. How many orders for cheese does the line plot show?

7. Which amount of cheese was ordered most often?

8. How many more orders for cheese were for $\frac{3}{4}$ pound or less than for 1 pound or more?

Data in a line plot can be shown with dots or Xs.

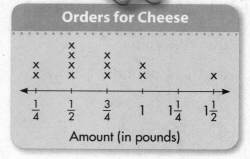

Orders for Cheese

Amount (in pounds)

*For another example, see Set A on page 447.

Topic 10 | Lesson 10-1   **431**

Problem Solving

In **9–11**, use the data set and line plot.

9. Jerome studied the feather lengths of some adult fox sparrows. How long are the longest feathers in the data set?

10. How many feathers are $2\frac{1}{4}$ inches or longer? Explain.

11. **Higher Order Thinking** Jerome found another feather that made the difference between the longest and shortest feather $1\frac{3}{4}$ inches. What could be the length of the new feather? Explain.

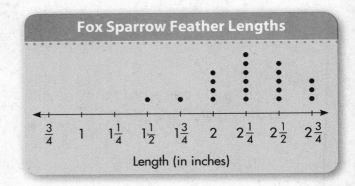

Fox Sparrow Feather Lengths (in inches)

DATA				
$2\frac{1}{2}$	$1\frac{3}{4}$	2	$2\frac{1}{2}$	$2\frac{3}{4}$
2	$2\frac{1}{2}$	$1\frac{1}{2}$	$2\frac{1}{4}$	$2\frac{1}{4}$
$2\frac{3}{4}$	2	$2\frac{1}{2}$	$2\frac{1}{2}$	$2\frac{3}{4}$
$2\frac{1}{4}$	$2\frac{1}{4}$	$2\frac{1}{4}$	2	$2\frac{1}{4}$

Fox Sparrow Feather Lengths

Length (in inches)

---

12. **Reasoning** How can you find the value that occurs most often by looking at a line plot?

13. Draw and label a rectangle with a perimeter of 24 inches.

Assessment Practice

14. Use the information shown in the line plot. What is the total weight of the 4 heaviest melons? **S.MD.2.2**

    Ⓐ 6 pounds

    Ⓑ $11\frac{1}{2}$ pounds

    Ⓒ $22\frac{1}{2}$ pounds

    Ⓓ 24 pounds

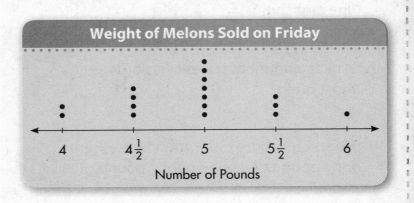

Weight of Melons Sold on Friday

Number of Pounds

© Pearson Education, Inc. 5

Name _____

Solve & Share

A fifth-grade class recorded the height of each student. How could you organize the data? If all the students in the class lay down in a long line, how far would it reach? **Make a line plot to solve this problem.**

I can ...
display data in a line plot.

MAFS.5.MD.2.2 Make a line plot to display a data set of measurements in fractions of a unit $\left(\frac{1}{2}, \frac{1}{4}, \frac{1}{8}\right)$. Use operations on fractions for this grade to solve problems involving information presented in line plots. **Also 5.NF.1.2** MAFS.K12.MP.1.1, MP.2.1, MP.8.1

Heights of Students in Grade 5
(to the nearest $\frac{1}{2}$ inch):

$55, 52, 50\frac{1}{2}, 50\frac{1}{2}, 55, 50\frac{1}{2},$

$50, 55, 50\frac{1}{2}, 55, 58\frac{1}{2}, 60, 52,$

$50\frac{1}{2}, 50\frac{1}{2}, 50, 55, 55, 58\frac{1}{2}, 60$

Organizing data makes it easier to understand and analyze.

Look Back! **Generalize** How does organizing the data help you see the height that occurs most often? Explain.

Essential Question

How Can You Use a Line Plot to Organize and Represent Measurement Data?

A

The dogs in Paulina's Pet Shop have the following weights. The weights are in pounds.

How can you organize this information in a line plot?

Measurement data that is organized is easier to use.

DATA

Weights of Dogs (in pounds)					
$8\frac{1}{2}$	$12\frac{1}{4}$	6	$11\frac{1}{2}$	$7\frac{1}{4}$	$12\frac{1}{4}$
$8\frac{1}{2}$	$12\frac{1}{4}$	$8\frac{1}{2}$	$12\frac{1}{4}$	$12\frac{1}{4}$	6

B **Organize the data.**

Write the weights from least to greatest.

$6, 6, 7\frac{1}{4}, 8\frac{1}{2}, 8\frac{1}{2}, 8\frac{1}{2}, 11\frac{1}{2}, 12\frac{1}{4}, 12\frac{1}{4}, 12\frac{1}{4}, 12\frac{1}{4}, 12\frac{1}{4}$

You can also organize the data in a frequency table. The frequency is how many times a given response occurs.

DATA

Dog Weight (pounds)	Tally	Frequency
6	II	2
$7\frac{1}{4}$	I	1
$8\frac{1}{2}$	III	3
$11\frac{1}{2}$	I	1
$12\frac{1}{4}$	IIII	5

C **Make a line plot.**

First draw the number line using an interval of $\frac{1}{4}$. Then mark a dot for each value in the data set. Write a title for the line plot.

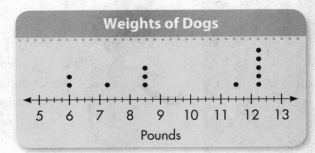

Weights of Dogs
Pounds

 Convince Me! **Reasoning** Which weight occurs most often? Which weight occurs least often? How can you tell from the line plot?

© Pearson Education, Inc. 5

Practice Tools Assessment

☆ Guided Practice *

Do You Understand?

1. In the line plot of dog weights on the previous page, what does each dot represent?

2. In a line plot, how do you determine the values to show on the number line?

Do You Know How?

3. Draw a line plot to represent the data.

Weights of Pumpkins	Tally	Frequency
$3\frac{1}{2}$ lb	II	2
$5\frac{1}{4}$ lb	III	3
7 lb	IIII	4
$8\frac{1}{2}$ lb	I	1

DATA

☆ Independent Practice ☆

In **4** and **5**, complete the line plot for each data set.

Double check that you have a dot for each value.

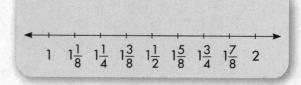

4. $11\frac{1}{4}$, $12\frac{1}{2}$, $11\frac{1}{4}$, $14\frac{3}{4}$, $10\frac{1}{2}$, $11\frac{1}{4}$, 12

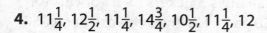

10   11   12   13   14   15

5. $1\frac{1}{8}$, 2, $1\frac{1}{2}$, $1\frac{1}{4}$, $1\frac{1}{8}$, 1, 2, $1\frac{1}{2}$, $1\frac{1}{4}$

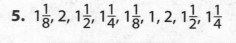

1   $1\frac{1}{8}$ $1\frac{1}{4}$ $1\frac{3}{8}$ $1\frac{1}{2}$ $1\frac{5}{8}$ $1\frac{3}{4}$ $1\frac{7}{8}$ 2

In **6** and **7**, construct a line plot for each data set.

6. $\frac{1}{2}$, $\frac{3}{4}$, $\frac{3}{4}$, 1, 1, 0, $\frac{1}{2}$, $\frac{1}{2}$, $\frac{3}{4}$

7. $5\frac{1}{2}$, 5, 5, $5\frac{1}{8}$, $5\frac{3}{4}$, $5\frac{1}{4}$, $5\frac{1}{2}$, $5\frac{1}{8}$, $5\frac{1}{2}$, $5\frac{3}{8}$

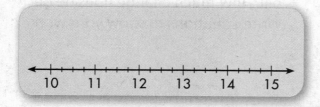

Problem Solving

In **8–10**, use the data set.

8. **Make Sense and Persevere** Martin's Tree Service purchased several spruce tree saplings. Draw a line plot of the data showing the heights of the saplings.

Heights of Saplings (in.)

$26\frac{1}{2}$	27	$26\frac{3}{4}$	$27\frac{1}{2}$	$26\frac{3}{4}$
$27\frac{1}{2}$	$27\frac{3}{4}$	$27\frac{1}{4}$	$27\frac{1}{2}$	$27\frac{1}{4}$
$27\frac{3}{4}$	$27\frac{1}{2}$	$26\frac{1}{2}$	$26\frac{1}{2}$	$27\frac{1}{2}$
$27\frac{1}{4}$	$27\frac{1}{4}$	$27\frac{1}{2}$	27	$26\frac{3}{4}$

9. How many more saplings with a height of $27\frac{1}{4}$ inches or less were there than saplings with a height greater than $27\frac{1}{4}$ inches?

10. **Higher Order Thinking** Suppose Martin's Tree Service bought two more saplings that were each $27\frac{1}{4}$ inches tall. Would the value that occurred most often change? Explain your answer.

11. Why is organizing data helpful?

12. Randall buys 3 tickets for a concert for $14.50 each. He gives the cashier a $50 bill. How much change does he get? Write equations to show your work.

13. Amy measured how many centimeters the leaves on her houseplants grew in July. Use the leaf growth data below to complete the line plot on the right. 5.MD.2.2

$2\frac{1}{2}, 4\frac{1}{2}, 4, 4, 3, 1, 3, 3\frac{1}{2}, 3\frac{1}{2}, 3\frac{1}{2}, 2\frac{1}{2}, 3, 3\frac{1}{2}, 3\frac{1}{2}, 5\frac{1}{2}$

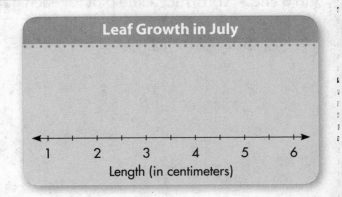

Leaf Growth in July

Length (in centimeters)

© Pearson Education, Inc. 5

Name _____

Activity

Solve & Share

Rainfall for the Amazon was measured and recorded for 30 days. The results were displayed in a line plot. What can you tell about the differences in the amounts of rainfall? *Use the line plot to solve this problem.*

I can ...
solve problems using data in a line plot.

MAFS.5.MD.2.2 Make a line plot to display a data set of measurements in fractions of a unit $\left(\frac{1}{2}, \frac{1}{4}, \frac{1}{8}\right)$. Use operations on fractions for this grade to solve problems involving information presented in line plots. Also 5.NF.1.2, 5.NF.2.6 MAFS.K12.MP.1.1, MP.2.1, MP.3.1

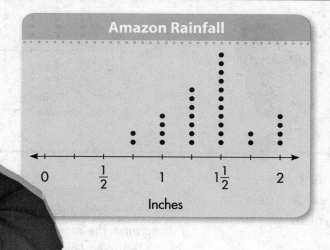

You can use a representation to analyze data. *Show your work!*

Look Back! Reasoning What is the difference between the greatest amount of rain in a day and the least amount of rain in a day? How can you tell?

How Can You Use Measurement Data Represented in a Line Plot to Solve Problems?

A

Bruce measured the daily rainfall while working in Costa Rica. His line plot shows the rainfall for each day in September. What was the total rainfall for the month?

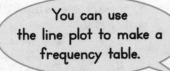

You can use the line plot to make a frequency table.

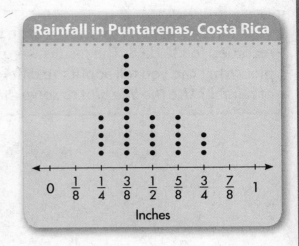

Rainfall in Puntarenas, Costa Rica

Inches

B Multiply each value by the frequency to find the amount of rain for that value. Then add the products to find the number of inches of rainfall for the month.

The table helps you organize the numerical data for your calculations.

Rainfall (inches)	Frequency	Multiplication
$\frac{1}{4}$	5	$5 \times \frac{1}{4} = 1\frac{1}{4}$
$\frac{3}{8}$	12	$12 \times \frac{3}{8} = 4\frac{1}{2}$
$\frac{1}{2}$	5	$5 \times \frac{1}{2} = 2\frac{1}{2}$
$\frac{5}{8}$	5	$5 \times \frac{5}{8} = 3\frac{1}{8}$
$\frac{3}{4}$	3	$3 \times \frac{3}{4} = 2\frac{1}{4}$

DATA

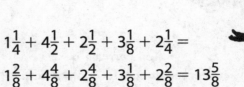

$1\frac{1}{4} + 4\frac{1}{2} + 2\frac{1}{2} + 3\frac{1}{8} + 2\frac{1}{4} =$

$1\frac{2}{8} + 4\frac{4}{8} + 2\frac{4}{8} + 3\frac{1}{8} + 2\frac{2}{8} = 13\frac{5}{8}$

The total rainfall was $13\frac{5}{8}$ inches.

Convince Me! **Critique Reasoning** Rosie says she can find the total rainfall in the example above without multiplying. Do you agree? Explain.

Name _____

☆ Guided Practice ☆

Do You Understand?

In **1–4**, use the line plot showing how many grams of salt were left after liquids in various containers evaporated.

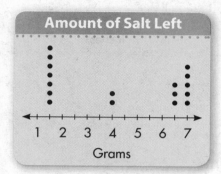

Amount of Salt Left

Grams

1. How could you find the difference between the greatest amount and the least amount of salt left?

Do You Know How?

2. Write a problem that can be answered using the line plot.

3. Write and solve an equation that represents the total number of grams of salt left.

4. How many grams of salt would be left if two of each container were used?

☆ Independent Practice ☆

In **5** and **6**, use the line plot Allie made to show the lengths of strings she cut for her art project.

5. Write an equation for the total amount of string.

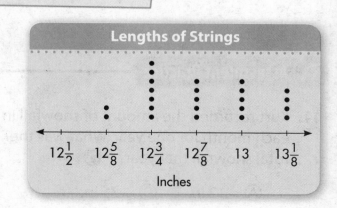

Lengths of Strings

$12\frac{1}{2}$ $12\frac{5}{8}$ $12\frac{3}{4}$ $12\frac{7}{8}$ 13 $13\frac{1}{8}$

Inches

6. What is the difference in length between the longest and the shortest lengths of string?

Problem Solving

In **7** and **8**, use the line plot Susannah made to show the amount of rainfall in one week.

7. **Algebra** Write and solve an equation for the total amount of rainfall, *r*, Susannah recorded.

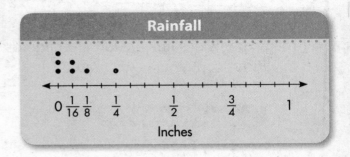

8. **Higher Order Thinking** Suppose the same amount of rain fell the following week, but the same amount of rain fell each day. How much rain fell each day?

9. **Make Sense and Persevere** The area of a square deck is 81 square feet. How long is each side of the deck?

How does knowing the shape of the deck help you?

10. Althea recorded the amount she earned from T-shirt sales each day for 14 days. She made a frequency table to organize the data. Write a problem that can be answered by using the frequency table.

Amount Earned (in $)	Frequency	Multiplication
7.50	3	$3 \times 7.50 = 22.50$
15.00	4	$4 \times 15.00 = 60.00$
22.50	5	$5 \times 22.50 = 112.50$
30.00	1	$1 \times 30.00 = 30.00$
37.50	1	$1 \times 37.50 = 37.50$

DATA

11. Kurt recorded the amount of snowfall in each month for one year. What was the total snowfall that year? **5.MD.2.2**

Ⓐ 12 in.   Ⓒ $7\frac{3}{4}$ in.

Ⓑ $10\frac{1}{4}$ in.   Ⓓ $7\frac{1}{2}$ in.

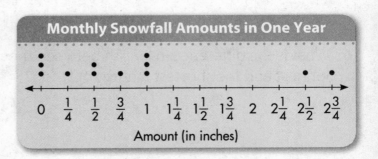

© Pearson Education, Inc. 5

Name _____

Activity

☆ Solve & Share ☆

A cross country coach recorded the team's practice runs and made the line plot below. The coach had each runner analyze the line plot and write an observation. Read the statements and explain whether you think each runner's reasoning makes sense.

I can ...
critique the reasoning of others by using what I know about line plots and fractions.

MAFS.K12.MP.3.1 Critique reasoning. **Also MP.1.1, MP.2.1, MP.4.1, MP.6.1** MAFS.5.MD.2.2 Make a line plot to display a data set of measurements in fractions of a unit $\left(\frac{1}{2}, \frac{1}{4}, \frac{1}{8}\right)$. Use operations on fractions for this grade to solve problems involving information presented in line plots. **Also 5.NF.1.2**

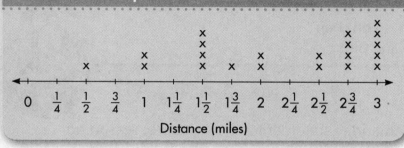

September Practice Runs

Distance (miles)

Olivia
The distance we ran the most often was 3 miles.

Michelle
The team ran different distances on different days. We usually ran for 2 miles or more.

Natalie
The team ran 8 different times, each time for a different distance.

Peter
Each day the team ran the same distance or a little farther than the day before.

Thinking Habits
Be a good thinker!
These questions can help you.

- What questions can I ask to understand other people's thinking?

- Are there mistakes in other people's thinking?

- Can I improve other people's thinking?

Look Back! **Critique Reasoning** Quinn said that to find the total distance the team ran in September, you add each number that has an X above it: $\frac{1}{2} + 1 + 1\frac{1}{2} + 1\frac{3}{4} + 2 + 2\frac{1}{2} + 2\frac{3}{4} + 3$. Do you agree? Explain why or why not.

Essential Question How Can You Critique the Reasoning of Others?

A

Ms. Kelly's class made a line plot showing how many hours each student spent watching television the previous evening. Amanda said, "No one watched TV for 3 hours." Drake said, "No, 3 of us watched no TV." Who is correct? Explain your reasoning.

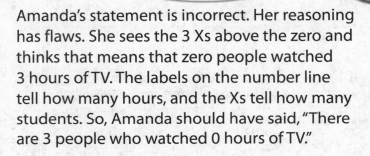

Time Spent Watching TV

Time (hours)

What information do Amanda and Drake use for reasoning?

Amanda and Drake base their reasoning on their analysis of the data displayed on the line plot.

B

How can I critique the reasoning of others?

I can

- decide if the statements make sense.

- look for mistakes in calculations.

- clarify or correct flaws in reasoning.

C

Here's my thinking...

Amanda's statement is incorrect. Her reasoning has flaws. She sees the 3 Xs above the zero and thinks that means that zero people watched 3 hours of TV. The labels on the number line tell how many hours, and the Xs tell how many students. So, Amanda should have said, "There are 3 people who watched 0 hours of TV."

Drake's statement is correct. Since there are 3 Xs above the 0, he is correct when he says that 3 people watched no TV.

Convince Me! **Critique Reasoning** Andre said, "More than half of us watched TV for less than 2 hours." Explain how you can critique Andre's reasoning to see if his thinking makes sense.

© Pearson Education, Inc. 5

Name _____

Renee works for a sand and gravel company. She made a line plot to show the weight of the gravel in last week's orders. She concluded that one third of the orders were for more than 6 tons.

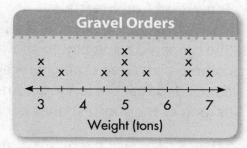

Gravel Orders

Weight (tons)

1. What is Renee's conclusion? How did she support it?

2. Describe at least one thing you would do to critique Renee's reasoning.

3. Does Renee's conclusion make sense? Explain.

Independent Practice

Critique Reasoning

Aaron made a line plot showing the weights of the heads of cabbage he picked from his garden. He said that since $1\frac{1}{2} + 2 + 2\frac{1}{4} + 2\frac{3}{4} = 8\frac{1}{2}$, the total weight of the cabbages is $8\frac{1}{2}$ pounds.

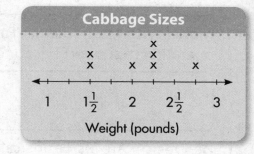

Cabbage Sizes

Weight (pounds)

4. Describe at least one thing you would do to critique Aaron's reasoning.

5. Is Aaron's addition accurate? Show how you know.

6. Can you identify any flaws in Aaron's thinking? Explain.

When you critique reasoning, you need to explain if someone's method makes sense.

7. Does Aaron's conclusion make sense? Explain.

Problem Solving

Television Commercials

Ms. Fazio is the manager of a television station. She prepared a line plot to show the lengths of the commercials aired during a recent broadcast. She concluded that the longest commercials were 3 times as long as the shortest ones because $3 \times \frac{1}{2} = 1\frac{1}{2}$.

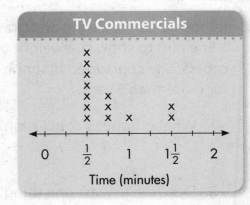

TV Commercials

8. **Make Sense and Persevere** Which information in the line plot did Ms. Fazio need to use in order to draw her conclusion? 🌀 5.MD.2.2, MP.1.1

9. **Reasoning** Did the number of Xs above the number line affect Ms. Fazio's conclusion? Explain. 🌀 5.MD.2.2, MP.2.1

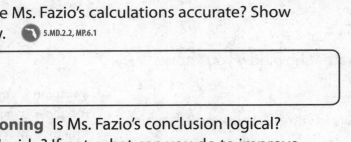

To use math precisely, you need to check that the words, numbers, symbols, and units you use are correct and that your calculations are accurate.

10. **Model With Math** Did Ms. Fazio use the correct operation to support her conclusion? Explain. 🌀 5.MD.2.2, MP.4.1

11. **Be Precise** Are Ms. Fazio's calculations accurate? Show how you know. 🌀 5.MD.2.2, MP.6.1

12. **Critique Reasoning** Is Ms. Fazio's conclusion logical? How did you decide? If not, what can you do to improve her reasoning? 🌀 5.MD.2.2, MP.3.1

© Pearson Education, Inc. 5

Follow the Path

Fluency Practice Activity

Solve each problem. Follow problems with an answer of 29,160 to shade a path from **START** to **FINISH**. You can only move up, down, right, or left.

I can ...
multiply multi-digit whole numbers.

 MAFS.5.NBT.2.5

Start				
729 × 40	2,430 × 12	360 × 81	1,620 × 18	540 × 54
1,234 × 25	712 × 55	704 × 40	596 × 50	1,215 × 24
663 × 45	454 × 65	810 × 36	3,645 × 8	486 × 60
740 × 27	1,816 × 15	405 × 72	430 × 71	412 × 70
731 × 40	1,164 × 25	1,080 × 27	972 × 30	648 × 45

Finish

TOPIC 10 **Vocabulary Review**

Glossary

A-Z

Word List

- bar graph
- data
- frequency table
- line plot

Understand Vocabulary

Choose the best term from the Word List. Write it on the blank.

1. Another name for collected information is _____.

2. A _____ uses tally marks to show how many times a data value occurs in a data set.

3. A(n) _____ is a display of responses on a number line with a dot or X used to show each time a response occurs.

Round the data to the nearest whole number and order from least to greatest.

4. 2.3, 8.6, 5.5, 4.9

5. 42.1, 50, 37.2, 76.5, 43.9

Order each data set from least to greatest.

6. $1\frac{1}{2}$, 0, $1\frac{3}{4}$, $13\frac{1}{2}$, $1\frac{2}{3}$

7. $\frac{6}{7}$, $2\frac{1}{2}$, $\frac{3}{4}$, 1, $1\frac{3}{4}$

Write **always**, **sometimes**, or **never**.

8. A line plot is _____ the best way to display data.

9. A data display _____ uses fractions or decimals.

10. Cross out the words that are **NOT** examples of items that contain *data*.

Encyclopedia   Alphabet   Email address   MP3 Player   Phone number   Grocery list

Use Vocabulary in Writing

11. Twenty students measured their heights for an experiment in their science class. How can a line plot help the students analyze their results?

© Pearson Education, Inc. 5

Set A pages 429–432

The data set below shows the number of cartons of milk drank by 20 students in a week.

2, 4, $3\frac{1}{2}$, $\frac{1}{2}$, $1\frac{1}{2}$, $1\frac{1}{2}$, $3\frac{1}{2}$, 2, 3, $\frac{1}{2}$, 1, $3\frac{1}{2}$, 3, 2, 1, $3\frac{1}{2}$, 1, 3, $3\frac{1}{2}$, 2

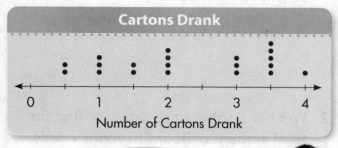

Cartons Drank

Number of Cartons Drank

The line plot shows how often each data value occurs.

Use the Cartons Drank line plot.

1. How many students drank $1\frac{1}{2}$ cartons?

2. How many students drank more than $2\frac{1}{2}$ cartons?

3. What was the greatest number of cartons drank by a student?

4. How many students drank only 1 carton?

5. What is the difference between the greatest and least number of cartons drank?

Set B pages 433–436

Twelve people were surveyed about the number of hours they spend reading books on a Saturday. The results are:

$\frac{3}{4}$ $1\frac{1}{2}$ 1 $\frac{1}{2}$ $1\frac{1}{2}$ $2\frac{3}{4}$

$1\frac{3}{4}$ $\frac{1}{2}$ $2\frac{1}{2}$ 2 $1\frac{1}{2}$ 2

Draw a number line from 0 to 3. Mark the number line in fourths because the survey results are given in $\frac{1}{4}$ hours. Then for each response, place a dot above the value on the number line.

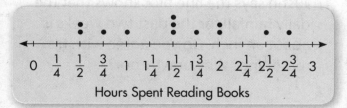

Hours Spent Reading Books

Remember that you can make a line plot to show and compare data.

Use the information below to make a line plot about Patrick's plants.

Patrick listed how many inches his plants grew in one week: 1 $\frac{1}{2}$ $\frac{3}{4}$ $1\frac{1}{2}$ $\frac{1}{2}$ $1\frac{1}{4}$ $1\frac{1}{4}$ $\frac{1}{2}$ 1

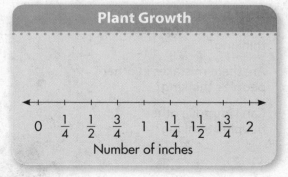

Plant Growth

Number of inches

1. Complete the line plot.

2. How many dots are on the line plot?

3. How many inches of plant growth was the most common?

Set C | pages 437–440

This line plot shows the amount of flour Cheyenne needs for several different recipes. She organizes the data in a frequency table to calculate the total amount of flour she needs.

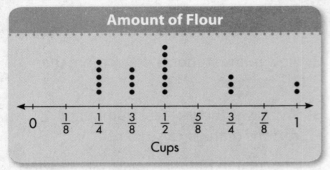

Amount of Flour

Cups

Amount of Flour (cups)	Frequency	Multiplication
$\frac{1}{4}$	5	$5 \times \frac{1}{4} = 1\frac{1}{4}$
$\frac{3}{8}$	4	$4 \times \frac{3}{8} = 1\frac{1}{2}$
$\frac{1}{2}$	7	$7 \times \frac{1}{2} = 3\frac{1}{2}$
$\frac{3}{4}$	3	$3 \times \frac{3}{4} = 2\frac{1}{4}$
1	2	$2 \times 1 = 2$

DATA

Remember that you can multiply each data value by its frequency to find the total amount.

Use the line plot and frequency table at the left.

1. What values are multiplied in the third column of the table?

2. Write and solve an equation to find the total amount of flour Cheyenne needs.

Set D | pages 441–444

Think about these questions to help you **critique the reasoning of others**.

Thinking Habits

- What questions can I ask to understand other people's thinking?

- Are there mistakes in other people's thinking?

- Can I improve other people's thinking?

Remember you need to carefully consider all parts of an argument.

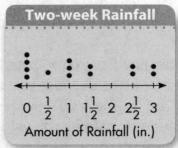

Two-week Rainfall

Amount of Rainfall (in.)

1. Justin says the line plot shows that the daily rainfall for the past two weeks is about an inch. Do you agree with his reasoning? Why or why not?

© Pearson Education, Inc. 5

Name _____

1. Which line plot shows the data?

8	$7\frac{1}{2}$	$8\frac{3}{4}$	$7\frac{1}{4}$	$7\frac{1}{4}$	$8\frac{3}{4}$	$8\frac{3}{4}$
$8\frac{3}{4}$	$8\frac{3}{4}$	8	$8\frac{3}{4}$	$9\frac{1}{4}$	$9\frac{1}{4}$	$7\frac{1}{4}$

Ⓐ
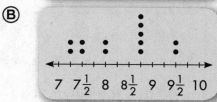

Ⓑ
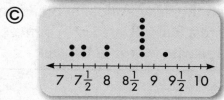

Ⓒ
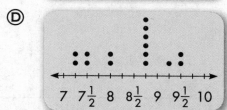

Ⓓ
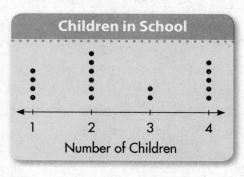

2. The line plot shows the results from a survey asking parents how many children they have in school. How many parents have two children in school?

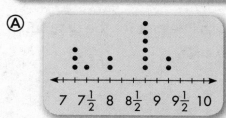

3. Georgiana made a line plot of the amount of time she spent practicing her violin each day in the past two weeks.

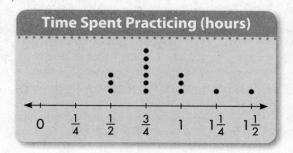

A. What is the difference between the greatest and least times spent practicing?

B. What is the most common amount of time she spent practicing?

C. What is the total amount of time Georgiana practiced? Write and solve an equation to show your work.

Ashraf and Melanie cut rope into different lengths for an art project. They made a line plot to display their data. Use the line plot to answer **4–6**.

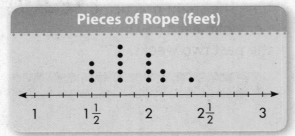

Pieces of Rope (feet)

4. Which is the most common length of rope?

Ⓐ $1\frac{5}{8}$ ft

Ⓑ $1\frac{3}{4}$ ft

Ⓒ $1\frac{7}{8}$ ft

Ⓓ $2\frac{3}{8}$ ft

5. Which is the total length of rope represented by the data?

Ⓐ $25\frac{1}{8}$ ft

Ⓑ $27\frac{5}{8}$ ft

Ⓒ $27\frac{7}{8}$ ft

Ⓓ 28 ft

6. Suppose 2 more pieces of rope are cut to be 2 feet. Would the value that occurred most often change? Explain your reasoning.

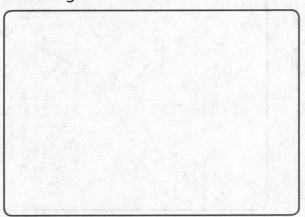

7. Terry works at a bakery. This morning he recorded how many ounces each loaf of bread weighed.

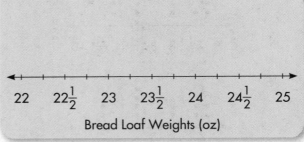

| $23\frac{1}{2}$ | 24 | $23\frac{3}{4}$ | $23\frac{1}{2}$ | $24\frac{1}{4}$ | $23\frac{1}{2}$ |
| 24 | $23\frac{1}{4}$ | $24\frac{1}{2}$ | $22\frac{3}{4}$ | $24\frac{1}{4}$ | $23\frac{1}{2}$ |

A. Make a line plot for the data set.

Bread Loaf Weights (oz)

B. Morgan said that the difference between the heaviest loaf of bread and the lightest loaf of bread is $1\frac{1}{2}$ ounces. Do you agree with Morgan? Explain.

C. What is the combined weight of all the loaves of bread? Show your work.

© Pearson Education, Inc. 5

Name _____

Measuring Bugs

Ms. Wolk's class measured the length and weight of
Madagascar Hissing Cockroaches.

1. The **Cockroach Lengths** line plot shows the lengths the class found.

Part A

Which length did the most students get? How
can you tell from the line plot? 🐾 5.MD.2.2

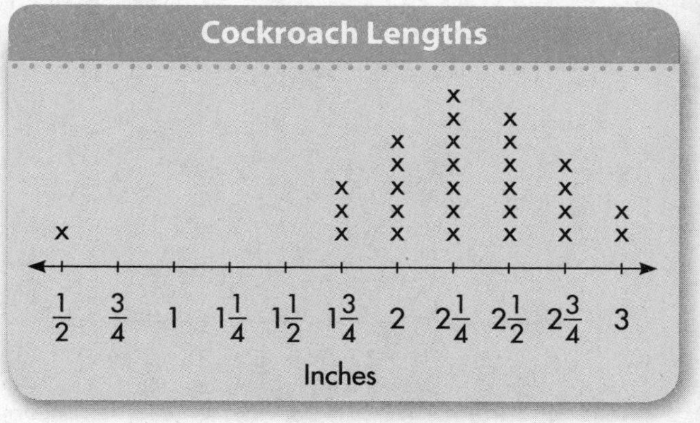

Cockroach Lengths

Part B

Jordan said that all of the Madagascar Hissing Cockroaches were
between 2 and 3 inches long. Is he correct? Explain your reasoning. 🐾 5.MD.2.2

Part C

Ginny said that twice as many students found a length of $2\frac{1}{2}$ inches as
found a length of $1\frac{3}{4}$ inches. Is she correct? Explain your reasoning. 🐾 5.MD.2.2

Part D

How many cockroaches were measured for the data set? How do you know? 🐾 5.MD.2.2

2. The **Cockroach Weights** table shows the weights the class found.

Part A

Complete the line plot to represent the cockroach weights. 5.MD.2.2

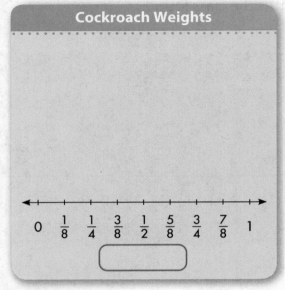

Cockroach Weights (In ounces)						
$\frac{3}{8}$	$\frac{5}{8}$	$\frac{1}{2}$	$\frac{3}{4}$	$\frac{5}{8}$	$\frac{1}{2}$	$\frac{5}{8}$
$\frac{1}{2}$	$\frac{3}{4}$	$\frac{3}{8}$	$\frac{3}{4}$	$\frac{1}{2}$	$\frac{3}{8}$	$\frac{3}{4}$
$\frac{3}{4}$	$\frac{3}{8}$	$\frac{3}{4}$	$\frac{5}{8}$	$\frac{1}{4}$	$\frac{3}{4}$	$\frac{1}{2}$
$\frac{5}{8}$	$\frac{1}{4}$	$\frac{1}{2}$	$\frac{1}{2}$	$\frac{3}{4}$	$\frac{3}{8}$	$\frac{5}{8}$

Part B

What is the total weight of all the cockroaches the students measured? Complete the table to help you. Show your work. 🐢 5.MD.2.2

Cockroach Weights (In ounces)		
Weight (ounces)	Frequency	Multiplication

© Pearson Education, Inc. 5

Understand Volume Concepts

Essential Questions: What is the meaning of volume of a solid? How can the volume of a rectangular prism be found?

Digital Resources

Solve Learn Glossary Practice Buddy

Tools Assessment Help Games

You use energy 24/7, from getting out of bed in the morning to texting your friends at night!

Chemical energy from food transforms to mechanical energy to get you out of bed.

MAFS.5.MD.3.3.a, 5.MD.3.3.b, 5.MD.3.5.a, 5.MD.3.5.b, 5.MD.3.5.c
MAFS.K12.MP.2.1, MP.3.1, MP.4.1, MP.5.1, MP.7.1

That's powerful! And, chemical and mechanical energy move the bus that takes me to school. Here's a project about everyday energy.

enVision STEM Project: Everyday Energy

Do Research Use the Internet and other sources to learn more about these five types of energy: electrical, light, mechanical, sound, and thermal. Make a table of the various types of energy you use every day. Include at least one example of how you use each type of energy.

Journal: Write a Report Include what you found. Also in your report:

- Draw a diagram of your classroom and label where and how 3 types of energy are used.

- Estimate how far your desk is from a light energy source and add this dimension to your sketch.

- Use your diagram to make up and solve problems involving measurements such as the volume of your classroom.

Name _____

Review What You Know

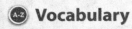

(A-Z) Vocabulary

Choose the best term from the box.
Write it on the blank.

> • compensation   • rectangle
> • partial products • unit fraction

1. Adjusting a number to make a computation easier and balancing the adjustment by changing another number is called _____.

2. A fraction with a numerator of 1 is called a _____.

3. A quadrilateral with 2 pairs of parallel sides that are the same length and 4 right angles is a _____.

Area

Find the area of each figure.

4.
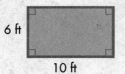
6 ft
10 ft

5.
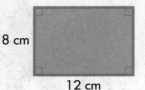
8 cm
12 cm

Operations

Find each product or quotient.

6. 16×6 **7.** 3×42 **8.** $216 \div 3$

9. $128 \div 4$ **10.** $(5 \times 6) \times 3$ **11.** $(6 \times 6) \times 6$

12. Joanie has two 12-inch-long wood pieces and two 16-inch-long wood pieces. What is the combined length of the wood pieces?

Ⓐ 28 inches   Ⓑ 32 inches   Ⓒ 56 inches   Ⓓ 192 inches

Finding Area

13. Niko used square tiles to make a rectangle with 2 rows and 7 tiles in each row. Explain how you can find the area of the rectangle.

       © Pearson Education, Inc. 5

PROJECT 11A

How big are skyscrapers?

Project: Build a Skyscraper with Unit Cubes

PROJECT 11B

Why do cats climb into boxes?

Project: Design a Cat Tree

PROJECT 11C

Why are trucks useful for transporting packages?

Project: Model a Truck's Capacity

Before watching the video, think:

Ice is frozen below 32°F (or 0°C), but most picnics and cookouts happen when it's warm out. The insulated walls of a cooler help keep ice from melting, which keeps my juice nice and cold!

MAFS.K12.MP.4.1 Model with math. **Also MAFS.K12.MP.2.1, MAFS.K12.MP.7.1**
MAFS.5.MD.3.5a Find the volume of a right rectangular prism with whole-number side lengths by packing it with unit cubes, and . . . by multiplying the edge lengths, equivalently by multiplying the height by the area of the base. Represent threefold whole-number products as volumes, e.g., to represent the associative property of multiplication. **Also MAFS.5.MD.3.3, MAFS.5.MD.3.4**

Lesson 11-1
Model Volume

I can ...
find the volume of solid figures.

MAFS.5.MD.3.3.a A cube with side length 1 unit, called a "unit cube," is said to have "one cubic unit" of volume, and can be used to measure volume. **Also 5.MD.3.3.b and 5.MD.3.4**
MAFS.K12.MP.2.1, MP.5.1

Solve & Share

Gina is building a rectangular prism out of sugar cubes for her art class project. She started by drawing a diagram of the rectangular prism that is 4 cubes high, 4 cubes long and 2 cubes wide. How many cubes does she use to make the prism? *Solve this problem any way you choose.*

Use Appropriate Tools
You can draw a picture to find the number of cubes in a rectangular prism. *Show your work!*

SUGAR CUBES

Side View

Front View

Top View

Look Back! Gina decided to change her art project and build a rectangular prism that is 3 cubes long, 4 cubes wide, and 2 cubes high. Use the picture to determine the number of cubes she used.

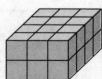

A

Volume is the number of cubic units needed to pack a solid figure without gaps or overlaps. A cubic unit is the volume of a cube measuring 1 unit on each edge. What is the volume of this rectangular prism?

Each cube of a solid figure is 1 cubic unit.

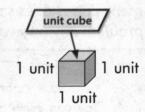

unit cube

1 unit 1 unit 1 unit

B Use unit cubes to make a model.

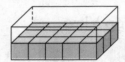

Count the number of cubes.

There are 15 unit cubes in the bottom layer. The volume of the bottom layer is 15 cubic units.

C There are two layers.

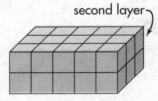

second layer

Multiply the volume of the bottom layer by 2.

The volume of the prism is 2 × 15 or 30 cubic units.

Convince Me! **Reasoning** In the picture below, how many unit cubes does it take to make the rectangular prism below without gaps or overlaps? How many 2-cube towers does it take to make the rectangular prism?

2-cube tower

© Pearson Education, Inc. 5

Name_____

☆ Guided Practice*

Do You Understand?

1. Make a model of a rectangular prism with a bottom layer that is 3 cubes long by 3 cubes wide. Make a top layer that is the same as the bottom layer. Then draw a picture of your model. What is the volume?

2. **A-Z Vocabulary** What is the difference between a unit cube and a cubic unit?

Do You Know How?

In **3** and **4**, use unit cubes to make a model of each rectangular prism. Find the volume.

3. 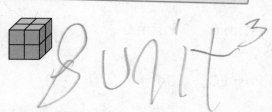 8 unit³

4. 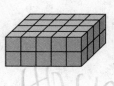 12 unit³

☆ Independent Practice ☆

In **5–13**, find the volume of each solid. Use unit cubes to help.

5. 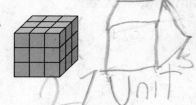 27 unit³

6. 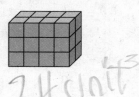 24 unit³

7. 40 unit³

8. 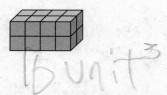 16 unit³

9.  10 unit³

10. 18 unit³

11. 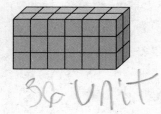 36 unit³

12. 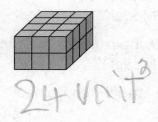 24 unit³

13. 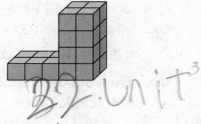 32 unit³

*For another example, see Set A on page 479.

Topic 11 | Lesson 11-1   **459**

Problem Solving

In **14–18**, use the table.

Compare the volumes of the prisms.
Write >, <, or = for each ◯.

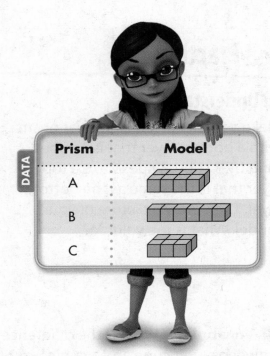

Prism	Model
A	
B	
C	

14. Prism A ◯ Prism B

15. Prism B ◯ Prism C

16. Prism C ◯ Prism A

17. If you added another layer of unit cubes on top of Prism A, what would the volume of the new solid be in cubic units?

18. If you put Prism C on top of Prism A, what would the volume of the new solid be in cubic units?

19. Reasoning In an election, 471 people voted. Candidate B received $\frac{2}{3}$ of the votes. How many votes did Candidate B receive?

20. Higher Order Thinking Ms. Kellson's storage closet is 3 feet long, 3 feet wide, and 7 feet high. Can she fit 67 boxes that each have a volume of 1 cubic foot in her closet? Explain your answer.

Assessment Practice

21. Natalie made the solid figures shown using unit cubes. Which statement about these models is true? 5.MD.3.3.a, 5.MD.3.3.b

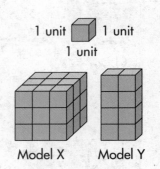

1 unit   1 unit
1 unit

Model X   Model Y

Ⓐ   Model X and Model Y have the same volume.

Ⓑ   The volume of Model X is 9 cubic units greater than the volume of Model Y.

Ⓒ   The volume of Model X is 19 cubic units greater than the volume of Model Y.

Ⓓ   The volume of Model X and Model Y combined is 45 cubic units.

© Pearson Education, Inc. 5

Name _____

Lesson 11-2
Develop a Volume Formula

☆ Solve & Share ☆

Kevin needs a new aquarium for his fish. The pet store has a fish tank in the shape of a rectangular prism that measures 5 feet long by 2 feet wide by 4 feet high. Kevin needs a fish tank that has a volume of at least 35 cubic feet. Will this fish tank be big enough? **Solve this problem any way you choose.**

I can ...
find the volume of rectangular prisms using a formula.

MAFS.5.MD.3.5.b Apply the formulas $V = l \times w \times h$ and $V = B \times h$ for rectangular prisms to find volumes of right rectangular prisms with whole-number edge lengths in the context of solving real world and mathematical problems. **Also 5.MD.3.5.a** **MAFS.K12.MP.2.1, MP.3.1**

Read the problem carefully to make sure that you understand what you are trying to find. *Show your work!*

Look Back! **Critique Reasoning** Malcolm says the volume of the aquarium would change if its dimensions were 2 feet long, 4 feet wide, and 5 feet high. Do you agree? Explain.

Essential Question **How Can You Use a Formula to Find the Volume of a Rectangular Prism?**

A

Remember that volume is the number of cubic units (units³) needed to pack a solid figure without gaps or overlaps.

Find the volume of the rectangular prism if each cubic unit represents 1 cubic foot.

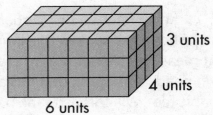

3 units

4 units

6 units

You can find the volume of a rectangular prism by counting cubes or using a formula.

A formula is a rule that uses symbols to relate two or more quantities.

B If the dimensions of a rectangular prism are given as length ℓ, width w, and height h, then use this formula to find the volume V:

Volume = length × width × height

$V = \ell \times w \times h$
$V = (6 \times 4) \times 3$
$V = 24 \times 3$
$V = 72$

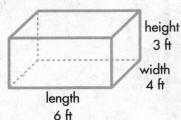

height
3 ft

width
4 ft

length
6 ft

The volume of the rectangular prism is 72 cubic feet or 72 ft³.

C Another formula for the volume of a rectangular prism is $V = B \times h$, where B is the area of the base.

$V = B \times h$
$V = 24 \times 3$
$V = 72$ ft³

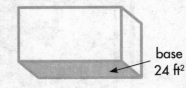

base
24 ft²

Convince Me! Reasoning Give the dimensions of a different rectangular prism that also has a volume of 72 ft³. Explain how you decided.

© Pearson Education, Inc. 5

Name _____

☆ Guided Practice*

Do You Understand?

1. In the example on page 462, could you first multiply the width by the height? Explain.

2. A wooden block measures 5 centimeters tall, 3 centimeters wide, and 2 centimeters long. The area of the base is 6 centimeters. Draw a rectangular prism to show the block and label it. What is the volume of the block?

Do You Know How?

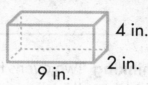
In **3** and **4**, find the volume of each rectangular prism.

3.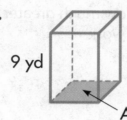
4 in.
2 in.
9 in.

4.
9 yd
Area of base: 24 yd²

☆ Independent Practice ☆

In **5–10**, find the volume of each rectangular prism.

5.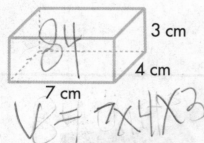
3 cm
4 cm
7 cm
V = 7×4×3

6.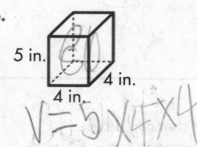
5 in.
4 in.
4 in.
V = 5×4×4

7.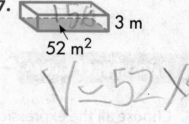
3 m
52 m²
V = 52×3

8.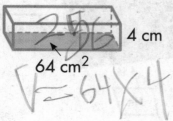
4 cm
64 cm²
V = 64×4

9.
7 m
7 m
7 m
V = 7×7×7

10.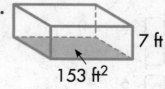
7 ft
153 ft²
V = 153×7

*For another example, see Set B on page 479.

Problem Solving

11. The dictionary is 3 inches thick. What is the volume of the dictionary?

9 in.

7 in.

---

12. Higher Order Thinking Two ovens have measurements as shown. Which oven has a greater volume? How much greater is its volume? Show your work.

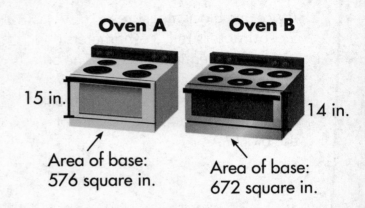

Oven A   **Oven B**

15 in.   14 in.

Area of base: Area of base:
576 square in.   672 square in.

---

13. The perimeter of an equilateral triangle is 51 feet. What is the length of one of its sides? Explain your work.

14. Reasoning Harry is in line at the store. He has three items that cost $5.95, $4.25, and $1.05. Explain how Harry can add the cost of the items mentally before he pays for them.

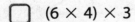 Assessment Practice

15. Choose all the expressions that can be used to find the volume of this wooden box. S.MD.3.5.b

- ☐ $(6 \times 4) \times 3$
- ☐ $(6 \times 4) + 3$
- ☐ 6×4
- ☐ $6 \times (4 \times 3)$
- ☐ 24×3

3 in.

4 in.

6 in.

© Pearson Education, Inc. 5

Name _____

☆ ⭐ ☆
Solve & Share

Ariel is thinking of a three-dimensional figure that is made by combining two rectangular prisms. What is the volume of this three-dimensional figure? *Solve this problem any way you choose.*

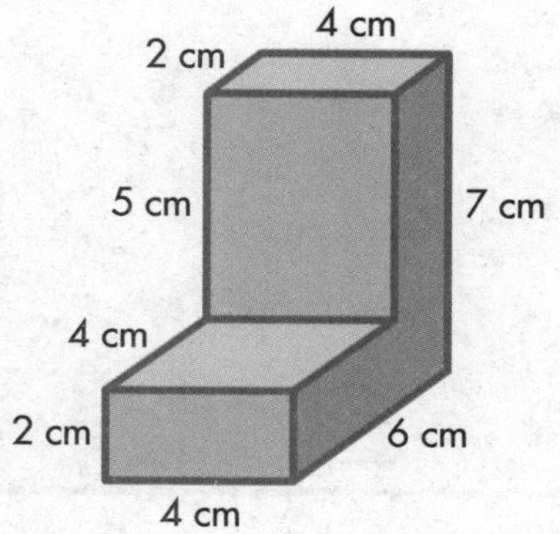

4 cm
2 cm
5 cm
7 cm
4 cm
2 cm
6 cm
4 cm

I can ...
find the volume of a solid figure that is the combination of two or more rectangular prisms.

MAFS.5.MD.3.5.c Recognize volume as additive. Find volume of solid figures composed of two non-overlapping right rectangular prisms by adding the volumes of the non-overlapping parts, applying this technique to solve real world problems. **MAFS.K12.MP.2.1, MP.4.1, MP.7.1**

Use Structure
You can find the volumes of the rectangular prisms that make up the solid figure. Show your work!

Look Back! How did you separate the solid into simpler rectangular prisms? Write the dimensions of each of the prisms.

Essential Question **How Can You Find the Volume of a Solid Figure Composed of Two Rectangular Prisms?**

A

The shape and size of a storage building are shown in the figure. The building supervisor wants to find the volume to determine how much storage space is available. What is the volume of the building?

You can find the volume of this figure by finding the volume of two rectangular prisms that make up the figure.

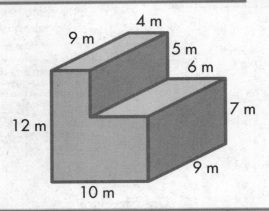

B The building can be separated into two rectangular prisms as shown. Identify the measurements for the length, width, and height of each prism.

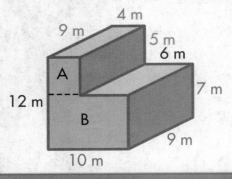

C Use the formula $V = \ell \times w \times h$ to find the volume of each rectangular prism.

Volume of Prism A	Volume of Prism B
$V = \ell \times w \times h$	$V = \ell \times w \times h$
$= 4 \times 9 \times 5$	$= 10 \times 9 \times 7$
$= 180$	$= 630$

Add to find the total volume.

$180 + 630 = 810$

The volume of the storage building is 810 cubic meters.

Convince Me! **Reasoning** What is another way to divide the solid above into two rectangular prisms? What are the dimensions of each prism?

© Pearson Education, Inc. 5

☆ Guided Practice ☆

Do You Understand?

In **1** and **2**, use the solid below. The dashed line separates it into two rectangular prisms, A and B.

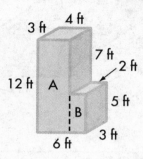

1. What are the length, width, and height of Prism A? What are the length, width, and height of Prism B?

2. What is another way you could separate the shape into two rectangular prisms? What are each prism's dimensions?

Do You Know How?

In **3** and **4**, find the volume of each solid figure.

3.

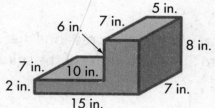

4.

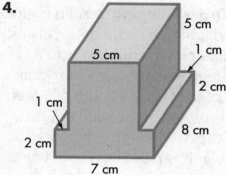

☆ Independent Practice ☆

In **5–7**, find the volume of each solid figure.

5.

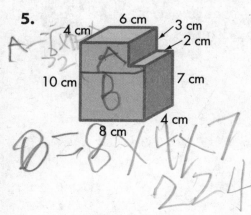

6.

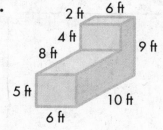

7.

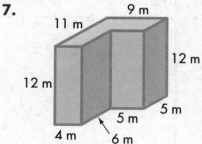

Problem Solving

For **8–10**, use the drawing of the solid figure.

8. How would you find the volume of the figure shown?

9. Algebra Write two expressions that can be added to find the volume of the solid figure.

10. What is the volume of the solid figure?

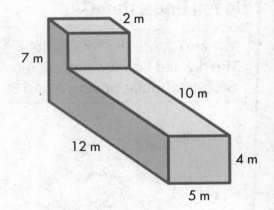

2 m

7 m

10 m

12 m

4 m

5 m

---

11. Higher Order Thinking A solid figure is separated into two rectangular prisms. The volume of Rectangular Prism A is 80 cubic feet. Rectangular Prism B has a length of 6 feet and a width of 5 feet. The total volume of the solid figure is 200 cubic feet. What is the height of Rectangular Prism B? Show your work.

12. Model with Math The Peters family will drive 615 miles to reach their vacation destination. If they drive 389 miles the first day, how many miles will they drive the second day? Complete the bar diagram to help.

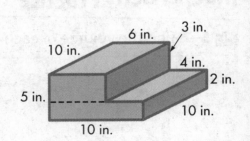

miles

| _____ miles | x |

Assessment Practice

13. A horizontal line separates the solid figure at the right into two rectangular prisms. Write an expression for the volume of the solid figure. **5.MD.3.5.c**

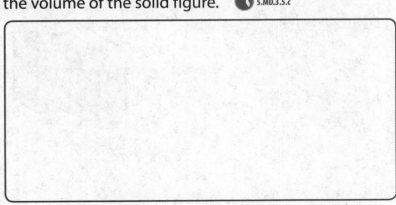

6 in.   3 in.

10 in.   4 in.

2 in.

5 in.

10 in.

10 in.

Name _____

⭐ Solve & Share

A school has two wings, each of which is a rectangular prism. The school district is planning to install air conditioning in the school and needs to know its volume. What is the volume of the school? *Solve this problem any way you choose.*

I can ...
solve word problems involving volume.

Model with Math Write a multiplication expression for the volume of each wing of the building.

MAFS.5.MD.3.5.c Recognize volume as additive. Find volume of solid figures composed of two non-overlapping right rectangular prisms by adding the volumes of the non-overlapping parts, applying this technique to solve real world problems. MAFS.K12.MP.3.1, MP.4.1

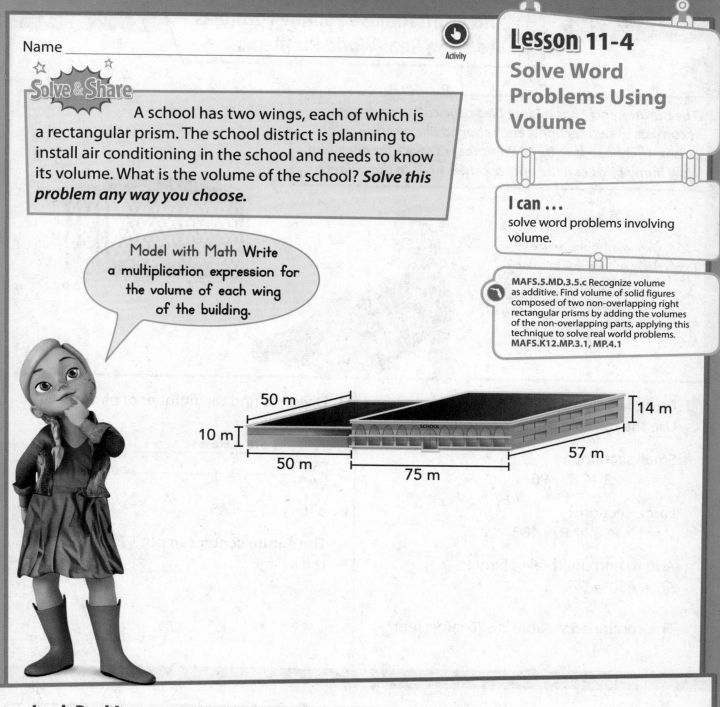

Look Back! Write a mathematical expression that can be used to find the total volume of the school.

Essential Question

How Can You Use Volume Formulas to Solve Real-World Problems?

A

The nature center has a large bird cage called an aviary. It consists of two sections, each shaped like a rectangular prism. There needs to be 10 cubic feet of space for each bird. How many birds can the nature center have in the aviary?

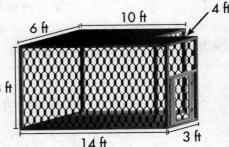

You can make sense of the problem by breaking it apart into simpler problems.

B Find the volume of each section. Use the formula $V = \ell \times w \times h$.

Small section:
$V = 4 \times 3 \times 8 = 96$

Large section:
$V = 10 \times 6 \times 8 = 480$

Add to find the total volume:
$96 + 480 = 576$

The combined volume is 576 cubic feet.

C Divide to find the number of birds that will fit.

576 cubic feet

| 10 cu ft | ? → |

$576 \div 10 = 57.6$

The nature center can put 57 birds in the aviary.

Convince Me! **Critique Reasoning** Tom solved the problem a different way. First he found the total area of the floor, and then he multiplied by the height. Does Tom's method work? Explain.

© Pearson Education, Inc. 5

Name _____

☆ Guided Practice *

Do You Understand?

1. How can you find the volume of the china cabinet?

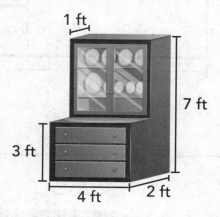

2. What is the height of the top section of the china cabinet? Explain.

3. Find the volume of the china cabinet.

Do You Know How?

4. Find the volume of the building below.

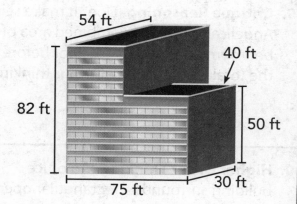

5. The nature center has a fish tank shaped like a rectangular prism that measures 6 feet long by 4 feet wide by 4 feet high. It can be stocked safely with 3 small fish in each cubic foot of water. How many small fish can safely fit in the tank?

☆ Independent Practice *

6. Sophie built a house out of building blocks. Find the volume of the house Sophie built.

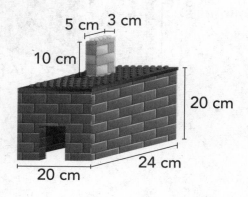

7. How many cubic inches of concrete would it take to make these stairs?

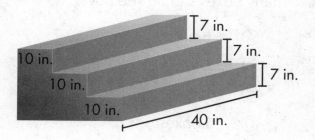

Problem Solving

8. A floor plan of Angelica's bedroom and closet is shown at the right. The height of the bedroom is 9 feet. The height of the closet is 7 feet. What is the total volume of the bedroom and the closet?

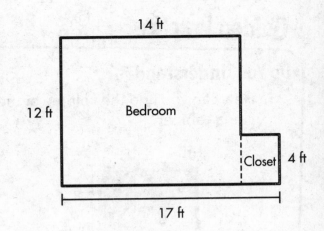

9. **Critique Reasoning** Does it make sense for Angelica to find the combined area of the bedroom floor and closet floor before finding the total volume? Explain your thinking.

10. **Higher Order Thinking** An office building surrounds a rectangular open-air courtyard. What is the volume of the building? How did you find the answer?

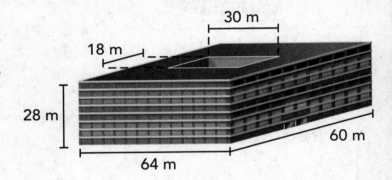

---

11. Mrs. Bhatia's closet consists of two sections, each shaped like a rectangular prism. She plans to buy mothballs to keep the moths away. She needs one box for every 32 cubic feet of space. How many boxes should she buy? 🔵 5.MD.3.5.c

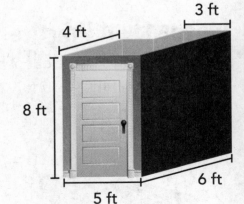

   (A) 6 boxes

   (B) 7 boxes

   (C) 8 boxes

   (D) 10 boxes

Name _____

Solve & Share

A space station is being built from 24 cubic modules. The space station can be any shape but the modules must be placed together so that entire faces match up with each other. Choose a tool to create two different plans for the space station. Explain why you chose the tool you selected.

I can ...
use appropriate tools to solve volume problems.

MAFS.K12.MP.5.1 Use appropriate tools. **Also MP.4.1, MP.7.1**
MAFS.5.MD.3.3a A cube with side length 1 unit, called a "unit cube," is said to have "one cubic unit" of volume, and can be used to measure volume.

Thinking Habits

Be a good thinker!
These questions can help you.

- Which tools can I use?

- Why should I use this tool to help me solve the problem?

- Is there a different tool I could use?

- Am I using the tool appropriately?

Look Back! **Use Appropriate Tools** How did you decide which tool to use?

A

Jeremiah needs to build a display of boxes that is 4 feet tall.

The boxes he uses are cubes that measure 1 foot on each edge. His display needs to look like a pyramid, with just one box in the top layer.

How many boxes will Jeremiah need to make his display?

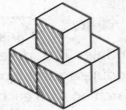

Top Layer   **Top 2 Layers**

What do I need to do?

I need to choose an appropriate tool to solve this problem.

 Here's my thinking...

B **How can I use appropriate tools strategically to help me solve this problem?**

I can

- decide which tool is appropriate.

- use cubes to solve this problem.

- use the tool correctly.

C I could use grid paper, but I will use cubes because building a display will make it easier to count the cubes.

Each cube represents 1 box in the display. My display will have 4 layers because it needs to be 4 feet tall, and each box is 1 foot high.

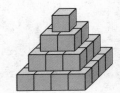

The display has $1 + 4 + 9 + 16 = 30$ cubes.

So, Jeremiah needs 30 boxes in all to make his display.

Convince Me! **Use Appropriate Tools** What tools other than cubes could you use to solve this problem? Explain.

© Pearson Education, Inc. 5

☆Guided Practice*

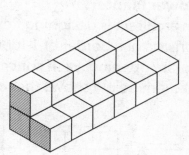

Use Appropriate Tools

A paint store manager is going to build a display with same-sized cubes. The display will look like a staircase with 5 steps. Each step in the display will be 6 cubes long. The store manager will build the staircase display with 1-foot plastic cubes.

1. What tool might the manager use to be sure that there is enough space for the display? Explain.

2. What is the volume of the display? Explain how you used tools to decide.

Independent Practice ☆

Use Appropriate Tools

Cindy plans to make a jewelry box shaped like a rectangular prism. She wants it to have a volume of 96 cubic inches.

Think about a tool you can use to help represent and solve the problem.

3. How can you find possible dimensions of the box?

4. What could the dimensions of that jewelry box be?

5. Can Cindy build the box so that it is twice as wide as it is tall?

6. Cindy has some ribbon to decorate the jewelry box. What tool might help her decide how much of the jewelry box she can decorate?

Problem Solving

Flower Planters

An architect is designing flower planters for a park. Each planter consists of a border of 1-foot concrete cubes surrounding a square opening. Each concrete cube weighs 120 pounds. The diagram below shows the top view of some of the planters.

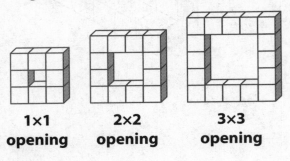

1×1 opening   **2×2 opening**   **3×3 opening**

> Remember to think about which tools make sense for these problems.

7. **Use Structure** What is the total volume of a planter that has a 6 × 6 opening? 5.MD.3.3a, MP.7.1

8. **Use Structure** What is the total volume of a planter that has an 8 × 8 opening? 5.MD.3.3a, MP.7.1

9. **Use Appropriate Tools** What will be the total volume of a planter that has a 12 × 12 opening? Can you determine this by just using paper and pencil? Explain. 5.MD.3.3a, MP.5.1

10. **Model with Math** Each concrete cube used to make the planters costs $3.00. What is the total cost of the cubes needed for two planters with 6 × 6 openings, two with 8 × 8 openings, and two with 12 × 12 openings? Write an expression that represents the total cost. 5.MD.3.3a, MP.4.1

© Pearson Education, Inc. 5

Name _____

Fluency Practice Activity

Find a Match

Work with a partner. Point to a clue.

Read the clue.

Look below the clues to find a match. Write the clue letter in the box above the match.

Find a match for every clue.

I can ...
fluently multiply multi-digit whole numbers.

MAFS.5.NBT.2.5

Clues

A The product is greater than 1,000,000.

B The product is 43,575.

C The product is 51,192.

D The product is between 150,000 and 200,000.

E The product is 550,000.

F The product is 550,055.

G The digit 7 appears twice in the product.

H The digit 2 appears twice in the product.

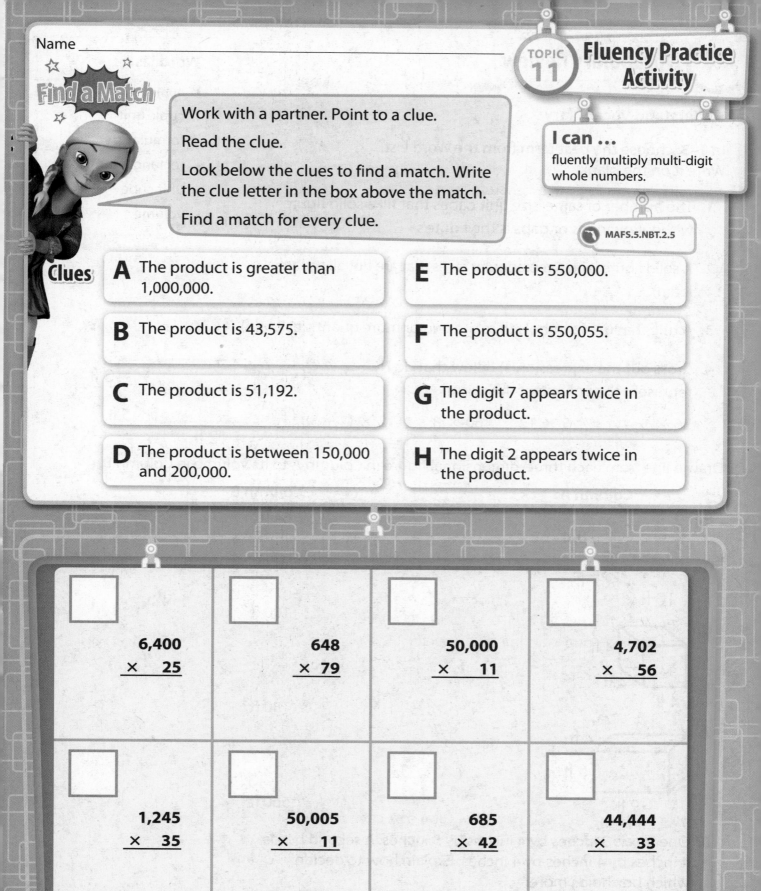

6,400 × 25	648 × 79	50,000 × 11	4,702 × 56
1,245 × 35	50,005 × 11	685 × 42	44,444 × 33

TOPIC 11 | Vocabulary Review

Glossary

Word List

- area
- cubic unit
- formula
- rectangular prism
- unit cube
- volume

Understand Vocabulary

In **1–3**, choose the best term from the Word List.
Write it on the blank.

1. The number of same-size unit cubes that fill a solid figure without overlaps or gaps is the figure's _____.

2. A solid figure with 6 rectangular faces that are not all squares is a(n) _____.

3. A rule that uses symbols to relate two or more quantities is a(n) _____.

4. Cross out the expression(s) below that do NOT represent the volume of the prism.

   36×5 $3 \times 5 \times 12$ 60×3 $12 \times (3 + 5)$

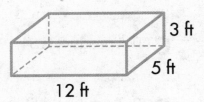

Draw a line from each three-dimensional figure in Column A to its volume in Column B.

Column A

5.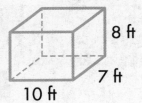

6.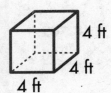

7.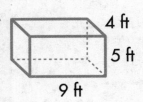

Column B

64 ft³

100 ft³

180 ft³

560 ft³

8. One box is 3 inches by 4 inches by 5 inches. A second box is 4 inches by 4 inches by 4 inches. Explain how to decide which box holds more.

    © Pearson Education, Inc. 5

Name _____

Set A pages 457–460

Find the number of cubes needed to make this rectangular prism.

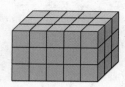

There are 3 rows of 5 cubes in the bottom layer. There are 3 layers.

Multiply to find the total number of cubes.

$3 \times 5 \times 3 = 45$

The volume is 45 cubic units.

Remember, you can multiply the numbers in any order!

Remember that you can find the number of cubes in each layer and then multiply by the number of layers.

Find each volume. You may use cubes to help.

1.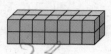
   28

2.
   20

3.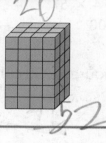
   32

Set B pages 461–464

Find the volume of this rectangular prism.

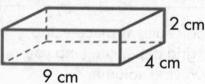

2 cm
4 cm
9 cm

Volume = length × width × height

$V = \ell \times w \times h$

$= 9 \text{ cm} \times 4 \text{ cm} \times 2 \text{ cm}$

$V = 72$ cubic centimeters or 72 cm³

The volume of the prism is 72 cm³.

Remember if you know the area of the base of a rectangular prism, use the formula $V = B \times h$, where B is the area of the base.

Find each volume. You may use cubes to help.

1. Area of the base, $B = 42$ square meters and height = 3 meters

2. Area of the base = 75 square inches and height = 15 inches

3.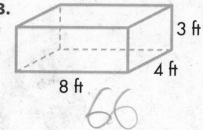
   3 ft
   4 ft
   8 ft
   66

Some solid figures can be separated into two rectangular prisms.

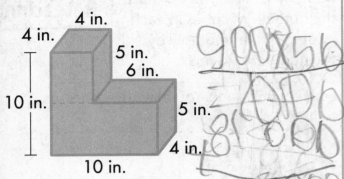

Add the volume of each prism to find the total volume of the solid figure.

$V = (4 \times 4 \times 5) + (10 \times 4 \times 5)$

$\quad = \qquad 80 \qquad + \qquad 200$

$\quad = 280$

The volume of the solid figure is 280 cubic inches.

Remember to identify the length, width, and height of each prism, so that you can calculate the volume of each part.

1. Find the volume.

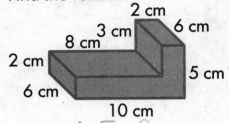

2. An office building has the dimensions shown. What is the volume of the building?

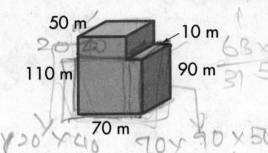

Think about these questions to help you **use appropriate tools strategically**.

Thinking Habits

- Which tools can I use?

- Why should I use this tool to help me solve the problem?

- Is there a different tool I could use?

- Am I using the tool appropriately?

Remember that tools such as place-value blocks, cubes, and grid paper can help you solve problems involving volume.

Molly used 1-inch cubes to build the structure shown. She left a 3-inch by 1-inch opening in both layers of the structure.

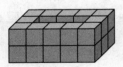

1. What tools could you use to model the problem?

2. What is the total volume of the structure?

© Pearson Education, Inc. 5

1. Julio used unit cubes to make a rectangular prism. What is the volume of the prism?

1 cube = 1 cubic unit

Ⓐ 18 cubic units   Ⓒ 72 cubic units

Ⓑ 54 cubic units   Ⓓ 108 cubic units

2. Select the possible dimensions for a prism with each given volume.

	3 cm, 4 cm, 5 cm	3 cm, 3 cm, 5 cm	2 cm, 4 cm, 9 cm	2 cm, 4 cm, 7 cm
45 cm³	❑	☑	❑	❑
56 cm³	❑	❑	❑	☑
60 cm³	☑	❑	❑	❑
72 cm³	❑	❑	☑	❑

3. A. A swimming pool is 50 meters long, 15 meters wide, and 3 meters deep. What is the volume of the pool?

Ⓐ 4,500 cubic meters

Ⓑ 2,250 cubic meters

Ⓒ 900 cubic meters

Ⓓ 750 cubic meters

B. After filling the pool for several minutes, the water is 1 meter deep. What is the volume of water in the pool?

750

4. A small building has the dimensions shown.

A. Write an expression for the total volume of the building.

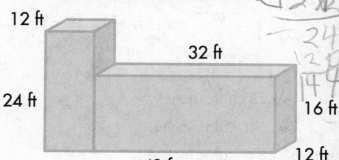

12 ft

32 ft

24 ft

16 ft

12 ft

40 ft

144 × 24 + 192 × 32

B. What is the volume of the building?

5. A. Choose all the expressions that could **NOT** be used to find the volume of the bale of hay.

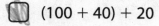

20 cm

40 cm

100 cm

❑ 100 × 40   ❑ (100 × 40) × 20

❑ 4,000 × 20   ☑ (100 × 40) + 20

☑ (100 + 40) + 20

B. Another 10 cm of hay is added to the top of the bale. What is the volume of the bale of hay now?

6. Madeline made the wooden steps shown. What is the volume of the steps?

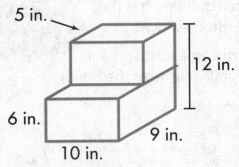

5 in.

12 in.

6 in.

9 in.

10 in.

- Ⓐ 72 cubic inches
- Ⓑ 540 cubic inches
- Ⓒ 840 cubic inches
- Ⓓ 1,080 cubic inches

7. A. What is the volume of the trunk shown?

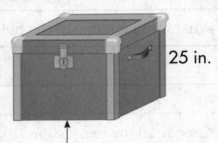

25 in.

Area of base: 750 in²

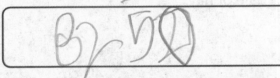

B. Which equation was used to find the volume of the trunk?

- Ⓐ $V = B \times h$
- Ⓑ $V = \ell \times w \times h$
- Ⓒ $V = \ell \times w$
- Ⓓ $V = B \times B \times h$

8. For her science project, Jada wants to build a rectangular prism out of foam blocks. The prism should have a volume of 350 cubic inches and a height of 5 inches.

What does the area of the base of the prism need to be for the given volume and height? Give one pair of possible whole-number dimensions for the base.

9. Martin's suitcase has a volume of 1,080 cubic inches. Lily's suitcase measures 9 inches wide, 13 inches long, and 21 inches high. What is the combined volume of the two suitcases?

10. Select all the expressions that can be used to find the volume of the box in cubic centimeters.

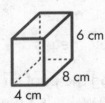

6 cm

8 cm

4 cm

- ☐ 8 × 6
- ☐ 32 × 6
- ☐ (4 × 8) + 6
- ☐ (4 × 8) × 6
- ☐ 46 × 8

© Pearson Education, Inc. 5

Name _____

Sporting Goods

Hiroto works in a sporting goods store.

1. Hiroto stacks identical boxes of golf balls to form a rectangular prism. Each box is a cube.

Golf Ball Display

Part A

How many boxes are in the **Golf Ball Display**? 5.MD.3.3.a, 5.MD.3.4, MP.5.1

Part B

Explain how the number of boxes you found in Part A is the same as what you would find by using the formula $V = \ell \times w \times h$. 5.MD.3.5.b, MP.3.1

Part C

Hiroto needs to restack the boxes so the display is 2 layers high, less than 14 inches wide, and less than 30 inches long. The size of each box is shown in at the right. What is one way Hiroto can stack the boxes? Justify your answer. 5.MD.3.5.b, MP.1.1

2 in.
2 in.
2 in.

Part D

What is the volume of the golf ball display in cubic inches? Explain how you solved. 🔖 5.MD.3.5.b, MP.6.1

2. Hiroto builds two displays using rectangular foam blocks.

Part A

What is the volume of the foam block used for the **Baseball Hats and Helmets Display**? Explain how to solve using the formula $V = B \times h$. 🔖 5.MD.3.5.b, MP.3.1

Baseball Hats and Helmets Display

30 in.
36 in.
58 in.

Part B

Hiroto used two blocks to build the **Baseball Uniforms Display**. What is the combined volume of the blocks? Explain how you solved. 🔖 5.MD.3.5.b, MP.1.1

Baseball Uniforms Display

8 in.
10 in.
28 in.
48 in.
24 in.

Part C

Explain how you knew which units to use for your answer to Part B. 🔖 5.MD.3.4, MP.3.1

© Pearson Education, Inc. 5

Convert Measurements

Essential Questions: What are customary measurement units and how are they related? What are metric measurement units and how are they related?

Digital Resources

Interactive Student Edition | Activity | Visual Learning | Video | Practice

Assessment | Games | Tools | Glossary

Wind and water carved out the Grand Canyon.

The flowing water of the Colorado River moved rock and soil to help form the canyon. This is called *water erosion*.

That's a lot of movement! Here's a project about the Grand Canyon.

MAFS.5.MD.1.1, 5.NBT.1.2, 5.NBT.2.5, 5.NBT.2.6
MAFS.K12.MP.1.1, MP.2.1, MP.3.1, MP.4.1, MP.6.1, MP.7.1, MP.8.1

enVision STEM Project: Grand Canyon

Do Research Use the Internet and other sources to learn about the Grand Canyon and the Colorado River. Where is the Grand Canyon? How was it formed? What do the different rock layers tell us? Predict how you think the canyon dimensions will change in a million years.

Journal: Write a Report Include what you found. Also in your report:

- Describe the canyon's dimensions.
- Describe the Colorado River's dimensions.
- Define erosion.
- Make up and solve problems involving measurement units and conversions.

Review What You Know

A-Z
Vocabulary

Choose the best term from the box.
Write it on the blank.

• customary   • multiplication
• exponent   • subtraction
• metric

1. A meter is a unit of length in the _____ system of measurement.

2. A foot is a unit of length in the _____ system of measurement.

3. Division has an inverse relationship with _____.

4. A(n) _____ shows the number of times a base is used as a factor.

Multiplication

Find each product.

5. 60×6

6. 24×10^3

7. 16×7

8. $10^2 \times 1.6$

9. 100×34

10. $10^4 \times 0.37$

11. 46.102×10^2

12. $10^1 \times 0.005$

Division

Find each quotient.

13. $1,000 \div 100$

14. $176 \div 16$

15. $3,600 \div 60$

16. $120 \div 24$

Measurement

Circle the more appropriate unit of measure for each item.

17. The capacity of a swimming pool: liters or milliliters

18. The length of an ear of corn: yards or inches

19. The mass of a gorilla: grams or kilograms

20. The weight of a tennis ball: ounces or pounds

21. Would you use more centimeters or meters to measure the length of car? Explain.

© Pearson Education, Inc. 5

Name

PROJECT 12A

What makes a treehouse so cool?

Project: Build a Model of a Treehouse

PROJECT 12B

What would you weigh on Mars?

Project: Make a Mobile Display of the Solar System

Have you ever heard of National Punch Day?

Project: Plan a Class Party

What are the characteristics of Florida panthers?

Project: Design a Zoo Space for Florida Panther Cubs

© Pearson Education, Inc. 5

Name _____

☆ ☆
Solve & Share

William has a piece of wire that measures 1 yard long. He will use wire to fix several electrical outlets in his house. How many inches long is the wire? *Solve this problem by using bar diagrams.*

I can ...
convert customary units of length.

MAFS.5.MD.1.1 Convert among different-sized standard measurement units (i.e., km, m, cm; kg, g; lb, oz.; l, ml; hr, min, sec) within a given measurement system (e.g., convert 5 cm to 0.05 m), and use these conversions in solving multi-step, real world problems. **Also 5.NBT.2.5, 5.NBT.2.6 MAFS.K12.MP.2.1, MP.8.1**

You can show the relationship between yards and inches in a bar diagram. *Show your work!*

1 yard

Look Back! **Generalize** How can you convert inches to yards? Would you multiply or divide when converting from a smaller unit to a larger unit? Explain.

Essential Question

How Do You Change from One Unit of Length to Another?

A

Some frogs can jump $11\frac{1}{4}$ feet. What are some other ways to describe the same distance?

The table shows equivalent measures.

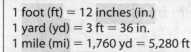

1 foot (ft) = 12 inches (in.)
1 yard (yd) = 3 ft = 36 in.
1 mile (mi) = 1,760 yd = 5,280 ft

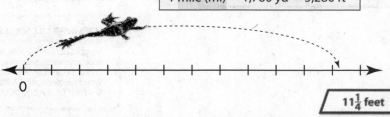

0

$11\frac{1}{4}$ feet

B To change larger units to smaller units, **multiply**.

$11\frac{1}{4}$ ft = ☐ in.

You know 1 foot equals 12 inches.

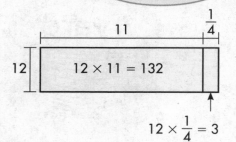

$$11\frac{1}{4} \times 12 = 132 + 3 = 135$$

So, $11\frac{1}{4}$ feet = 135 inches.

C To change smaller units to larger units, **divide**.

Ed's frog jumped 11 feet. How many yards is this?

11 ft = ☐ yd ☐ ft

You know 3 feet is equal to 1 yard.

1 ft

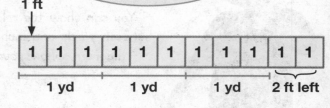

1 yd   1 yd   1 yd   2 ft left

$11 \div 3 = 3$ R2   So, 11 feet = 3 yards, 2 feet.

Convince Me! Generalize In the example above, explain how you could use a mixed number to write 11 feet as an equivalent measure in yards.

© Pearson Education, Inc. 5

☆ Guided Practice

Do You Understand?

1. If you want to convert yards to feet, what operation would you use?

2. If you want to convert feet to miles, what operation would you use?

3. What are some tools you could select to measure length? Explain when you would use them.

Do You Know How?

In **4–8**, convert each unit of length.

4. 9 ft = _____ yd

5. 8 ft 7 in. = _____ in.

6. $5\frac{1}{2}$ ft = _____ in.

7. 288 in. = _____ yd

8. 219 in. = _____ ft _____ in. or _____ ft

Independent Practice ☆

In **9** and **10**, complete the table to show equivalent measures.

Will the number in your answer be greater than or less than the number in the given measurement?

9.

Feet	Inches
1	
2	
	36
4	

10.

Yards	Feet
1	
	6
3	
4	

In **11–16**, convert each unit of length.

11. 3 yd = _____ in.

12. 324 ft = _____ yd

13. $2\frac{2}{3}$ mi = _____ ft

14. 56 ft = _____ yd _____ ft

15. $12\frac{1}{2}$ ft = _____ in.

16. 6 in. = _____ ft

In **17–19**, compare lengths. Write >, <, or = for each ◯.

17. 100 ft ◯ 3 yd

18. 74 in. ◯ 2 yd 2 in.

19. 5,200 ft 145 in. ◯ 1 mi 40 in.

Problem Solving

20. Number Sense Which number would be greater, the height of a tree in feet or the height of the same tree in yards?

21. Reasoning The dimensions of the nation's smallest post office are 8 feet 4 inches by 7 feet 3 inches. Why would you use the measurement 8 feet 4 inches instead of 7 feet 16 inches?

---

22. Roger earns $24 a week mowing lawns. He spends $\frac{1}{6}$ of his earnings on lunch and $\frac{2}{3}$ of his earnings on music. He saves the rest. How many dollars does Roger save? Tell how you found the answer.

23. Ariana has 144 peaches. She has to pack 9 boxes with an equal number of peaches. How many peaches should she pack in each box?

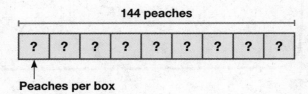

Peaches per box

---

24. Higher Order Thinking How do you convert 108 inches to yards?

25. (A-Z) **Vocabulary** What is an appropriate customary unit to use when measuring the length of a driveway? Justify your answer.

---

26. Select all of the measurements greater than 7 feet. 5.MD.1.1

- [ ] 2 yards
- [ ] 2 yards 2 inches
- [ ] 2 yards 2 feet
- [ ] 3 yards

27. Select all of the measurements less than 435 inches. 5.MD.1.1

- [ ] 37 feet
- [ ] 36 feet 2 inches
- [ ] 12 yards 3 inches
- [ ] 12 feet 3 inches

© Pearson Education, Inc. 5

Name _____

Lesson 12-2
Convert Customary Units of Capacity

Solve & Share

A recipe makes 16 cups of soup. How many quarts does the recipe make? Remember, there are 2 cups in a pint and 2 pints in a quart. **Solve this problem any way you choose!**

____ cups = 1 quart

16 cups = ____ quarts

I can ...
convert customary units of capacity.

MAFS.5.MD.1.1 Convert among different-sized standard measurement units (i.e., km, m, cm; kg, g; lb, oz.; l, ml; hr, min, sec) within a given measurement system (e.g., convert 5 cm to 0.05 m), and use these conversions in solving multi-step, real world problems. **Also 5.NBT.2.5, 5.NBT.2.6 MAFS.K12.MP.2.1, MP.8.1**

You can use reasoning to help you convert between different units.

Look Back! Is the number of cups greater than or less than the number of quarts? Why do you think that is?

How Do You Convert Customary Units of Capacity?

A

Sue is making punch. She needs $3\frac{3}{4}$ cups of orange juice and 5 pints of lemonade. How many fluid ounces of orange juice and how many quarts of lemonade does she need?

1 gallon (gal) = 4 quarts (qt)
1 quart = 2 pints (pt)
1 pint = 2 cups (c)
1 cup = 8 fluid ounces (fl oz)

You can multiply or divide to convert one unit of capacity to a different one.

| 1 cup | 1 pint | 1 quart |

B **To change a larger unit to a smaller unit, multiply.**

$3\frac{3}{4}$ c = $\square$ fl oz

$3\frac{3}{4}$ c

| 8 fl oz | 8 fl oz | 8 fl oz | 6 fl oz |

$3\frac{3}{4} \times 8 = (3 \times 8) + \left(\frac{3}{4} \times 8\right)$

$= 24 + 6 = 30$

So, $3\frac{3}{4}$ cups = 30 fluid ounces.

C **To change a smaller unit to a larger unit, divide.**

 5 pt = $\square$ qt

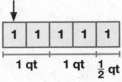 2 pints equals 1 quart.

1 pt

| 1 | 1 | 1 | 1 | 1 |

1 qt   1 qt $\frac{1}{2}$ qt

Find 5 ÷ 2.

$5 \div 2 = \frac{5}{2} = 2\frac{1}{2}$

So, 5 pints = $2\frac{1}{2}$ quarts.

 Convince Me! **Generalize** When you convert from pints to quarts, why do you divide?

© Pearson Education, Inc. 5

Name_____

☆ Guided Practice *

Do You Understand?

1. Why would you change 4 gallons 5 quarts to 5 gallons 1 quart?

2. Why is $\frac{1}{8}$ cup equal to 1 fluid ounce?

Do You Know How?

In **3–8**, convert each unit of capacity.

3. 32 c = _____ gal   **4.** $\frac{1}{2}$ qt = _____ gal

5. 48 qt = _____ pt   **6.** $6\frac{1}{8}$ qt = _____ c

7. 3 qt 1 pt = _____ pt

8. 9 pt = _____ qt _____ pt or _____ qt

☆ Independent Practice ☆

In **9–20**, convert each unit of capacity.

9. 10 pt = _____ qt   **10.** 48 fl oz = _____ c   **11.** $\frac{1}{2}$ c = _____ pt

You may need to convert more than once.

12. $9\frac{1}{4}$ pt = _____ c   **13.** 36 pt = _____ qt   **14.** 30 qt = _____ gal _____ qt

15. 1 qt = _____ gal   **16.** 5 gal = _____ c   **17.** 1 gal 1 c = _____ fl oz

18. 7 c = _____ fl oz   **19.** 72 pt = _____ gal   **20.** $\frac{1}{3}$ pt = _____ c

21. Complete the table to show equivalent measures.

Gallons	Quarts	Pints	Cups	Fluid Ounces
1		8		
2				256

Problem Solving

For **22–24**, use the aquarium.

22. The class aquarium holds 2 gallons of water. How many cups is this? How many fluid ounces is this?

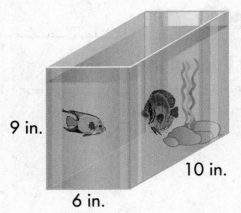

9 in.

10 in.

6 in.

23. Susan finds that 2 pints 1 cup of water has evaporated from the class aquarium. How many pints of water are left in the aquarium?

24. If all of the dimensions of the aquarium were doubled, what would be the volume of the new aquarium?

25. Carrie has 3 gallons of paint. Bryan has 10 quarts of paint. How many more pints of paint does Carrie have than Bryan?

26. **Reasoning** Lorelei filled her 5-gallon jug with water. How many times could she fill her 2-quart canteen with water from the jug? Explain.

27. **Higher Order Thinking** A recipe calls for 3 tablespoons of pineapple juice. A can of pineapple juice is 12 fluid ounces. How many teaspoons of juice are in the can?

DATA

| 1 tablespoon (tbsp) = 3 teaspoons (tsp) |
| 1 fluid ounce (fl oz) = 2 tablespoons (tbsp) |

Assessment Practice

28. Choose all the measurements that are greater than 4 cups. 5.MD.1.1

- ☐ 30 fluid ounces
- ☐ 2 pints
- ☐ 3 pints
- ☐ 1 quart
- ☐ 1 gallon

29. Choose all the statements that are true. 5.MD.1.1

- ☐ 15 pt < 2 gal
- ☐ 1 gal < 5 qt
- ☐ 12 fl oz > 2 c
- ☐ 2 qt 1 cup > 10 cups
- ☐ 20 pints = 10 quarts

© Pearson Education, Inc. 5

Name _____

Solve & Share

Maria adopted 4 dogs. All together they eat $1\frac{3}{4}$ pound of food each day. One pound is equal to 16 ounces. How many ounces of food will the dogs eat in 5 days? **Solve this problem any way you choose.**

I can ...
convert customary units of weight.

Use Appropriate Tools You can use drawings or equations to solve the problem. *Show your work!*

MAFS.5.MD.1.1 Convert among different-sized standard measurement units (i.e., km, m, cm; kg, g; lb, oz.; l, ml; hr, min, sec) within a given measurement system (e.g., convert 5 cm to 0.05 m), and use these conversions in solving multi-step, real world problems. Also 5.NBT. 2.5, 5.NBT.2.6 MAFS.K12.MP.5.1, MP.6.1, MP.8.1

Look Back! Which is the larger unit of weight, an ounce or a pound? How can you use this relationship to find the number of ounces in 5 pounds?

Essential Question **How Can You Convert Units of Weight?**

A

An adult African elephant weighs about 5 tons. A baby African elephant weighs about 250 pounds. How many pounds does the adult elephant weigh? How can you convert 250 pounds to tons?

1 ton (T) = 2,000 pounds (lb)
1 pound (lb) = 16 ounces (oz)

To convert from one unit of weight to another, you can use multiplication or division.

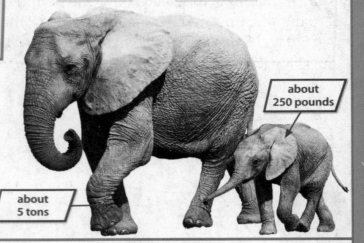

about 250 pounds

about 5 tons

B **To convert from larger units to smaller units, multiply.**

$5 \text{ T} = \square \text{ lb}$

1 ton equals 2,000 pounds.

5 T				
2,000 lb	2,000 lb	2,000 lb	2,000 lb	2,000 lb

Find $5 \times 2,000$.

$5 \times 2,000 = 10,000$

So, 5 tons = 10,000 pounds.

C **To convert from smaller units to larger units, divide.**

$250 \text{ lb} = \square \text{ T}$

2,000 pounds equals 1 ton.

? T → 250 lb

1 T → 2,000 lb

Find $\frac{250}{2,000}$.

$\frac{250 \div 250}{2,000 \div 250} = \frac{1}{8}$ So, 250 pounds = $\frac{1}{8}$ ton.

Convince Me! **Generalize** When you convert 16 pounds to ounces, do you multiply or divide? Explain.

© Pearson Education, Inc. 5

☆ Guided Practice ☆

Do You Understand?

1. Would it be best to measure the weight of an egg in tons, pounds, or ounces? Explain.

2. What types of tools do people select to measure weight? Explain your example.

Do You Know How?

In **3–6**, convert each unit of weight.

3. 2,000 lb = _____ T **4.** 48 oz = _____ lb

5. 6,500 lb = _____ T **6.** $\frac{1}{2}$ lb = _____ oz

In **7** and **8**, compare. Write $>$, $<$, or $=$ for each ◯.

7. 2 T ◯ 45,000 lb **8.** 4 lb ◯ 64 oz

☆ Independent Practice ☆

In **9–14**, convert each unit of weight.

9. 240 oz = _____ lb **10.** $7\frac{1}{10}$ T = _____ lb **11.** 8 lb = _____ oz

Will your answer be greater than or less than the number you started with?

12. 4 oz = _____ lb **13.** 250 lb = _____ T **14.** 1 T = _____ oz

In **15–17**, compare. Write $>$, $<$, $=$ for each ◯.

15. 5,000 lb ◯ 3 T **16.** 24 lb ◯ 124 oz **17.** 64,000 oz ◯ 2 T

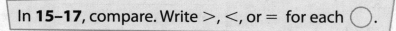

In **18** and **19**, complete each table to show equivalent measures.

18.

pounds	$\frac{1}{2}$		5
ounces		32	

19.

tons	$\frac{1}{2}$	2	
pounds			12,000

Problem Solving

20. Be Precise The perimeter of the rectangular playground shown below is 160 feet. What is the area of the playground?

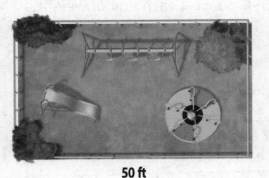

50 ft

21. enVision® STEM Humans exploring space have left behind bags of trash, bolts, gloves, and pieces of satellites. There are currently about 4,000,000 pounds of litter in orbit around Earth. Julia says that this amount using number names is four billion. Do you agree? Explain your thinking.

In **22–25**, use the table.

22. What would be the most appropriate unit to measure the combined weight of 4 horses?

23. About how much would 4 horses weigh? Write the weight two different ways.

24. How many more ounces does the sheep weigh than the ape?

25. Higher Order Thinking What is the difference in weight between the horse and the combined weight of the dolphin and the ape? Write your answer in tons.

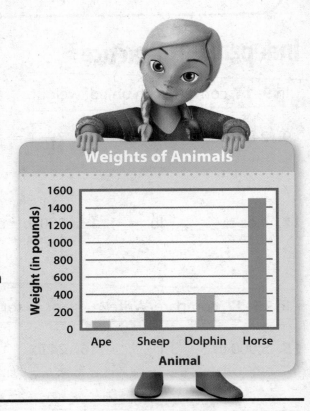

Weights of Animals

Assessment Practice

26. Part A

The world's heaviest lobster weighed 44 pounds 6 ounces. Write the lobster's weight in ounces below.

44 lb 6 oz = _____ ounces   5.MD.1.1

Part B

Describe the steps you took to find your answer.   5.MD.1.1

© Pearson Education, Inc. 5

Name _____

Activity

Solve & Share

Measure the length of your book in centimeters. Then measure it in millimeters. What do you notice about the two measurements?

1 cm = ____ mm

length of book: ____ cm

length of book: ____ mm

I can ...
convert metric units of length.

MAFS.5.MD.1.1 Convert among different-sized standard measurement units (i.e., km, m, cm; kg, g; lb, oz.; l, ml; hr, min, sec) within a given measurement system (e.g., convert 5 cm to 0.05 m), and use these conversions in solving multi-step, real world problems. **Also 5.NBT.1.2 MAFS.K12.MP.2.1, MP.3.1, MP.7.1**

You can select appropriate units and tools to measure the length of objects!

Look Back! **Use Structure** How many meters long is your textbook? How do you know?

A

The most commonly used metric units of length are the kilometer (km), meter (m), centimeter (cm), and millimeter (mm).

$1 \text{ km} = 10^3 \text{ m} = 1,000 \text{ m}$
$1 \text{ m} = 10^2 \text{ cm} = 100 \text{ cm}$
$1 \text{ m} = 10^3 \text{ mm} = 1,000 \text{ mm}$
$1 \text{ cm} = 10 \text{ mm}$

DATA

1 kilometer	1 hectometer	1 decameter	1 meter	1 decimeter	1 centimeter	1 millimeter
10^3 m	10^2 m	10 m	1 m	0.1 m	0.01 m	0.001 m

Every metric unit is 10 times as great as the next smaller unit.

B

The distance between two towns is 3 kilometers. How many meters apart are they?

$3 \text{ km} = \boxed{} \text{ m}$

To change from larger units to smaller units, multiply.

One kilometer equals 1,000 meters.

Find 3×10^3.
$3 \text{ km} = 3,000 \text{ m}$

So, the towns are 3,000 meters apart.

C

The distance between a kitchen and living room is 1,200 centimeters. How many meters apart are they?

$1,200 \text{ cm} = \boxed{} \text{ m}$

To change from smaller units to larger units, divide.

Find $1,200 \div 10^2$.
$1,200 \text{ cm} = 12 \text{ m}$

So, the kitchen and the living room are 12 meters apart.

Convince Me! **Critique Reasoning** Elena says that 25 cm is equal to 250 mm. Do you agree? Why or why not?

Name _____

☆ Guided Practice ☆

Do You Understand?

1. To find the number of meters in six kilometers, why do you multiply 6×10^3?

2. Convert 12.5 centimeters to millimeters. Explain.

Do You Know How?

In **3–6**, convert each unit of length.

3. 10^3 cm = _____ m

4. 58 m = _____ mm

5. 1,000 mm = _____ cm

6. 3 km = _____ m

In **7** and **8**, compare lengths. Write >, <, or = for each ◯.

7. 9,000 m ◯ 20 km

8. 400 cm ◯ 4 m

☆ Independent Practice ☆

In **9–14**, convert each unit of length.

9. 7.5 cm = _____ mm

10. 6 m = _____ cm

11. 0.8 km = _____ cm

12. 17,000 m = _____ km

13. 48,000 mm = _____ m

14. 4 km = _____ m

In **15–20**, compare lengths. Write >, <, or = for each ◯.

15. 25,365 cm ◯ 30 m

16. 3.6 km ◯ 3,600 m

17. 1,200 mm ◯ 12 m

18. 52,800 cm ◯ 1 km

19. 7,500,000 m ◯ 750 km

20. 800 m ◯ 799,999 mm

In **21** and **22**, complete each table.

21.

km	1		0.1
m		500	

22.

m		5	0.5
cm	5,000		

Problem Solving

23. Number Sense Let x = the length of an object in meters and y = the length of the same object in millimeters. Which is a smaller number, x or y?

24. Higher Order Thinking How many millimeters are equal to one kilometer? Show your work.

---

25. Reasoning Which fraction is greater: $\frac{7}{8}$ or $\frac{9}{12}$? Explain how you know.

How do you compare fractions?

26. A week ago, Trudy bought the pencil shown. Now the pencil measures 12.7 centimeters.

How many centimeters of the pencil have been used?

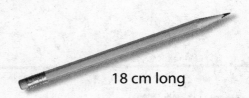

18 cm long

---

27. enVision® STEM Mount St. Helens, located in Washington, erupted on May 18, 1980. Before the eruption, the volcano was 2.95 kilometers high. After the eruption, the volcano was 2.55 kilometers high. Use the bar diagram to find the difference in height of Mount St. Helens before and after the eruption. Convert the difference to meters.

2.95 km	
2.55 km	?

---

28. Eileen plants a tree that is 2 meters tall in her yard. Which of the following is equivalent to 2 meters? 5.MD.1.1

- Ⓐ 200 mm
- Ⓑ 20 cm
- Ⓒ 200 km
- Ⓓ 2,000 mm

29. Which of these number sentences is **NOT** true? 5.MD.1.1

- Ⓐ 600 cm = 6 m
- Ⓑ 1 m < 9,000 mm
- Ⓒ 900 mm = 9 cm
- Ⓓ 10 km > 5,000 m

 © Pearson Education, Inc. 5

Name _____

Activity

☆ **Solve & Share** ☆

A pitcher holds 4 liters of water. How many milliliters does the pitcher hold? *Solve this problem any way you choose.*

I can ...
convert metric units of capacity.

MAFS.5.MD.1.1 Convert among different-sized standard measurement units (i.e., km, m, cm; kg, g; lb, oz.; l, ml; hr, min, sec) within a given measurement system (e.g., convert 5 cm to 0.05 m), and use these conversions in solving multi-step, real world problems. Also 5.NBT.1.2 MAFS.K12.MP.2.1, MP.7.1

You can convert metric units of capacity using multiplication or division. *Show your work!*

1 liter = _____ milliliters

4 liters = _____ milliliters

Look Back! **Look for Relationships** Juanita shares a one-liter bottle of water equally with 3 friends. How much water does each person get? Give your answer in liters and milliliters.

Essential Question **How Do You Convert Metric Units of Capacity?**

A

The most commonly used units of capacity in the metric system are the liter (L) and the milliliter (mL).

Can you find a liter or milliliter in the real world?

1 liter equals 1,000 milliliters

B Susan has 1.875 liters of water. How many milliliters is this?

$$1.875 \text{ L} = \boxed{} \text{ mL}$$

To change a larger unit to a smaller unit, multiply.

Find 1.875×10^3.
$1.875 \times 10^3 = 1,875$
$1.875 \text{ L} = 1,875 \text{ mL}$

So, Susan has 1,875 milliliters of water.

C Jorge has 3,500 milliliters of water. How many liters is this?

$$3,500 \text{ mL} = \boxed{} \text{ L}$$

To change a smaller unit to a larger unit, divide.

Find $3,500 \div 10^3$.
$3,500 \div 10^3 = 3.5$
$3,500 \text{ mL} = 3.5 \text{ L}$

So, Jorge has 3.5 liters of water.

Convince Me! **Reasoning** Order these measurements from greatest to least. Explain how you decided.

2,300 L   500 mL   3,000 mL   2 L   22 L

© Pearson Education, Inc. 5

Name _____

☆ Guided Practice*

Do You Understand?

1. Explain how you can convert milliliters to liters.

2. What types of tools would you select to measure capacity? Give an example and explain how that tool could be used.

Do You Know How?

In **3–8**, convert each unit of capacity.

3. 2.75 L =
_____ mL

4. 3,000 mL =
_____ L

5. 5 L =
_____ mL

6. 250 mL =
_____ L

7. 0.027 L =
_____ mL

8. 400 mL =
_____ L

☆ Independent Practice ☆

In **9–20**, convert each unit of capacity.

9. 5,000 mL =
_____ L

10. 45,000 mL =
_____ L

11. 4.27 L =
_____ mL

12. 13 L =
_____ mL

13. 3,700 mL =
_____ L

14. 0.35 L =
_____ mL

15. 2,640 mL =
_____ L

16. 314 mL =
_____ L

17. 0.06 L =
_____ mL

18. 2,109 mL =
_____ L

19. 85 mL =
_____ L

20. 9.05 L =
_____ mL

In **21** and **22**, complete each table to show equivalent measures.

21.

liters	0.1	1	10
milliliters			

22.

milliliters	500	5,000	50,000
liters			

Problem Solving

23. Reasoning Carla's famous punch calls for 3 liters of mango juice. The only mango juice she can find is sold in 500-milliliter cartons. How many cartons of mango juice does Carla need to buy?

24. Carla makes 6 liters of punch. She pours the punch into 800 mL bottles. How many bottles can she fill?

25. Bobby filled the jug with water for soccer practice. If each player gets 250 milliliters of water, how many players will the water jug serve?

holds 5 L

26. Higher Order Thinking One cubic centimeter will hold 1 milliliter of water. How many milliliters will the aquarium below hold? How many liters will it hold?

30 cm

20 cm

40 cm

27. Terry is buying juice. He needs 3 liters. A half-liter of juice costs $2.39. A 250-milliliter container of juice costs $1.69. What should Terry buy so he gets 3 liters at the lowest price? Explain.

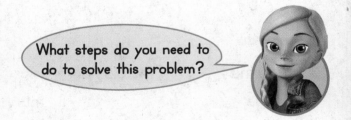

What steps do you need to do to solve this problem?

28. A birdbath holds 4 liters of water. How many milliliters of water does it hold? 🔲 5.MD.1.1

   Ⓐ 400 mL

   Ⓑ 800 mL

   Ⓒ 4,000 mL

   Ⓓ 8,000 mL

29. You are filling a 2-liter bottle with liquid from full 80-milliliter containers. How many containers will it take to fill the 2-liter bottle? 🔲 5.MD.1.1

   Ⓐ 400

   Ⓑ 250

   Ⓒ 40

   Ⓓ 25

© Pearson Education, Inc. 5

Name _____

Solve & Share

In chemistry class, Rhonda measured 10 grams of a substance. How many milligrams is this? *Solve this problem any way you choose.*

I can ...
convert metric units of mass.

MAFS.5.MD.1.1 Convert among different-sized standard measurement units (i.e., km, m, cm; kg, g; lb, oz.; l, ml; hr, min, sec) within a given measurement system (e.g., convert 5 cm to 0.05 m), and use these conversions in solving multi-step, real world problems. **Also 5.NBT.1.2 MAFS.K12.MP.1.1, MP.7.1**

Look for Relationships
You can use patterns to help you see a relationship between the units.

Look Back! How many kilograms did Rhonda measure? Write an equation to model your work.

Essential Question **How Do You Convert Metric Units of Mass?**

A

about 5 g

The three most commonly used units of mass are the milligram (mg), the gram (g), and the kilogram (kg).

Converting metric units of mass is like converting other metric units.

$$10^3 \text{ mg} = 1 \text{ g}$$
$$10^3 \text{ g} = 1 \text{ kg}$$

about 100 kg

B A whistle has a mass of about 5 grams. How many milligrams is this?

To change from a larger unit to a smaller unit, multiply.

Find 5×10^3.
$5 \times 10^3 = 5 \times 1{,}000 = 5{,}000$
So, 5 g = 5,000 mg.

So, a whistle has a mass of about 5,000 milligrams.

C How many kilograms is the whistle?

To change from a smaller unit to a larger unit, divide.

Find $5 \div 10^3$.
$5 \div 10^3 = 5 \div 1{,}000 = 0.005$
So, 5 g = 0.005 kg.

So, a whistle has a mass of about 0.005 kilogram.

Convince Me! **Use Structure** In the picture above, what is the football player's mass in grams and in milligrams? How can you tell?

© Pearson Education, Inc. 5

Name _____

☆Guided Practice*

Do You Understand?

1. **A-Z Vocabulary** How does the relationship between meters and millimeters help you understand the relationship between grams and milligrams?

2. Which has the greater mass: 1 kilogram or 137,000 milligrams? Explain how you made your comparison.

Do You Know How?

In **3** and **4**, convert each unit of mass.

3. 9.25 g = _____ mg

4. 190 g = _____ kg

In **5** and **6**, compare. Write >, <, or = for each ○.

5. 7,000 mg ○ 7,000 g

6. 10^2 kg ○ 10^4 g

Independent Practice*

In **7–12**, convert each unit of mass.

7. 17,000 g =

_____ kg

8. 18 kg =

_____ g

9. 4,200 mg =

_____ g

10. 0.276 g =

_____ mg

11. 4.08 kg =

_____ g

12. 43 mg =

_____ g

In **13–18**, compare. Write >, <, or = for each ○.

13. 2,000 g ○ 3 kg

14. 4 kg ○ 4,000 g

15. 10^4 mg ○ 13 g

16. 7 kg ○ 7,000 g

17. 9,000 g ○ 8 kg

18. 8,000 g ○ 5 kg

In **19** and **20**, complete each table.

19.

grams		10	
milligrams	1,000		100,000

20.

grams	500		50,000
kilograms		5	

*For another example, see Set F on page 528.

Topic 12 | Lesson 12-6 **511**

Problem Solving

21. Make Sense and Persevere Sheryl has a recipe for pasta with vegetables. The recipe calls for 130 grams of vegetables and twice as much pasta as vegetables. What is the total mass in grams of the recipe?

22. Terri is beginning a science experiment in the lab. The instructions call for 227 milligrams of potassium. Calculate the difference between this amount and 1 gram.

23. Number Sense One of the world's heaviest hailstones weighed 2.2 pounds. Which is more appropriate to express its mass, 1 kilogram or 1 gram?

24. Higher Order Thinking A cook has 6 onions that have a total mass of 900 grams and 8 apples that have a total mass of 1 kilogram. All onions are the same size, and all apples are the same size. Which has the greater mass, an onion or an apple? Explain.

In **25** and **26**, use the given information and the picture.

enVision® STEM If a man weighs 198 pounds on Earth, his mass on Earth is 90 kilograms.

25. What is this man's weight on the Moon?

26. What is his mass in grams?

The weight of a person on the Moon is about $\frac{1}{6}$ his or her weight on Earth.

27. Write the following masses on the lines from least to greatest. 🐢 5.MD.1.1
500 g   50 kg   5,000 mg

_____ < _____ < _____

28. If you convert grams to milligrams, what operation would you use? 🐢 5.MD.1.1

Ⓐ Addition

Ⓑ Subtraction

Ⓒ Multiplication

Ⓓ Division

Name _____

Solve & Share

Emily played softball all weekend. She was wondering the difference in time between the shortest game and the longest game. Can you help her figure it out?

Game	Length of Game
Game 1	78 minutes
Game 2	1 hour, 10 minutes
Game 3	1 hour, 8 minutes
Game 4	85 minutes
Game 5	1.5 hours

I can ...
solve problems that involve conversions between seconds and minutes, and between minutes and hours

MAFS.5.MD.1.1 Convert among different-sized standard measurement units (i.e., km, m, cm; kg, g; lb, oz.; l, ml; hr, min, sec) within a given measurement system (e.g., convert 5 cm to 0.05 m), and use these conversions in solving multi-step, real world problems. **Also 5.NBT.2.5, 5.NBT.2.6**
MAFS.K12.MP.1.1, MP.3.1

60 minutes = 1 hour

Select a common unit of time to help compare game times.

Look Back! **Make Sense and Persevere** Mateo saw a professional baseball game, which lasted $2\frac{1}{2}$ hours. How many minutes longer was the professional game than Emily's Game 3? Explain.

Essential Question

How Do You Solve Problems that Involve Different Units of Time?

A

Kendall's family is driving to the theater to see a 2-hour movie. Kendall notices this sign at the parking lot closest to the theater. Do you think they should park there?

You can convert one of these times so you are comparing like units.

90 MINUTES PARKING

1 hour = 60 minutes
1 minute = 60 seconds

B One Way:

Convert 2 hours to minutes. Then compare.

To change from larger units to smaller units, multiply.

Remember, 1 hour equals 60 minutes.

2 × 60 minutes = 120 minutes

120 minutes > 90 minutes, so Kendall's family should not park in that lot.

C Another Way:

Convert 90 minutes to hours. Then compare.

To change from smaller units to larger units, divide.

$90 \div 60 = \frac{90}{60} = 1\frac{1}{2}$ hours

$1\frac{1}{2}$ hours < 2 hours, so Kendall's family should not park in that lot.

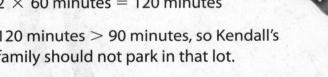

Convince Me! **Make Sense and Persevere** Explain how to convert 4 hours, 15 minutes to minutes.

© Pearson Education, Inc. 5

Another Example!

There is often more than one way to show converted units of time. Find the missing numbers.

Remember, 1 minute equals 60 seconds.

210 seconds = ____ minutes, ____ seconds

Divide. Write the quotient with a remainder.

$210 \div 60 = 3\ R\ 30$

So, 210 seconds = 3 minutes, 30 seconds

210 seconds = ____ minutes

Divide. Write the quotient as a mixed number.

$\frac{210}{60} = 3\frac{30}{60} = 3\frac{1}{2}$

So, 210 seconds = $3\frac{1}{2}$ minutes

☆ Guided Practice☆

Do You Understand?

1. Which is the longer time: 5 minutes, 25 seconds or 315 seconds? Explain.

2. How many minutes are in a quarter hour? How do you know?

Do You Know How?

In **3–6**, convert each time.

3. 240 seconds = ____ minutes

4. 2 hours, 18 minutes = ____ minutes

5. $4\frac{1}{2}$ minutes = ____ seconds

6. 80 minutes = ____ hour
        ____ minutes

Independent Practice ☆

In **7–10**, convert each time.

7. 6 hours = ____ minutes

8. 390 seconds = ____ minutes

9. 208 minutes = ____ hours, ____ minutes

10. 7 minutes, 12 seconds = ____ seconds

In **11–12**, compare. Write >, <, or = for each ◯.

11. 330 minutes ◯ 7.5 hours

12. 45 minutes ◯ $\frac{3}{4}$ hour

Problem Solving

13. Brock spends 15 minutes walking to school and 15 minutes walking home each day. By the end of the school week (5 days) how many hours has Brock spent traveling between home and school?

14. A television station shows commercials for $7\frac{1}{2}$ minutes each hour. How many 45-second commercials can it show per hour?

---

15. Leslie is making these two recipes. Which takes longer to make, the strawberry bread or the spaghetti sauce? How many minutes longer?

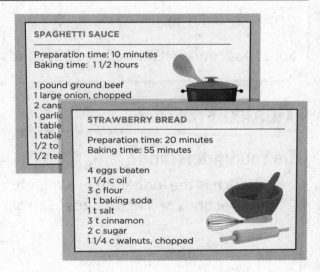

SPAGHETTI SAUCE

Preparation time: 10 minutes
Baking time: 1 1/2 hours

1 pound ground beef
1 large onion, chopped
2 cans
1 garli
1 table
1 table
1/2 to
1/2 tea

STRAWBERRY BREAD

Preparation time: 20 minutes
Baking time: 55 minutes

4 eggs beaten
1 1/4 c oil
3 c flour
1 t baking soda
1 t salt
3 t cinnamon
2 c sugar
1 1/4 c walnuts, chopped

---

16. Critique Reasoning The school day is 6 hours, 15 minutes long. Jenna says that it's $6\frac{1}{4}$ hours. Henry says it's 6.25 hours. Can they both be correct? Explain.

17. Higher Order Thinking How many seconds are there in 1 hour? In 10 hours? Explain.

Assessment Practice

18. Three hikers reported how long it took to hike a trail. Write the names of the hikers from fastest to slowest. 🏵 5.MD.1.1

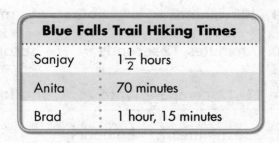

Blue Falls Trail Hiking Times	
Sanjay	$1\frac{1}{2}$ hours
Anita	70 minutes
Brad	1 hour, 15 minutes

_____ _____

© Pearson Education, Inc. 5

Name _____

Solve & Share

Amy wants to frame a poster that has a width of 8 inches and a length of 1 foot. What is the perimeter of the poster? **Solve this problem any way you choose.**

Make Sense and Persevere You can use measurement conversions in real-world situations. *Show your work!*

1 foot = _____ inches

I can ...
solve real-world problems with measurement conversions.

MAFS.5.MD.1.1 Convert among different-sized standard measurement units (i.e., km, m, cm; kg, g; lb, oz.; l, ml; hr, min, sec) within a given measurement system (e.g., convert 5 cm to 0.05 m), and use these conversions in solving multi-step, real world problems. **Also 5.NBT.2.5**
MAFS.K12.MP.1.1, MP.2.1, MP.6.1

Look Back! Which measurement did you convert? Can you find the perimeter by converting to the other unit of measurement?

Essential Question

How Can You Convert Units of Measurement to Solve a Problem?

Visual Learning Bridge

A

A city pool is in the shape of a rectangle with the dimensions shown. What is the perimeter of the pool?

You can convert one of the measures so that you are adding like units.

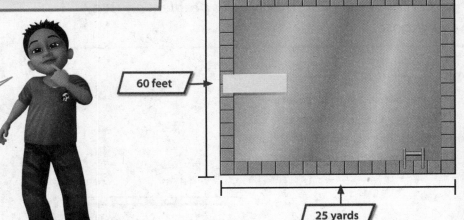

60 feet

25 yards

B *What do you know?*

The dimensions of the pool:
ℓ = 25 yards
w = 60 feet

What are you asked to find?

The perimeter of the pool

 You can use feet for perimeter.

C Convert 25 yards to feet so you can add like units.

1 yard = 3 feet

To change from larger units to smaller units, multiply.

25 × 3 feet = 75 feet

So, 25 yards = 75 feet.

D Substitute like measurements into the perimeter formula.

Perimeter = (2 × length) + (2 × width)

$P = (2 \times \ell) + (2 \times w)$

$P = (2 \times 75) + (2 \times 60)$

$P = 150 + 120$

$P = 270$ feet

The perimeter of the pool is 270 feet.

Convince Me! **Be Precise** If the width of the pool is increased by 3 feet, what would be the new perimeter of the pool? Explain.

© Pearson Education, Inc. 5

Name _____

☆ Guided Practice *

Do You Understand?

1. In the example on the previous page, how could you find the perimeter by converting all measurements to yards?

2. Write a real-world multiple-step problem that involves measurement.

Do You Know How?

3. Stacia needs enough ribbon to wrap around the length (ℓ) and height (h) of a box. If the length is 2 feet and the height is 4 inches, how much ribbon will she need?

4. If ribbon is sold in whole number yards and costs $1.50 per yard, how much will it cost Stacia to buy the ribbon?

☆ Independent Practice ☆

> In **5–7**, use conversions to solve each problem.

5. Becca wants to edge her hexagonal garden with brick. All sides are equal. The brick costs $6 per yard. What is the perimeter of the garden? How much will it cost to buy the edging she needs?

Edging means she will put bricks around the perimeter of the hexagon.

Becca's Garden

12 feet

6. Isaac buys milk to make milkshakes for his friends. He buys 1 quart of milk and $\frac{1}{2}$ gallon of milk. How many cups of milk does he buy?

7. Maggie buys $1\frac{1}{2}$ pounds of walnuts, 8 ounces of pecans, and $\frac{3}{4}$ pound of almonds. How much do the nuts weigh in all?

Problem Solving

8. **Reasoning** Matt's family is thinking about buying a family pass to the city pool. The pass is $80 for a family of 4. Individual passes are $25 each. How much money can Matt's family save by purchasing a family pass instead of 4 individual passes?

9. Marcia walked 900 meters on Friday. On Saturday, she walked 4 kilometers. On Sunday, she walked 3 kilometers, 600 meters. How many kilometers did Marcia walk over all three days?

10. **Higher Order Thinking** Raul wants to put wood shavings in his rabbit's cage. The floor of the cage measures 1 yard wide by 5 feet long. One bag of shavings covers 10 square feet.

    How many bags will Raul have to buy to cover the floor of the cage? Explain.

11. Cheryl's fish tank is 2 yards long by 24 inches wide by 3 feet high. What is the volume of Cheryl's tank in cubic inches?

Remember,
Volume = ℓ × w × h

12. Some statistics about a typical adult Royal antelope are shown in the data table.

    a What is a typical Royal antelope's tail length in millimeters?

    b How many centimeters high can a typical Royal antelope jump?

    c What is the mass of a typical Royal antelope in grams?

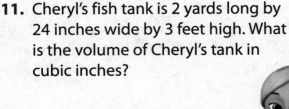

An Adult Royal Antelope	
Head and body length	43 cm
Tail length	6 cm
Mass	2.4 kg
Vertical leap	2 m

13. Joann wants to put a wallpaper border around her room. The border costs $3 per foot. The diagram shows Joann's room. How much money will the border cost? **5.MD.1.1**

    Ⓐ $120

    Ⓑ $102

    Ⓒ $84

    Ⓓ $60

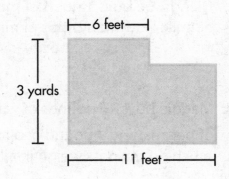

├─ 6 feet ─┤

3 yards

├──── 11 feet ────┤

   © Pearson Education, Inc. 5

Name _____

★ ☆ ★
Solve & Share

Beth wants to make a picture frame like the one pictured below. She recorded the outside dimensions as 5 cm by 7 cm. Measure the outside dimensions of the frame in millimeters. Compare your measurements to Beth's. Do you think her measurements are precise enough? Explain.

I can ...
be precise when solving measurement problems.

MAFS.K12.MP.6.1 Be precise. **Also MP.1.1, MP.4.1**
MAFS.5.MD.1.1 Convert among different-sized standard measurement units (i.e., km, m, cm; kg, g; lb, oz.; l, ml; hr, min, sec) within a given measurement system (e.g., convert 5 cm to 0.05 m), and use these conversions in solving multi-step, real world problems. **Also 5.NBT.2.5**

Thinking Habits

Think about these questions to help you attend to precision.

- Am I using numbers, units, and symbols appropriately?

- Am I using the correct definitions?

- Am I calculating accurately?

- Is my answer clear?

Look Back! **Be Precise** What is the difference between the perimeter based on the measurements Beth made and the perimeter based on the measurements you made? Explain how you found the answer.

Essential Question ## How Can You Be Precise When Solving Math Problems?

A

Chad and Rhoda are hanging a swing. Chad cut a piece of chain 6 feet 2 inches long. Rhoda cut a piece of chain 72 inches long. When they hung the swing, it was crooked.

Use precise language to explain why.

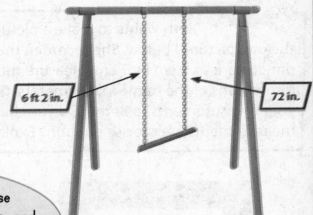

6 ft 2 in.   72 in.

Be Precise means that you use appropriate math words, symbols, and units as well as accurate calculations when you solve problems.

B **How can I be precise in solving this problem?**

I can

- calculate accurately.
- give a clear answer.
- use the correct units.

C   Here's my thinking...

Convert 6 ft 2 inches to inches to see if Chad and Rhoda cut equal lengths of chain.

6 ft 2 in. = ☐ in.

$6 \times 12 = 72$, so 6 ft = 72 in.

6 ft 2 in. = $72 + 2 = 74$ in.

Chad's chain is 74 inches long, but Rhoda's chain is only 72 inches long. Since Chad and Rhoda used unequal lengths of chain, the swing is crooked.

Convince Me! **Be Precise** What recommendations would you make to Chad and Rhoda so that the swing hangs level?

Name _____

☆ Guided Practice *

Mary needs a board 4 feet 8 inches long. She cut a board 56 inches long.

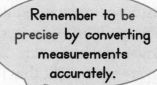

Remember to be precise by converting measurements accurately.

1. What measurements are given? Are the same units used for each measurement? Explain.

   no

2. Explain how you can convert one of the measurements so that both use the same unit.

   To see how many inches in a yard

3. Is the board Mary cut the right length? Give a clear and appropriate answer.

   no

Independent Practice *

Be Precise

Sean is making meat loaf. He used the amount of catsup shown in the measuring cup.

Meat Loaf
2 lb ground beef
1 egg
6 fl oz catsup
$\frac{1}{2}$ c bread crumbs
salt and pepper to taste

4. Are the units that Sean used to measure the catsup the same as those given in the recipe? Explain.

5. How can you convert one of the measurements so that both use the same unit?

6. Did Sean use the right amount of catsup? Give a clear and appropriate answer.

Problem Solving

Shipping a Package

A customer is using regular delivery to ship a package. Northside Shipping Company discovered that its old scale is not very accurate. It registers a weight that is 2 ounces too heavy. A new, accurate scale shows that the actual weight of the customer's package is 2 pounds 11 ounces.

```
┌─────────────────────────────────────────┐
│ Northside Shipping Company               │
│  Regular Delivery                        │
│ $0.75 first ounce                        │
│ $0.60 each additional ounce              │
│                                          │
│ Rush Delivery                            │
│ $1.45 first ounce                        │
│ $0.75 each additional ounce              │
└─────────────────────────────────────────┘
```

7. **Make Sense and Persevere** Which information do you need to determine the total shipping cost using either scale? 5.NBT.2.5

8. **Be Precise** Why do you need to convert measurements to determine total shipping costs? 5.MD.1.1

> To be precise, you need to check that the words, numbers, symbols, and units you use are correct and that your calculations are accurate.

9. **Model with Math** Show how to convert the measurements you described in Exercise 8. 5.MD.1.1

10. **Be Precise** What would the total cost be if the package is weighed on the new scale? What would the total cost be if the package is weighed on the old scale? Show your work. 5.NBT.2.5

 © Pearson Education, Inc. 5

Name _____

Find a partner. Get paper and a pencil. Each partner chooses light blue or dark blue.

At the same time, Partner 1 and Partner 2 each point to one of their black numbers. Both partners find the product of the two numbers.

The partner who chose the color where the product appears gets a tally mark. Work until one partner has seven tally marks.

I can ...
multiply multi-digit whole numbers.

MAFS.5.NBT.2.5

Partner 1					Partner 2
1,000	14,250	275,937	363,075	4,841,000	**570**
25	67,650	18,750	652,700	121,025	**750**
57	6,527,000	750,000	57,000	22,550	**902**
75	42,750	56,250	163,175	75,000	**4,841**
100	484,100	90,200	372,039	489,525	**6,527**
	32,490	51,414	570,000	902,000	

Tally Marks for Partner 1	Tally Marks for Partner 2

A-Z
Glossary

Word List

- capacity
- centimeter
- cup
- fluid ounce
- foot
- gallon
- gram
- inch
- kilogram
- kilometer
- liter
- mass
- meter
- mile
- milligram
- milliliter
- millimeter
- ounce
- pint
- pound
- quart
- ton
- weight
- yard

Understand Vocabulary

Choose the best term from the Word List. Write it on the blank.

1. One _____ is equivalent to twelve _____.

2. The measure of the amount of matter in an object is known as _____.

3. The volume of a container measured in liquid units is its _____.

4. There are 1,000 meters in one Ki lometer.

5. Finding how light or how heavy an object is means measuring its _____.

6. There are 2 cups in one _____.

For each of these objects, give an example and a non-example of a unit of measure that could be used to describe it.

	Example	Non-example
7. Milk	✓	
8. Person's height	✓	
9. Shoe length	✓	

Use Vocabulary in Writing

10. Explain the relationship among the metric units of mass in the Word List.

© Pearson Education, Inc. 5

Name _____

Set A pages 489–492, 517–520 _____

Convert 3 yards to inches.

1 foot (ft) = 12 inches (in.)
1 yard (yd) = 3 ft = 36 in.
1 mile (mi) = 1,760 yd = 5,280 ft

1 yard = 36 inches. To change larger units to smaller units, multiply: $3 \times 36 = 108$.

So, 3 yards = 108 inches.

Remember to divide when changing smaller units to larger units.

Convert.

1. 7 ft = 84 in.   **2.** 7,920 ft = 1½ mi

3. Max wants to put a fence around his triangular garden. If each side is 6 yards, how many feet of fencing does Max need?   216 F

Set B pages 493–496 _____

Convert 16 cups to pints.

2 cups = 1 pint. To change smaller units to larger units, divide: $16 \div 2 = 8$.

So, 16 cups = 8 pints.

Remember that 1 gal = 4 qt, 1 qt = 2 pt, 1 pt = 2 c, and 1 c = 8 fl oz.

Convert.

1. 36 c = _____ gal   **2.** 7 pt = _____ qt

3. $1\frac{1}{2}$ gal = _____ fl oz   **4.** 6 pt = _____ c

Set C pages 497–500 _____

Convert 6 pounds to ounces.

1 pound = 16 ounces. To change larger units to smaller units, multiply: $6 \times 16 = 96$.

So, 6 pounds = 96 ounces.

Remember that 2,000 pounds = 1 ton.

Convert.

1. $2\frac{3}{4}$ lb = _____ oz   **2.** 56 oz = _____ lb

3. 4,000 lb = _____ T   **4.** $6\frac{1}{2}$ T = _____ lb

Set D pages 501–504 _____

Convert 2 meters to centimeters.

1 km = 1,000 m   1 m = 100 cm
1 m = 1,000 mm   1 cm = 10 mm

1 meter = 100 centimeters. To change larger units to smaller units, multiply:
$2 \times 100 = 200$.

So, 2 meters = 200 centimeters.

Remember to multiply or divide by a power of 10 to convert metric measurements.

Convert.

1. 5.4 m = _____ cm   **2.** 2.7 km = _____ m

3. 0.02 km = _____ cm   **4.** 0.025 m = _____ mm

5. 675 mm = _____ m   **6.** 7,435 cm = _____ m

Set E pages 505–508

Convert 6,000 milliliters to liters.

1,000 milliliters = 1 liter. To change milliliters to larger units, divide: 6,000 ÷ 1,000 = 6.

So, 6,000 milliliters = 6 liters.

Remember that the most commonly used metric units of capacity are the liter and milliliter.

Convert.

1. 6 L = _6000_ mL   2. 0.15 L = _150_ mL

3. 2,000 mL = _2_ L   4. 900 mL = _9.0_ L

Set F pages 509–512

Convert 6 kilograms (kg) to grams (g).

1 kilogram = 1,000 grams. To change larger units to smaller units, multiply: 6 × 1,000 = 6,000.

So, 6 kg = 6,000 g.

Remember that to convert metric units, you can annex zeros and move the decimal point.

Convert.

1. 30 kg = _30000_ g   2. 3,000 mg = _3_ g

3. 560 g = _56_ kg   4. 0.17 g = _170_ mg

Set G pages 513–516

The choir concert is scheduled to last 90 minutes. The band concert is scheduled from 7:00–8:45. Which concert is scheduled to be longer? By how many minutes?

The choir concert will last 90 minutes = 1 hour, 30 minutes. The band concert will last 1 hour, 45 minutes. The band concert will be 15 minutes longer.

Remember to check if the units in the problem are the same.

Convert.

1. 8 minutes = _480_ seconds
2. 86 minutes = _1_ hour, _26_ minutes
3. A movie starts at 7:10 and ends at 9:03. How long does the movie last?
   _1_ hour, _53_ minutes

Set H pages 521–524

Think about these questions to help you **be precise** in your work.

Remember that the problem might have more than one step.

Solve. Show your work.

Thinking Habits

- Am I using numbers, units, and symbols appropriately?
- Am I using the correct definitions?
- Am I calculating accurately?
- Is my answer clear?

1. Monica bought a 40-pound bag of dog food. Twice a day, she gives her dog 6 ounces of food. How many pounds of dog food will she use in 1 week? Explain.

5 1/4

© Pearson Education, Inc. 5

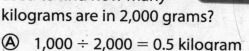

1. Which of the following are equivalent to 7 grams? Select all that apply.

- ☑ 0.007 kilogram $= 7g$
- ☐ 70 milligrams
- ☐ 7,000 kilograms
- ☑ 7,000 milligrams
- ☐ 0.007 milligram

2. Justin's garden is shown below.

6 yards 2 | 6 inches

288 inches 6 inches

8 yards

A. How can you convert the dimensions of Justin's garden from yards to inches?

B. What is the perimeter of Justin's garden in inches?

1604 in

3. Which of the following equations can be used to find how many kilograms are in 2,000 grams?

- Ⓐ 1,000 ÷ 2,000 = 0.5 kilogram
- Ⓑ 2,000 ÷ 1,000 = 2 kilograms
- Ⓒ 2,000 × 1,000 = 2,000,000 kilograms
- Ⓓ 2,000 × 100 = 200,000 kilograms

4. A. 10 bales of cotton weigh approximately 5,000 pounds. How can you convert 5,000 pounds to tons?

$1 P = \dfrac{1}{2000}$ ton

$5000 P = \dfrac{5000}{2000} = \dfrac{5}{2}$ ton $= 2\frac{1}{2}$ ton

B. Which comparison is true?

- Ⓐ 5,000 pounds > 10,000 tons
- Ⓑ 5,000 pounds = 3 tons
- Ⓒ 5,000 pounds < 3 tons
- Ⓓ 5,000 pounds > 3 tons

5. Tyrell bought 4 liters of fruit punch for a party. He will serve the punch in glasses that can hold 200 milliliters. How many full glasses of fruit punch can he serve?

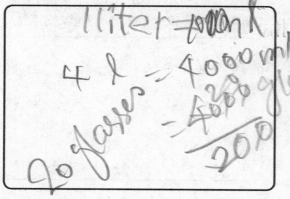

1 liter = 1000 ml

4 l = 4000 ml

20 glasses $= \dfrac{4000}{200}$ glasses

$= 20$ glasses

6. Select each equation that the number 10^3 will make true.

- [ ] ? km = 1 mm ✗
- [x] ? mm = 1 m
- [ ] ? cm = 1 m
- [x] ? m = 1 km
- [ ] ? dm = 1 m

1000 mm = 1 m

7. Match each measurement on the left to its equivalent measurement.

	2 cups	2 pints	8 fl oz	4 quarts
1 gallon	☐	☐	☐	☑
1 cup	☐	☐	☑	☐
1 quart	☐	☑	☐	☐
1 pint	☑	☐	☐	☐

8. Select all lengths that are equal to 6 feet 12 inches.

- [ ] 3 yd 1 ft
- [x] 7 ft
- [ ] 7 ft 2 in.
- [x] 2 yd 1 ft   *6 ft 12 inches.*
- [x] 1 yd 4 ft

9. Write and solve an equation to find how many milliliters are in 3.4 liters.

$1\ell = 1000 \text{ ml}$
$3.4\ell = 3400 \text{ ml}$
$3.4 \times 1000 = 3400 \text{ ml}$

10. Mason made 5 quarts of salsa. Which of the following can be used to find the number of cups of salsa Mason made?

- Ⓐ $5 \times 2 \times 2$
- Ⓑ $5 \times 4 \times 4$
- Ⓒ $5 \div 2 \div 2$
- Ⓓ $5 \times 4 \div 2$

11. Alicia bought 5 pounds of potting soil. She wants to put 10 ounces of soil in each flower pot.

A. How can she convert 5 pounds to ounces?

B. How many flower pots can she fill?

12. The tail of a Boeing 747 is $63\frac{2}{3}$ feet tall. How many inches tall is the tail?

13. Write and solve an equation to convert 0.38 meter to centimeters.

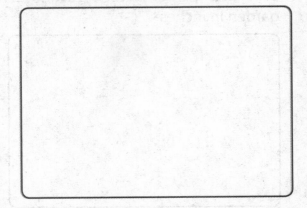

© Pearson Education, Inc. 5

Name _____

Orange Juice

Heidi sells freshly-squeezed orange juice in **Heidi's Orange Juice** cups.

1. Use the **Information About Oranges**. Answer the questions below to find how many pounds of oranges Heidi needs for her orange juice.

Heidi's Orange Juice

   Part A

   How many oranges does Heidi need to make one large orange juice? Show your work. 5.MD.1.1

   Large = $2\frac{1}{4}$ cups

   Information About Oranges

   Part B

   How many pounds of oranges does Heidi need to make one large orange juice? Show your work. 5.MD.1.1

   One medium orange has about 2 fl oz of juice and weighs about 5 ounces.

2. Answer the following to find the area of **Heidi's Display Shelf**.

   Part A

   What units can you use for the area? Explain. 5.MD.1.1

   Heidi's Display Shelf

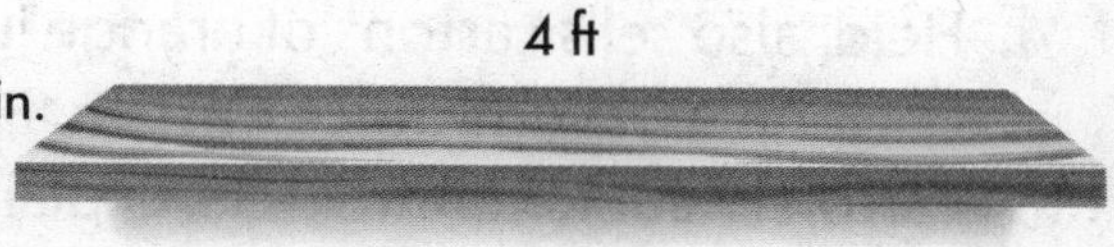

   4 ft

   15 in.

Part B

What is the area of **Heidi's Display Shelf**? Show your work. ⓕ 5.MD.1.1

3. The **Orange Nutrition** table shows nutrients in one medium-sized orange that weighs 5 ounces or 140 grams. All the nutrients in the orange are also in Heidi's orange juice.

Part A

How many grams of potassium are in one large cup of Heidi's orange juice? Explain how you solved. ⓦ 5.MD.1.1

Orange Nutrition	
Nutrient	**Amount**
Carbohydrates	16 g
Fiber	3.5 g
Potassium	250 mg

Part B

How many milligrams of fiber are in one large cup of Heidi's orange juice? Use an exponent when you explain the computation you used to solve. ⓦ 5.MD.1.1

4. Heidi also sells cartons of orange juice. Use the picture of **Heidi's Orange Juice Carton.** Find the volume of the carton in cubic centimeters. Explain. ⓦ 5.MD.1.1

Heidi's Orange Juice Carton

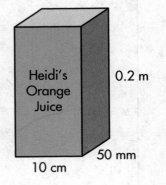

Heidi's Orange Juice
0.2 m
50 mm
10 cm

© Pearson Education, Inc. 5

Write and Interpret Numerical Expressions

Essential Question: How is the value of a numerical expression found?

Digital Resources

Interactive Student Edition · Activity · Visual Learning · Video · Practice

Assessment · Games · Tools · Glossary

MAFS.5.OA.1.1, 5.OA.1.2
MAFS.K12.MP.1.1, MP.2.1, MP.3.1, MP.4.1, MP.6.1, MP.7.1

So when I drink milk, I am part of that food chain. Yum! Here's a project on food chains and food webs.

A *food chain* shows a path of energy moving through an ecosystem.

For example, plants capture the Sun's energy and convert it into food energy. Cows eat plants.

ēnVision STEM Project: Food Chains and Food Webs

Do Research Use the Internet or other sources to find out more about food chains and food webs. Investigate the roles of producers, consumers, and decomposers. Explain how energy from sunlight is transferred to consumers.

Journal: Write a Report Include what you found. Also in your report:

- Draw a food web from an ecosystem near your home.

- Draw arrows on your food web to show how energy moves. Explain why the order is important.

- On one food chain of your food web, label each organism as a producer, consumer, or decomposer.

Review What You Know

A-Z Vocabulary

Choose the best term from the box.
Write it on the blank.

| • difference | • product | • sum |
| • equation | • quotient | |

1. The answer to a division problem is the _____.

2. The _____ of 5 and 7 is 12.

3. To find the _____ between 16 and 4, you subtract.

4. A number sentence that shows two equivalent values is a(n) _____.

Mixed Review

Find each answer.

5. $648 \div 18$

6. 35×100

7. $47.15 + 92.9$

8. $\frac{1}{4} + \frac{1}{4} + \frac{1}{4}$

9. $3.4 - 2.7$

10. $1.9 + 7$

11. $3\frac{2}{5} + \frac{1}{2}$

12. $75 \div \frac{1}{5}$

13. $\$3.75 + \$2.49$

14. $8\frac{5}{8} - 1\frac{2}{8}$

15. 31.8×2.3

16. $9 - 4.6$

17. Jackson bought 2 tickets to the state fair. Each ticket cost $12. He spent $15 on rides and $8.50 on food. How much did Jackson spend in all?

18. A baker has 3 pounds of dried fruit. Each batch of a recipe she is making uses $\frac{1}{2}$ pound of the fruit. How many batches can she make?

   Ⓐ 9 batches   Ⓑ 6 batches   Ⓒ 2 batches   Ⓓ $1\frac{1}{2}$ batches

Multiplication

19. What equation comes next in the pattern below? Explain.

   $7 \times 10 = 70$
   $7 \times 100 = 700$
   $7 \times 1,000 = 7,000$

   © Pearson Education, Inc. 5

Name _____

PROJECT 13A

What's been recovered from the wreck of the *Atocha*?

Project: Write a Treasure Adventure Mystery Story

PROJECT 13B

Do you like to play games?

Project: Design a Game Using Dominos

PROJECT 13C

What happens when a calculation is incorrect?

Project: Program a Robot

Math Modeling

Measure Me!

LOLA 1|5|14

LOLA 8-12-13

LOLA 2|5|13

LOLA 10|8|12

LOLA 7|5|11
LOLA 6-3-10

lola 1|20|10

Lola 7|5|9

Lola 6-2-8

Lola 1-8-8

LUCA 1|5|14
LUCA 8-12-13
LUCA 2|5|13
LUCA 10|8|12
LUCA 7|5|11
LUCA 6-3-10

Before watching the video, think:

A *conjecture* is a statement someone believes is true based on observations. You can usually either prove or disprove a conjecture. Keep an eye out for the conjecture in this video.

MAFS.K12.MP.4.1 Model with math. **Also MAFS.K12.MP.5.1, MAFS.K12.MP.8.1**
MAFS.5.OA.1.2 Write simple expressions that record calculations with numbers, and interpret numerical expressions without evaluating them. . . . **Also MAFS.5.MD.1.1**

Name _____

Solve & Share

Jordan and Annika are working on $15 + 12 \div 3 + 5$. Jordan says the answer is 14 and Annika says the answer is 24. Who is right?

$$15 + 12 \div 3 + 5$$

I can ...
evaluate expressions with parentheses, brackets, and braces.

MAFS.5.OA.1.1 Use parentheses, brackets, or braces in numerical expressions, and evaluate expressions with these symbols. MAFS.K12.MP.3.1, MP.6.1

Solve this problem any way you choose.

Look Back! **Construct Arguments** Do you think two students, who made no computation errors, would get different values for this numerical expression? Explain.

$(4 \times 35) + (36 \times 8)$

What Order Should You Use When You Evaluate an Expression?

Essential Question

A

Jack evaluated
$[(7 \times 2) - 3] + 8 \div 2 \times 3$.

To avoid getting more than one answer, he used the order of operations given at the right.

Parentheses, brackets, and braces are all used to group numbers in numerical expressions.

Order of Operations

1. Evaluate inside parentheses ( ), brackets [ ], and braces { }.

2. Multiply and divide from left to right.

3. Add and subtract from left to right.

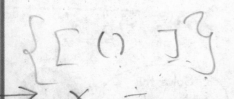

B ## Step 1

First, do the operations inside the parentheses.

$[(7 \times 2) - 3] + 8 \div 2 \times 3$

$[14 - 3] + 8 \div 2 \times 3$

Then, evaluate the terms inside the brackets.

$[14 - 3] + 8 \div 2 \times 3$

$11 + 8 \div 2 \times 3$

C ## Step 2

Next, <u>multiply and divide</u> in order from left to right.

$11 + 8 \div 2 \times 3$

$11 + 4 \times 3$

$11 + 12$

D ## Step 3

Finally, add and subtract in order from left to right.

$11 + 12 = 23$

So, the value of the expression is 23.

Convince Me! **Construct Arguments** Would the value of $\{2 + [(15 - 3) - 6]\} \div 2$ change if the braces were removed? Explain.

 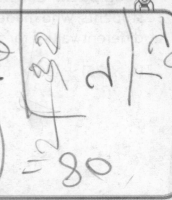

© Pearson Education, Inc. 5

Practice   Tools   Assessment

☆ Guided Practice

Do You Understand?

1. Explain the steps involved in evaluating the expression $[(4 + 2) - 1] \times 3$.

[6 - 1] × 3
5 × 3 = 1.5

2. Would the value of $(12 - 4) \div 4 + 1$ change if the parentheses were removed? Explain.

= 8 ÷ 4 + 1
= 2 + 1
= 3

Do You Know How?

In **3–6**, use the order of operations to evaluate the expression.

3. $[7 \times (6 - 1)] + 100$

[7 × 5] + 100 = 35 + 100 = 135

4. $17 + 4 \times 3$

17 + 12 = 29

5. $(8 + 1) + 9 \times 7$

9 + 9 × 7 = 72   *= 9 + 63*

6. $\{[(4 \times 3) \div 2] + 3\} \times 6$

{12 ÷ 2} × 3 × 6

☆ Independent Practice ☆

Leveled Practice In **7–21**, use the order of operations to evaluate the expression.

Remember to evaluate inside parentheses, brackets, and braces first.

7. $8 \times (3 + 4) \div 2$

$8 \times 7 \div 2$

$56 \div 2 = 28$

8. $39 + 6 \div 2$

$39 + 3 = 42$

9. $24 \div [(3 + 1) \times 2]$

$24 \div [4 \times 2]$

$24 \div 8 = 3$

10. $5 \div 5 + 4 \times 12$

1 + 48 = 49

11. $[6 - (3 \times 2)] + 4$

12. $(4 \times 8) \div 2 + 8$

32   *16*   *= 24*

13. $(18 + 7) \times (11 - 7)$

14. $2 + [4 + (5 \times 6)]$

36

15. $(9 + 11) \div (5 + 4 + 1)$

20   *2*

16. $90 - 5 \times 5 \times 2$

40

17. $120 - 40 \div 4 \times 6$

10   *= 60*

18. $22 + (96 - 40) \div 8$

29

19. $(7.7 + 0.3) \div 0.1 \times 4$

8 ÷ 0.1 × 4 = 88 × 4 = 320

20. $32 \div (12 - 4) + 7$

= 11

21. $\{8 \times [1 + (20 - 6)]\} \div \frac{1}{2}$

= 240

Problem Solving

22. Dan and his 4 friends want to share the cost of a meal equally. They order 2 large pizzas and 5 small drinks. If they leave a tip of $6.30, how much does each person pay?

Menu	
Small pizza	$8.00
Large pizza	$12.00
Small drink	$1.50
Large drink	$2.25

{(12×2)}+(5×1.50) + 6.30}÷4
24+7.50+6.30 = 37.80 ÷ 4 = 9.45$

---

23. **Higher Order Thinking** Use the operation signs +, −, ×, and ÷ once each in the expression below to make the number sentence true.

6 × (3 ÷ 1) + 5 − 1 = 17

12 + 5 = 17

24. **Be Precise** Carlotta needs $12\frac{1}{2}$ yards of ribbon for a project. She has $5\frac{1}{4}$ yards of ribbon on one spool and $2\frac{1}{2}$ yards on another spool. How much more ribbon does she need?

$12\frac{1}{2} - 7\frac{3}{4} = 4\frac{3}{4}$ yards.

---

25. Theresa bought three containers of tennis balls at $2.98 each. She had a coupon for $1 off. Her mom paid for half of the remaining cost. How much did Theresa pay? Evaluate the expression $[(3 × 2.98) − 1] ÷ 2$.

(2.98 × 3) − 1 ÷ 2 = 3.92$

3.92

 Evaluate the expression in the parentheses first. Then subtract inside the brackets.

2.98 × 3
6 | 7.94
  | 9
2.98 × 3
18 9 4
14

26. **enVision®** STEM Giraffes are *herbivores*, or plant eaters. A giraffe can eat up to 75 pounds of leaves each day. Write and evaluate an expression to find how many pounds of leaves 5 giraffes can eat in a week.

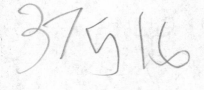

---

27. Which expression has a value of 8?

5.OA.1.1

- Ⓐ 11 − 6 − 3
- Ⓑ 4 + 30 ÷ 6
- Ⓒ (9 + 7) ÷ 2 = 8
- Ⓓ 1 + 1 × (2 + 2)

28. Using the order of operations, which operation should you perform last to evaluate this expression? 5.OA.1.1

$(1 × 2.5) + (52 ÷ 13) + (6.7 − 5) − (98 + 8)$

- Ⓐ Addition
- Ⓑ Subtraction
- Ⓒ Multiplication
- Ⓓ Division

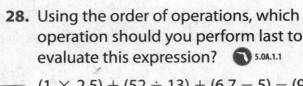

© Pearson Education, Inc. 5

Name _____

Solve & Share

A baker packages 12 cupcakes to a box. Sean orders 5 boxes for his sister's graduation party and 3.5 boxes for the Variety Show party. Write an expression that shows the calculations you could use to find the number of cupcakes Sean orders.

I can ...
write simple expressions that show calculations with numbers.

MAFS.5.OA.1.2 Write simple expressions that record calculations with numbers, and interpret numerical expressions without evaluating them. Also 5.OA.1.1
MAFS.K12.MP.2.1, MP.4.1

Model with Math
You can write a numerical expression to model this situation.

$$9.45$$
$$4\overline{)37.8}$$
$$36$$
$$18$$
$$16$$
$$20$$
$$0$$

Look Back! Write a different expression to model Sean's order. Evaluate both expressions to check that they are equivalent. How many cupcakes does Sean order?

How Can You Write a Numerical Expression to Record Calculations?

A

The school auditorium has 546 seats on the main floor and 102 in the balcony. Every seat is filled for all of the Variety Show performances. Write an expression that shows the calculations you could use to determine how many tickets were sold.

Variety Show
Tickets $4.50

Performances:
·Friday, March 18, 7:00 P.M.
·Saturday, March 19, 2:00 P.M.
·Saturday, March 19, 7:00 P.M.
·Sunday, March 20, 2:00 P.M.

B Think about how you would calculate the total number of tickets.

Add 546 + 102 to find the total number of seats.
Then **multiply** by the number of performances, 4.

So, you need to write a numerical expression that represents:

"Find 4 times the sum of 546 and 102."

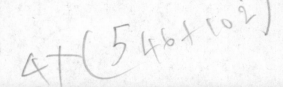

C Use numbers and symbols to write the numerical expression.

The sum of 546 and 102: 546 + 102

4 times the sum: 4 × (546 + 102)

Remember, parentheses show which calculation to do first.

The expression 4 × (546 + 102) shows the calculations for the number of tickets sold.

Convince Me! **Reasoning** Two students wrote different expressions to find the total number of tickets sold.
Is their work correct? Explain.

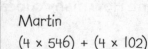

Martin
(4 × 546) + (4 × 102)

Ashley
4 × 546 + 102

© Pearson Education, Inc. 5

Name _____

Guided Practice

Do You Understand?

1. Why do some numerical expressions contain parentheses?

2. Show how to use a property to write an equivalent expression for $9 \times (7 + 44)$. Can you use a different property to write another equivalent expression? Explain.

$= 9 \times 7 + 9 \times 44$

$=$

Do You Know How?

In **3–6**, write a numerical expression for each calculation.

3. Add 8 and 7, and then multiply by 2.

$(8 + 7) \times 2$

4. Find triple the difference between 44.75 and 22.8.

$(44.75 - 22.8) \times 3$

5. Multiply 4 times $\frac{7}{8}$ and then add 12.

$4 \times \frac{7}{8} + 12$

6. Add 49 to the quotient of 125 and 5.

$49 + 125 \div 5$

Independent Practice

In **7–11**, write a numerical expression for each calculation.

7. Add 91, 129, and 16, and then divide by 44.

$(91 + 129 + 16) \div 44$

8. Find 8.5 times the difference between 77 and 13.

$(77 - 13) \times 8.5$

9. Subtract 55 from the sum of 234 and 8.

$(234 + 8) - 55$

10. Multiply $\frac{2}{3}$ by 42, and then multiply that product by 10.

$2/3 \times 42 \times 10$

11. Write an expression to show the calculations you could use to determine the total area of the rectangles at the right.

$18 \times 22 \times 3$

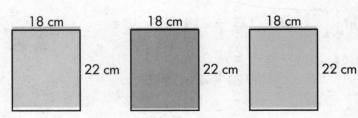

18 cm   18 cm   18 cm

22 cm   22 cm   22 cm

For another example, see Set B on page 555.

Topic 13 | Lesson 13-2   **543**

Problem Solving

12. Model with Math Ronnie's Rentals charges $25 plus $15 per hour to rent a chain saw. David rented a chain saw for 5 hours. Write an expression to show how you could calculate the total amount David paid.

$(25 + 15) \times 5$

13. Fourteen students bought their art teacher a new easel for $129 and a set of blank canvases for $46. Sales tax was $10.50. They shared the cost equally. Write an expression to show how you could calculate the amount each student paid.

$(46 + 129 + 10.50) \div 14$

---

14.  **Vocabulary** When evaluating an expression, why is it important to use the **order of operations**?

Yes

15. A storage shed is shaped like a rectangular prism. The width is 8 yards, the height is 4 yards, and the volume is 288 cubic yards. Explain how to find the length of the storage shed.

$l = \dfrac{288}{(4 \times 8)}$

---

16. Higher Order Thinking Danielle has a third of the amount needed to pay for her choir trip expenses. Does the expression $(77 + 106 + 34) \div 3$ show how you could calculate the amount of money Danielle has? Explain.

Yes.

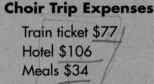

Choir Trip Expenses
Train ticket $77
Hotel $106
Meals $34

---

17. Which expression represents the following phrase?

Subtract 214 from 721 and then divide by 5. 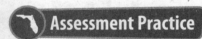 5.OA.1.2

Ⓐ $(721 \div 214) - 5$

Ⓑ $721 - 214 \div 5$

Ⓒ $(721 \div 5) - 214$

Ⓓ $(721 - 214) \div 5$

$(721 - 214)$
$\div 5$

18. What is the first step in evaluating this expression?

$2 \times (47 + 122) - 16$ 5.OA.1.1

Ⓐ Multiply 2 and 47

Ⓑ Multiply 2 and 16

Ⓒ Add 47 and 122

Ⓓ Add 2 and 47

© Pearson Education, Inc. 5

Name _____

Solve & Share

Mrs. Katz is planning her family's trip to the museum. She made a list of the expenses. Then she wrote the following expression to show how she can calculate the total cost.

$6 \times (4.20 + 8 + 12 + 3.50)$

How many people do you think are in the family? How can you tell?

Lesson 13-3
Interpret Numerical Expressions

I can ...
interpret numerical expressions without evaluating them.

MAFS.5.OA.1.2 Write simple expressions that record calculations with numbers, and interpret numerical expressions without evaluating them. MAFS.K12.MP.3.1, MP.7.1

Use Structure
You can interpret the relationships in numerical expressions without doing any calculations.

Museum Trip Expenses (per person)

Roundtrip bus fare: $4.20

Buffet lunch: $8

Entrance fee: $12

Dinosaur lecture: $3.50

Look Back! While they are at the museum, the family decides to watch a movie about earthquakes for $2.75 per person. Jana and Kay disagree as to how they should adjust Mrs. Katz's expression to find the total expenses for the trip.

Jana says the expression should be $6 \times (4.20 + 8 + 12 + 3.50) + 2.75$.
Kay says the expression should be $6 \times (4.20 + 8 + 12 + 3.50 + 2.75)$.

Who is correct? Explain.

Essential Question

How Can You Interpret Numerical Expressions Without Evaluating Them?

A

Jimmy's clown costume requires $\frac{7}{8} + \frac{1}{2} + 1\frac{3}{4}$ yards of fabric.

His dad's matching clown costume requires $3 \times \left(\frac{7}{8} + \frac{1}{2} + 1\frac{3}{4}\right)$ yards.

How does the amount of fabric needed for the dad's costume compare to the amount needed for Jimmy's costume?

Child's Clown Costume

Fabric

Blue	$\frac{7}{8}$ yd
Yellow	$\frac{1}{2}$ yd
Polka Dot	$1\frac{3}{4}$ yd

You can compare the expressions and solve the problem without doing any calculations.

B Interpret the part of each expression that is the same.

$$\frac{7}{8} + \frac{1}{2} + 1\frac{3}{4}$$
$$3 \times \left(\frac{7}{8} + \frac{1}{2} + 1\frac{3}{4}\right)$$

Both expressions contain the sum $\frac{7}{8} + \frac{1}{2} + 1\frac{3}{4}$. This is the amount of fabric needed for Jimmy's costume.

C Interpret the part of each expression that is different.

$$\frac{7}{8} + \frac{1}{2} + 1\frac{3}{4}$$
$$3 \times \left(\frac{7}{8} + \frac{1}{2} + 1\frac{3}{4}\right)$$

Remember, multiplying by 3 means "3 times as much."

The second expression shows that the sum is multiplied by 3.

So, the dad's costume requires 3 times as much fabric as Jimmy's costume.

Convince Me! Reasoning The 7 students in a sewing class equally share the cost of fabric and other supplies. Last month, each student paid ($167.94 + $21.41) ÷ 7. This month, each student paid ($77.23 + $6.49) ÷ 7. Without doing any calculations, in which month did each student pay more? Explain.

© Pearson Education, Inc. 5

Practice Tools Assessment

☆ Guided Practice*

Do You Understand?

1. The number of yards of fabric needed for Rob's costume is $\left(\frac{7}{8} + \frac{1}{2} + 1\frac{3}{4}\right) \div 2$. How does the amount of fabric needed for Rob's costume compare to the amount needed for Jimmy's costume? Explain.

2. Without doing any calculations, explain why the following number sentence is true.

$14 + (413 \times 7) > 6 + (413 \times 7)$

Yes.

Do You Know How?

Without doing any calculations, describe how Expression A compares to Expression B.

3. **A** $8 \times (41,516 - 987)$
   B $41,516 - 987$

$A > B$

In **4** and **5**, without doing any calculations, write $>$, $<$, or $=$.

4. $7 \times \left(4\frac{3}{8} + 3\frac{1}{2}\right)$ ⬰ $22 \times \left(4\frac{3}{8} + 3\frac{1}{2}\right)$

5. $8.2 + (7.1 \div 5)$ ⬰ $(7.1 \div 5) + 8.2$

$P(A+B) = PA + PB$

☆ Independent Practice ☆

In **6** and **7**, without doing any calculations, describe how Expression A compares to Expression B.

6. **A** $(613 + 15,090) \div 4$
   B $613 + 15,090$

$B > A$

7. **A** $\left(418 \times \frac{1}{4}\right) + \left(418 \times \frac{1}{2}\right) = 418\left(\frac{1+1}{4\ 2}\right)$
   B $418 \times \frac{3}{4}$

$A = B$

In **8–11**, without doing any calculations, write $>$, $<$, or $=$.

8. $(284 + 910) \div 30$ ⬰ $(284 + 7,816) \div 30$

9. $\frac{1}{3} \times (5,366 - 117)$ ⬰ $5,366 - 117$

10. $71 + (13,888 - 4,296)$ ⬰ $70 + (13,888 - 4,296)$

11. $15 \times (3.6 + 9.44)$ ⬰ $(15 \times 3.6) + (15 \times 9.44)$

$15(3.6 + 9.44)$

Problem Solving

12. A four-story parking garage has spaces for 240 + 285 + 250 + 267 cars. While one floor is closed for repairs, the garage has spaces for 240 + 250 + 267 cars. How many spaces are there on the floor that is closed? Explain.

13. Use Structure Peter bought $4 \times \left(2\frac{1}{4} + \frac{1}{2} + 2\frac{7}{8}\right)$ yards of ribbon. Marilyn bought $4 \times \left(2\frac{1}{4} + \frac{1}{2} + 3\right)$ yards of ribbon. Without doing any calculations, determine who bought more ribbon. Explain.

14. Brook's score in a card game is 713 + 102 + 516. On her next turn, she draws one of the cards shown. Now her score is (713 + 102 + 516) ÷ 2. Which card did Brook draw? Explain.

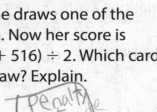

BONUS Double your score!

PENALTY Cut your score in half!

BONUS Add 200 points to your score!

PENALTY Lose 200 points!

15. Marta bought a 0.25-kilogram box of fish food. She uses 80 grams a week. Is one box of fish food enough for 4 weeks? Explain.

16. Higher Order Thinking How can you tell that (496 + 77 + 189) × 10 is twice as large as (496 + 77 + 189) × 5 without doing complicated calculations?

 Assessment Practice

17. Which statement describes the expression (21 + 1.5) × 12 − 5? 🔲 5.OA.1.2

Ⓐ The sum of 21 and 1.5 times the difference of 12 and 5

Ⓑ Five less than the sum of 21 and 1.5 multiplied by 12

Ⓒ Five less than the product of 12 and 1.5 added to 21

Ⓓ Subtract the product of 12 and 5 from the sum of 21 and 1.5

© Pearson Education, Inc. 5

Name _____

Activity

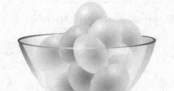

The camp cook has 6 dozen eggs. He uses 18 eggs to bake some brownies. Then he uses twice as many eggs to make pancakes. How many eggs does the cook have left? Use reasoning to write and evaluate an expression that represents the problem.

I can ...

make sense of quantities and relationships in problem situations.

MAFS.K12.MP.2.1 Reason abstractly and quantitatively. **Also, MP.1.1, MP.4.1** MAFS.5.OA.1.1 Use parentheses, brackets, or braces in numerical expressions, and evaluate expressions with these symbols.

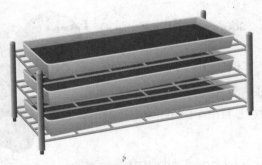

Thinking Habits

Be a good thinker! These questions can help you.

- What do the numbers and symbols in the problem mean?

- How are the numbers or quantities related?

- How can I represent a word problem using pictures, numbers, or equations?

Look Back! Reasoning Explain how the numbers, symbols, and operations in your expression represent this problem.

Essential Question

How Can You Use Reasoning to Solve Problems?

A

Rose has 3 albums for her soccer cards. She gets 7 more cards for each of her albums for her birthday. How many cards does Rose have in all?

22 cards in each album

What do I need to do to solve the problem?

I need to find how many cards, including Rose's new cards, will be in each album. Then I need to multiply to find the number of cards in 3 albums.

You can use tools or draw a diagram to help solve the problem.

B

How can I use reasoning to solve this problem?

I can

- identify the quantities I know.

- use mathematical properties, symbols, and operations to show relationships.

- use diagrams to help.

C

Here's my thinking...

I need to find how many cards Rose has in all.

I can use a diagram to show how the quantities in the problem are related. Then I can write an expression.

There are 22 cards in each of her 3 albums. She gets 7 more cards for each of her 3 albums.

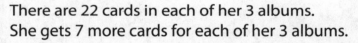

| 22 | 7 | | 22 | 7 | | 22 | 7 |

$$3 \times (22 + 7) = 3 \times 29$$
$$= 87$$

Rose has 87 cards.

Convince Me! **Reasoning** How can you use the Distributive Property to write an expression equivalent to the one given above? Use reasoning to explain how you know the expressions are equivalent.

© Pearson Education, Inc. 5

Name _____

☆ Guided Practice*

Reasoning

Todd has 4 baseball card albums like the one pictured. He lets his best friend Franco choose 5 cards from each album. How many cards does Todd have now?

4

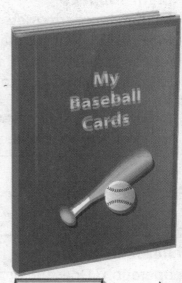

My Baseball Cards

42 cards in each album

1. Write an expression to represent the total number of cards in Todd's albums before he gives some cards to Franco. Explain how your expression represents the quantities and the relationship between the quantities.

   4 × 42 — 20

2. Write an expression to represent the total number of cards in Todd's albums after he gives some cards to Franco.

   4 × 42 — 20

3. How many cards does Todd have after he gives some cards to Franco? Explain how you solved the problem.

☆ Independent Practice ☆

Reasoning

Brandon is filling a flower order for a banquet. He needs 3 large arrangements and 12 small arrangements. The large arrangements each contain 28 roses. The small arrangements each contain 16 roses. How many roses does Brandon need in all?

> Remember to think about the meaning of each number before solving the problem.

4. Write an expression to represent the total number of roses Brandon needs. You can use a diagram to help.

5. Explain how the numbers, symbols, and operations in your expression represent the problem.

6. How many roses does Brandon need? Explain how you solved the problem.

Problem Solving

Math Supplies

Ms. Kim is ordering sets of place-value blocks for the 3rd, 4th, and 5th graders. She wants one set for each student, and there are 6 sets of blocks in a carton. How many cartons should Ms. Kim order?

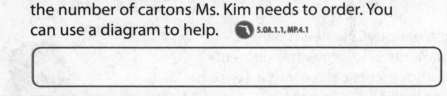

	Grade	Number of Students
DATA	3rd	48
	4th	43
	5th	46
	6th	50

7. **Make Sense and Persevere** What information in the problem do you need? 🏴 5.OA.1.1, MP.1.1

8. **Reasoning** Does this problem require more than one operation? Does the order of the operations matter? Explain. 🏴 5.OA.1.1, MP.2.1

9. **Model with Math** Write an expression to represent the number of cartons Ms. Kim needs to order. You can use a diagram to help. 🏴 5.OA.1.1, MP.4.1

Use reasoning to make sense of the relationship between the numbers.

10. **Construct Arguments** Did you use grouping symbols in your expression? If so, explain why they are needed. 🏴 5.OA.1.1, MP.3.1

11. **Be Precise** Find the total number of cartons Ms. Kim should order. Explain how you found the answer. 🏴 5.OA.1.1, MP.6.1

© Pearson Education, Inc. 5

Find a Match

Work with a partner. Point to a clue. Read the clue.

Look below the clues to find a match. Write the clue letter in the box next to the match.

Find a match for every clue.

I can ...
multiply multi-digit whole numbers.

MAFS.5.NBT.2.5

Clues

A The product is 3,456.

B The product is 100,000.

C The product is 123,321.

D The product is 225,000.

E The product is 45,432.

F The product has a 6 in the thousands place.

G The product has a 9 in the thousands place.

H The product has a 3 in the hundred thousands place.

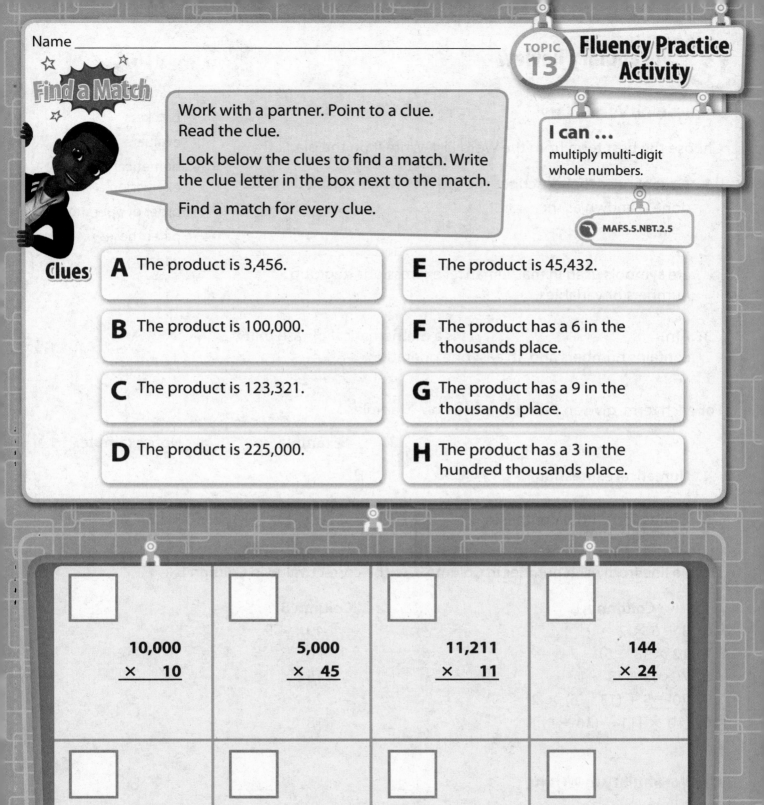

10,000 × 10	5,000 × 45	11,211 × 11	144 × 24
5,038 × 63	2,643 × 87	327 × 21	1,262 × 36

Vocabulary Review

Word List

- braces
- brackets
- evaluate
- numerical expression
- order of operations
- parentheses
- variable

Understand Vocabulary

Choose the best term from the Word List. Write it on the blank.

1. A set of rules that describes the order in which calculations are done is known as the _____.

2. _____, _____, and _____ are symbols used in mathematical expressions to group numbers or variables.

3. A(n) _____ is a mathematical phrase that contains numbers and at least one operation.

For each term, give an example and a non-example.

	Example	Non-example
4. Numerical expression	_____	_____
5. Expression with parentheses	_____	_____

Draw a line from each number in Column A to the correct value in Column B.

Column A	Column B
6. $3 + 6 \times 2$	49
7. $12 \times (8 - 5) - 7$	20
8. $7 \times [5 + (3 - 1)]$	15
9. $20 \div 5 + (13 - 6) \times 2$	29
10. $\{10 \times [11 - (36 \div 4)]\}$	18

Use Vocabulary in Writing

11. Explain why the order of operations is important. Use at least three terms from the Word List in your explanation.

© Pearson Education, Inc. 5

Name _____

Set A | pages 537–540

Use the order of operations to evaluate
$50 + (8 + 2) \times (14 - 4)$.

Order of Operations

1. Calculate inside parentheses, brackets, and braces.
2. Multiply and divide from left to right.
3. Add and subtract from left to right.

Perform the operations inside the parentheses, brackets, and braces.

$50 + (8 + 2) \times (14 - 4) = 50 + 10 \times 10$

Multiply and divide in order from left to right.

$50 + 10 \times 10 = 50 + 100$

Add and subtract in order from left to right.

$50 + 100 = 150$

Remember that if the parentheses are inside brackets or braces, perform the operations inside the parentheses first.

Evaluate each expression.

1. $(78 + 47) \div 25$

2. $4 + 8 \times 6 \div 2 + 3$

3. $[(8 \times 25) \div 5] + 120$

4. $312 \times (40 + 60) \div 60$

5. $80 - (0.4 + 0.2) \times 10$

6. $(18 - 3) \div 5 + 4$

7. $8 \times 5 + 7 \times 3 - (10 - 5)$

8. $22 - \{[(87 - 32) \div 5] \times 2\}$

Set B | pages 541–544

Write a numerical expression for the phrase: "Subtract 15 from the product of 12 and 7".

Think:

Sum → Addition (+)

Difference → Subtraction (−)

Product → Multiplication (×)

Quotient → Division (÷)

Product of 12 and 7: 12×7

Subtract 15 from the product: $(12 \times 7) - 15$

So, a numerical expression for the phrase is: $(12 \times 7) - 15$.

Remember that you can use parentheses to show which calculation to do first.

Write a numerical expression for each phrase.

1. Add 15 to the product of $\frac{3}{4}$ and 12.

2. Find the difference of 29 and 13, and then divide by 2.

3. Add $1\frac{1}{2}$ and $\frac{3}{4}$, and then subtract $\frac{1}{3}$.

4. Multiply 1.2 by 5 and then subtract 0.7.

5. Add the quotient of 120 and 3 to the product of 15 and 10.

The expressions below show how many miles each student ran this week. How does Alex's distance compare to Kim's distance?

Kim: $\left(4 \times 3\frac{1}{2}\right)$

Alex: $\left(4 \times 3\frac{1}{2}\right) + 2\frac{1}{2}$

What is the **same** about the expressions? Both contain the product $4 \times 3\frac{1}{2}$.

What is **different** about the expressions? $2\frac{1}{2}$ is added in Alex's expression.

So, Alex ran $2\frac{1}{2}$ miles farther than Kim this week.

Remember that sometimes you can compare numerical expressions without doing any calculations.

> Without doing any calculations, write $>$, $<$, or $=$.

1. $72 \times (37 - 9) \bigcirc 69 \times (37 - 9)$

2. $(144 \div 12) - 6 \bigcirc 144 \div 12$

3. $\left(4 + \frac{1}{2} + 3\right) \times 2 \bigcirc 2 \times \left(4 + \frac{1}{2} + 3\right)$

4. Describe how Expression A compares to Expression B.

   A $\$3.99 + (\$9.50 \times 2)$ **B** $\$9.50 \times 2$

Think about these questions to help you **reason abstractly and quantitatively**.

Thinking Habits

- What do the numbers and symbols in the problem mean?

- How are the numbers or quantities related?

- How can I represent a word problem using pictures, numbers, or equations?

Remember that you can use diagrams to help solve problems.

1. Kerry has 5 metal and 3 wood paperweights in her collection. She has twice as many glass paperweights as metal paperweights. Write an expression to represent the total number of paperweights in her collection. Then find the total number of paperweights.

2. Reese had 327 baseball cards. Then he lost 8 of them and gave 15 of them to his brother. Write an expression to represent the number of baseball cards he has left. Then find how many baseball cards he has left.

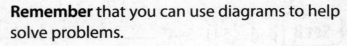

© Pearson Education, Inc. 5

Name _____

1. Which of the following is equal to 10?

Ⓐ $2 \times (45 \div 9)$

Ⓑ $24 - (7 \times 3)$

Ⓒ $1 + (4 \times 2)$

Ⓓ $(2 \times 25) \times 5$

2. Select all of the expressions that are equal to 8×65.

☐ $3 + 5 \times 60$

☐ $8 \times (60 + 5)$

☐ $8 \times (50 + 15)$

☐ $(8 + 60) \times (8 + 5)$

☐ $(8 \times 60) + (8 \times 5)$

3. Which is the value of the expression $7 + (3 \times 4) - 2$?

Ⓐ 38

Ⓑ 20

Ⓒ 17

Ⓓ 12

4. Which expression represents the following calculation?

Add 16 to the quotient of 72 and 8.

Ⓐ $(72 - 8) + 16$

Ⓑ $(72 \div 8) + 16$

Ⓒ $(16 + 72) \div 8$

Ⓓ $(16 + 72) + 8$

5. What is the value of $(100 \times 15) + (10 \times 15)$?

6. Describe how the value of Expression A compares to the value of Expression B.

A $1\frac{1}{2} \times \left(54 \div \frac{2}{5}\right)$

B $54 \div \frac{2}{5}$

7. Write $>$, $<$, or $=$ in the circle to make the statement true.

$(368 \times 19) - 24 \bigcirc (368 \times 19) - 47$

8. Insert parentheses to make the statement true.

$7 + 6 \times 14 - 9 = 37$

9. Which expression represents the following calculation?

Subtract 2 from the product of 7 and 3.

Ⓐ $(7 + 3) - 2$

Ⓑ $7 \times (3 - 2)$

Ⓒ $(7 \times 3) - 2$

Ⓓ $(7 \times 2) - 3$

10. What is the value of the expression $(6 + 3) \times 2$?

11. Evaluate the expression $(6 + 12 \div 2) + 4$. Show your work.

12. Write $>$, $<$, or $=$ in the circle to make the statement true.

$(249 + 1{,}078) \times \frac{1}{3}$ ◯ $(249 + 1{,}078) \div 3$

13. Write an expression to find the product of 3 and 28 plus the product of 2 and 15. Then solve.

14. Evaluate the expression.

$6 + (24 - 4) + 8 \div 2$

A. What step do you perform first in evaluating this expression?

B. What step do you perform second in evaluating this expression?

C. What is the value of the expression?

© Pearson Education, Inc. 5

Name _____

Decorating

Jackie is decorating her room. She wants to put a border around the ceiling. She will put wallpaper on one wall and paint the other three walls.

1. The drawing of **Jackie's Room** shows the width of the room. The expression $[13.2 - (2 \times 2.8)] \div 2$ represents the length of her room.

Part A

How much border does Jackie need to go around the entire ceiling of her room? Explain how you can tell from the expression. 🔵 5.0A.1.1; 5.0A.1.2; MP.1.1

Jackie's Room

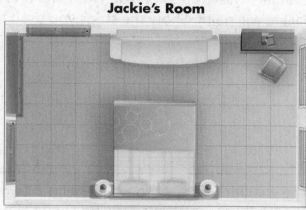

2.8 m

Part B

What is the length of Jackie's room? Show the steps you use to evaluate the expression. 🔵 5.0A.1.1; MP.2.1

2. The **Painted Walls** drawing shows the three walls Jackie wants to paint. One wall is 2.8 meters long. The length of each of the other walls is the answer you found in Question 1, Part B.

Painted Walls

2 m

?

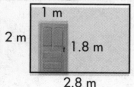

2 m   1 m   1.8 m

2.8 m

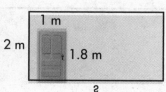

2 m   1 m   1.8 m

?

Part A

Write an expression to represent how many square meters Jackie will paint. 5.OA.1.2, MP.1.1

Part B

Evaluate the expression you wrote in Part A to find how many square meters Jackie will paint. Show the steps you used to evaluate the expression. 5.OA.1.1, MP.6.1

3. The wall Jackie wants to wallpaper has two windows. The **Wallpapered Wall** drawing shows the lengths and widths of the wall and the windows. Each roll of wallpaper covers 0.8 square meter.

Wallpapered Wall

2 m   1.5 m

0.8 m   0.8 m

2.8 m

Part A

What does the expression $2 \times (1.5 \times 0.8)$ represent? What does the expression $(2.8 \times 2) - [2 \times (1.5 \times 0.8)]$ represent?

5.OA.1.2, MP.2.1

Part B

Write an expression to find how many rolls of wallpaper Jackie needs to buy. Show the steps you used to evaluate the expression. 5.OA.1.1, 5.OA.1.2, MP.1.1

   © Pearson Education, Inc. 5

Graph Points on the Coordinate Plane

Essential Questions: How are points plotted? How are relationships shown on a graph?

Digital Resources

Interactive Student Edition · Activity · Visual Learning · Video · Practice

Assessment · Games · Tools · Glossary

MAFS.5.G.1.1, 5.G.1.2
MAFS.K12.MP.1.1, MP.2.1, MP.3.1, MP.4.1, MP.5.1, MP.7.1

> Day and night are caused by Earth spinning.

> The imaginary line through Earth's center is Earth's *axis*. The spinning of Earth on its axis is called *rotation*.

> I'm getting dizzy thinking about it! Here's a project about Earth's rotation.

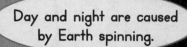 STEM Project: Earth's Rotation

Do Research Use the Internet or other sources to find out more about Earth's rotation. Investigate why it appears that the Sun is moving across the sky. Design a model to explain Earth's day/night cycle. Compare Earth's rotation to another planet's rotation.

Write a Report: Journal Include what you found. Also in your report:

- Write a step-by-step procedure of how to use a ball and a flashlight to represent the day/night cycle.

- Explain what happens if the ball rotates slowly. What happens if the ball rotates quickly?

- Make up and solve problems for plotting points and using graphs to show relationships.

Review What You Know

A-Z Vocabulary

Choose the best term from the Word List.
Write it on the blank.

| • equation |
| • factor |
| • line plot |
| • numerical expression |
| • variable |

1. A(n) _____
   contains numbers and at least one operation.

2. A letter or symbol that represents an
   unknown amount is a(n) _____.

3. A number sentence that uses the = symbol is a(n) _____.

4. A display that shows Xs or dots above a number line is a(n) _____.

Evaluate Expressions

Evaluate each numerical expression.

5. $3 \times 4 \times (10 - 7) \div 2$

6. $(8 + 2) \times 6 - 4$

7. $8 + 2 \times 6 - 4$

8. $40 \div 5 + 5 \times (3 - 1)$

9. $15 \div 3 + 2 \times 10$

10. $21 \times (8 - 6) \div 14$

Write Expressions

Write a numerical expression for each word phrase.

11. Three less than the product of eight and six

12. Thirteen more than the quotient of twenty divided by four

13. Four times the difference between seven and two

Compare Expressions

14. Use < or > to compare $13 \times (54 + 28)$ and $13 \times 54 + 28$ without
    calculating. Explain your reasoning.

Name _____

**PROJECT
14A**

What does a city planner do?

Project: Plan a City

**PROJECT
14B**

What are some of the oldest childhood games?

Project: Make Your Own Game

PROJECT
14C

How can dogs help rescue people?

Project: Write a Story of a Missing Hiker

PROJECT
14D

How can artists use grids in their work?

Project: Draw a Picture Using a Grid

© Pearson Education, Inc. 5

Name _____

☆ ☆
Solve & Share

On the first grid, plot a point where two lines intersect. Name the location of the point. Plot and name another point. Work with a partner. Take turns describing the locations of the points on your first grid. Then plot the points your partner describes on your second grid. Compare your first grid with your partner's second grid to see if they match. **Use the grids below to solve this problem.**

I can ...
locate points on a coordinate grid.

MAFS.5.G.1.1 Use a pair of perpendicular number lines, called axes, to define a coordinate system, with the intersection of the lines (the origin) arranged to coincide with the 0 on each line and a given point in the plane located by using an ordered pair of numbers, called its coordinates....
MAFS.K12.MP.2.1, MP.3.1

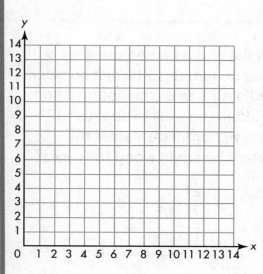
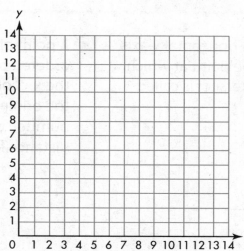

You can use grid paper to graph ordered pairs. *Show your work!*

Look Back! **Construct Arguments** Why does the order of the two numbers that name a point matter? Explain your thinking.

How Do You Name a Point on a Coordinate Grid?

A

A map shows the locations of landmarks and has guides for finding them. In a similar way, a coordinate grid is used to graph and name the locations of points in a plane.

You can use ordered pairs to locate points on a coordinate grid.

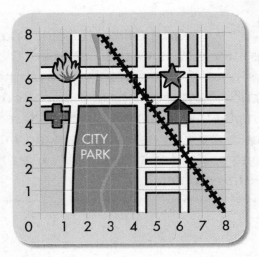

B A coordinate grid has a horizontal *x*-axis and a vertical *y*-axis. The point at which the *x*-axis and *y*-axis intersect is called the origin.

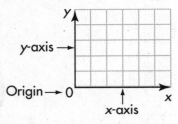

C A point on the grid is named using an ordered pair of numbers. The first number, the *x*-coordinate, names the distance from the origin along the *x*-axis. The second number, the *y*-coordinate, names the distance from the origin along the *y*-axis.

$A\ (1, 3)$

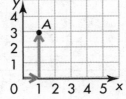

Convince Me! **Reasoning** In the example above, name the ordered pair for Point *B* if it is 3 units to the right of Point *A*. Tell how you decided.

© Pearson Education, Inc. 5

Practice Tools Assessment

☆ Guided Practice*

Do You Understand?

1. You are graphing Point *E* at (0, 5). Do you move to the right zero units, or up zero units? Explain.

2. (A-Z) **Vocabulary** What ordered pair names the origin of any coordinate grid?

3. Describe how to graph Point *K* at (5, 4).

Do You Know How?

In **4** and **5**, write the ordered pair for each point. Use the grid.

4. B   3,2

5. A

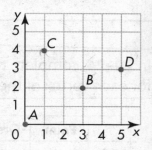

In **6** and **7**, name the point for each ordered pair on the grid above.

6. (5, 3)   **7.** (1, 4)

Independent Practice ☆

In **8–13**, write the ordered pair for each point. Use the grid.

8. T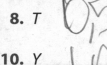

9. X   4,3

10. Y   40

11. W   3,2

12. Z   14

13. S   5,2

In **14–18**, name the point for each ordered pair on the grid above.

14. (2, 2)   **15.** (5, 4)   **16.** (1, 5)   **17.** (0, 3)   **18.** (4, 0)

          ←   M   P

Problem Solving

19. Higher Order Thinking Describe to a friend how to find and name the ordered pair for Point *R* on the grid.

Over 4
Up 5

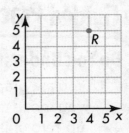

In **20–24**, complete the table. List the point and ordered pair for each vertex of the pentagon at the right.

	Point	Ordered Pair
20.		
21.		
22.		
23.		
24.		

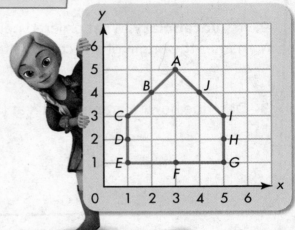

25. Reasoning Why is the order important when naming or graphing the coordinates of a point?

26. How are the *x*-axis and the *y*-axis related on a coordinate grid?

27. Which of the following points is located at (4, 2)? 5.G.1.1

Ⓐ Point *A*

Ⓑ Point *M*

Ⓒ Point *B*

Ⓓ Point *P*

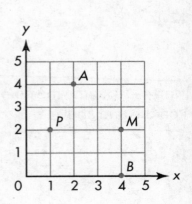

Name _____

Lesson 14-2
Graph Data Using Ordered Pairs

☆ Solve & Share ☆

Graph and label the point for each ordered pair below on the grid. Then connect the points with line segments to form a shape. What shape did you draw?

I can ...
graph points on a coordinate grid.

MAFS.5.G.1.2 Represent real world and mathematical problems by graphing points in the first quadrant of the coordinate plane, and interpret coordinate values of points in the context of the situation. **Also 5.G.1.1** MAFS.K12.MP.2.1, MP.5.1

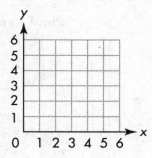

Use Appropriate Tools
You can graph points on a coordinate grid. Show your work!

A (2, 1) B (5, 1) C (5, 4) D (2, 4)

Look Back! What tool could you use to help connect points *A*, *B*, *C*, and *D*? Explain.

Essential Question

How Do You Graph a Point on a Coordinate Grid?

A

The table below shows the growth of a plant over a period of several days. Graph ordered pairs to show the plant's growth.

Let *x* be the number of days and let *y* be the height of the plant in centimeters.

Time (days)	1	3	5	7	9
Height (cm)	4	8	10	11	14

The ordered pairs are (1, 4), (3, 8), (5, 10), (7, 11), and (9, 14).

B ## Step 1

Graph the first point (1, 4).

Start at (0, 0). Move 1 unit to the right along the *x*-axis. Then move 4 units up.

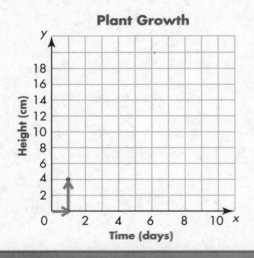

C ## Step 2

Plot the rest of the ordered pairs from the table. Use a ruler to connect the points.

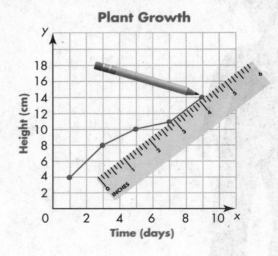

Convince Me! Reasoning Based on the data, about how tall was the plant on day 4? Day 8?

© Pearson Education, Inc. 5

Practice Tools Assessment

☆Guided Practice☆

Do You Understand?

1. Natalie is graphing Point *T* at (1, 8). Should she move to the right 8 units or up 8 units? Explain.

2. Describe how to graph the point (*c*, *d*).

Do You Know How?

In **3–6**, graph each point on the grid and label it with the appropriate letter.

3. *E* (1, 3)

4. *F* (4, 4)

5. *G* (5, 2)

6. *H* (0, 2)

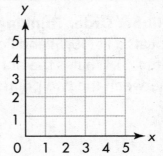

Independent Practice ☆

In **7–18**, graph and label each point on the grid at the right.

7. *J* (2, 6)   **8.** *K* (6, 2)

9. *L* (4, 5)   **10.** *M* (0, 8)

11. *N* (3, 9)   **12.** *V* (6, 6)

13. *P* (1, 4)   **14.** *Q* (5, 0)

15. *R* (7, 3)   **16.** *S* (7, 8)

17. *T* (8, 1)   **18.** *U* (3, 3)

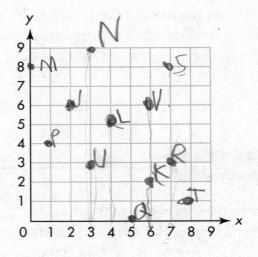

Problem Solving

19. Reasoning How is graphing (0, 2) different from graphing (2, 0)?

20. Number Sense Shane took a test that had a total of 21 items. He got about $\frac{3}{4}$ of the items correct. About how many items did he get correct?

21. Higher Order Thinking Point C is located at (10, 3) and Point D is located at (4, 3). What is the horizontal distance between the two points? Explain.

22. Laurel buys 3 balls of yarn. Each ball of yarn costs $4.75. She also buys 2 pairs of knitting needles. Each pair costs $5.75. She pays for her purchase with two 20-dollar bills. What is her change?

23. Graph the points below on the grid at the right.

A (2, 4)   B (1, 2)   C (2, 0)
D (3, 0)   E (4, 2)   F (3, 4)

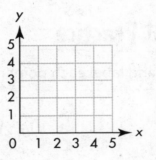

24. Alejandro wants to connect the points to form a shape. What would be the most appropriate tool for him to use? Use the tool to connect the points.

Assessment Practice

25. Talia draws a map of her neighborhood on a coordinate grid. Her map shows the school at S (1, 6), her house at H (4, 3), and the library at L (7, 2). Graph and label each location on the grid at the right. 5.G.1.2

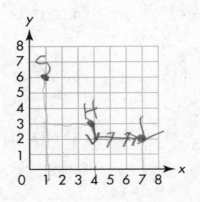

© Pearson Education, Inc. 5

Name _____

Activity

Solve & Share

    The table below uses number patterns to describe changes in the width and length of a rectangle. Let *x* be the width and *y* be the length. Then plot each of the four ordered pairs in the table on the coordinate grid. What do you think the length is if the width is 5?

I can ...
solve real-world problems by graphing points.

MAFS.5.G.1.2 Represent real world and mathematical problems by graphing points in the first quadrant of the coordinate plane, and interpret coordinate values of points in the context of the situation.
MAFS.K12.MP.7.1

	Rule	Start			
Width	Add 1	1	2	3	4
Length	Subtract 1	11	10	9	8

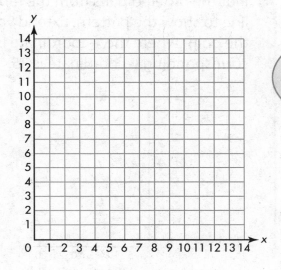

You can make a graph to help solve the problem. *Show your work!*

Look Back! **Look for Relationships** What pattern do the points form on your graph?

How Can You Use Ordered Pairs to Solve Problems?

A

Both Ann and Bill earn the amount shown each week. Ann starts with no money, but Bill starts with $5. How much will Bill have when Ann has $30? Represent this situation using a table and a graph.

You know that when Ann has $0, Bill has $5.

B Make a table showing how much money Ann and Bill have after each week.

DATA	Week	Start	1	2	3	4	5
	Ann's earnings in $	0	3	6	9	12	15
	Bill's earnings in $	5	8	11	14	17	20

Let x = Ann's earnings and y = Bill's earnings.

C Plot the ordered pairs from the table. Draw a line to show the pattern. Extend your line to the point where the x-coordinate is 30. The corresponding y-coordinate is 35.

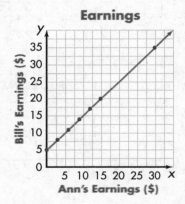

Earnings

So, Bill has $35 when Ann has $30.

Convince Me! **Look for Relationships** What is the relationship between Bill's earnings and Ann's earnings?

© Pearson Education, Inc. 5

☆ **Guided Practice**

Do You Understand?

1. In the example on page 574, find another point on the line. What does this point represent?

2. **Algebra** In the example on page 574, write an equation to show the relationship between Ann's earnings and Bill's earnings. Remember to let x = Ann's earnings and y = Bill's earnings.

Do You Know How?

Write the missing coordinates and tell what the point represents.

3.

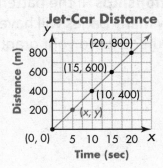

Jet-Car Distance

Independent Practice ☆

In **4** and **5**, find the missing coordinates and tell what the point represents.

4.

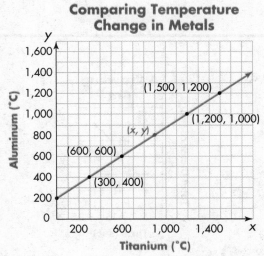

Comparing Temperature Change in Metals

5.

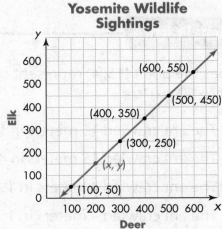

Yosemite Wildlife Sightings

6. For Exercise 5, find two other points on the line. Then graph and label them. Describe the relationship between deer sightings and elk sightings.

Problem Solving

In **7** and **8**, use the table at the right.

7. Graph the points in the table on the grid at the right. Then draw a line through the points.

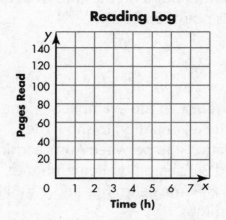

DATA	Reading Log				
Time (h)	1	2	3	4	5
Pages Read	20	40	60	80	100

8. **Look for Relationships** If the pattern continues, how many pages will have been read after 6 hours? Extend your graph to solve.

Reading Log

9. **Higher Order Thinking** Suppose you have a graph of speed that shows a lion can run four times as fast as a squirrel. Name an ordered pair that shows this relationship. What does this ordered pair represent?

10. **Number Sense** Candace drives a total of 48 miles each day to get to work and back home. She works 5 days a week. Her car gets 21 miles per gallon of gas. About how many gallons of gas does she need to drive to work and back home each week?

Assessment Practice

11. What does the point (15, 4) represent on the graph at the right? 5.6.1.2

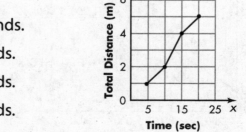

A Crawling Ant

Ⓐ The ant crawled 15 meters in 19 seconds.

Ⓑ The ant crawled 15 meters in 4 seconds.

Ⓒ The ant crawled 4 meters in 19 seconds.

Ⓓ The ant crawled 4 meters in 15 seconds.

12. What does the point (20, 5) represent on the graph? 5.6.1.2

Ⓐ In 20 seconds, the ant crawled 5 centimeters.

Ⓑ In 20 seconds, the ant crawled 5 meters.

Ⓒ In 5 seconds, the ant crawled 20 meters.

Ⓓ In 5 seconds, the ant crawled 15 meters.

© Pearson Education, Inc. 5

Name _____

☆ Solve & Share ☆

Six clowns apply for a circus job. The specific job requires the clown to have a clown shoe size less than 15 inches and to be shorter than 5 ft 8 in. tall.

How many clowns meet the size requirements for the job? Complete the graph below to help you decide.

I can ...
use reasoning to solve problems.

MAFS.K12.MP.2.1 Reasoning. **Also MP.1.1, MP.4.1, MP.5.1, MP.7.1**
MAFS.5.G.1.2 Represent real world and mathematical problems by graphing points in the first quadrant of the coordinate plane, and interpret coordinate values of points in the context of the situation. **Also 5.G.1.1**

Clown	Tippy	Yippy	Dippy	Zippy	Fippy	Gippy
Shoe	15	13	13	16	12	16
Height	5'9"	5"10"	5'3"	5'2"	5'4"	5'11"

DATA

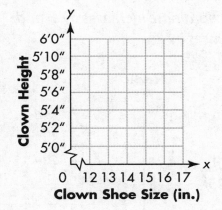

Thinking Habits

Be a good thinker!
These questions can help you.

• What do the numbers and symbols in the problem mean?

• How are the numbers or quantities related?

• How can I represent a word problem using pictures, numbers, or equations?

Look Back! **Reasoning** How can you use reasoning about the completed graph to find the number of clowns that meet the requirements? Explain.

How Can You Use Reasoning to Solve Mathematical Problems?

A

In 1705, a ship sank in the ocean at the point shown. Every year the ocean currents moved the ship 1 mile east and 2 miles north. Where was the ship located after 4 years? Where was the ship located after 10 years? Tell how you decided.

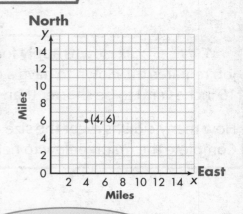

What do I need to do to solve the problem?

I need to find the ship's location after 4 years and after 10 years.

B How can I use reasoning to solve this problem?

I can

- use what I know about graphing points.

- graph ordered pairs.

- look for relationships in the coordinates.

- decide if my answer makes sense.

C

Here's my thinking...

I will use the graph to show the location each year for 4 years. Each point is 1 mile east and 2 miles north from the previous point.

After 4 years the ship was at (8, 14).

I see a pattern. The x-coordinate increases by 1, and the y-coordinate increases by 2:

(4, 6), (5, 8), (6, 10), (7, 12), (8, 14)

I can continue the pattern for another 6 years:

(9, 16), (10, 18), (11, 20), (12, 22), (13, 24), (14, 26)

After 10 years, the ship was at (14, 26).

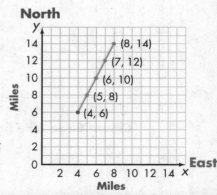

 Convince Me! **Make Sense and Persevere** How could you decide if your answers make sense?

© Pearson Education, Inc. 5

Name _____

☆ Guided Practice *

Tanya marked a grid in her garden. She planted a rose bush at (3, 1). She moved 2 feet east and 1 foot north and planted the second rose bush. She continued planting rose bushes so that each bush is 2 feet east and 1 foot north of the previous bush.

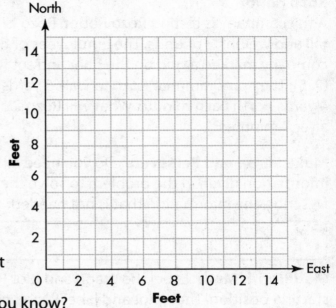

1. How can a coordinate grid help you reason about the problem?

2. Draw and label the locations of the first four bushes on the grid. Do Tanya's bushes lie on a straight line? How do you know?

3. What are the locations of the fifth and ninth rose bushes?

Independent Practice ☆

Reasoning

A marching band uses a grid to determine the members' positions. Juan starts at (2, 2). Every 15 seconds, he moves 4 yards east and 3 yards north.

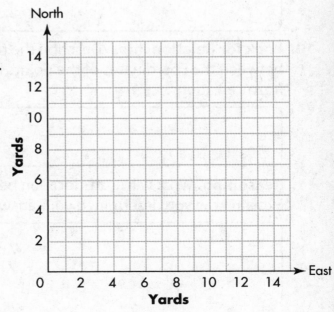

4. How can you model this problem?

5. Draw and label the locations of Juan's first four positions. Do the points form a pattern? How can you tell?

6. What will Juan's location be after 60 seconds? 90 seconds? How does the coordinate grid help you reason about the locations?

Problem Solving

Rozo Robot

A toy company is testing Rozo Robot. Rozo is 18 inches tall and weighs 2 pounds. The employees of the company marked a grid on the floor and set Rozo at (2, 5). They programmed Rozo to walk 3 yards east and 4 yards north each minute. What will Rozo's location be after 7 minutes?

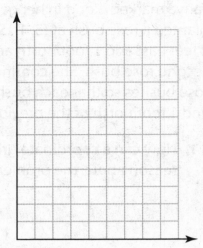

7. **Make Sense and Persevere** Do you need all of the information given in the problem to solve the problem? Describe any information that is not needed. 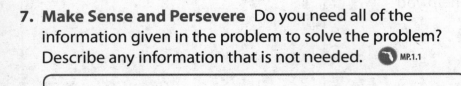 MP.1.1

8. **Model with Math** Label the graph and plot Rozo's starting position. Then plot and label Rozo's position at the end of each of the first 4 minutes. 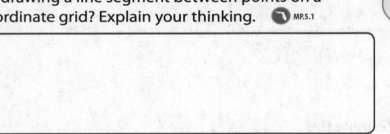 MP.4.1, 5.G.1.2

9. **Use Appropriate Tools** What tool would you choose for drawing a line segment between points on a coordinate grid? Explain your thinking.  MP.5.1

> You can use the coordinate grid to reason about relationships between the points

10. **Look for Relationships** Describe the relationships between the coordinates of the points that represent Rozo's locations.  MP.7.1

11. **Reasoning** What will Rozo's location be after 7 minutes? Explain how you determined your answer. MP.2.1, 5.G.1.2

© Pearson Education, Inc. 5

Name _____

Point & Tally

Find a partner. Get paper and a pencil. Each partner chooses light blue or dark blue.

At the same time, Partner 1 and Partner 2 each point to one of their black numbers. Both partners find the product of the two numbers.

The partner who chose the color where the product appears gets a tally mark. Work until one partner has seven tally marks.

I can ...
multiply multi-digit whole numbers.

MAFS.5.NBT.2.5

Partner 1					Partner 2
85	24,024	94,435	11,616	90,100	264
79	101,101	8,712	20,856	11,682	198
91	30,345	18,018	22,440	83,740	357
44	15,576	87,769	21,063	28,203	1,060
59	15,642	62,540	32,487	96,460	1,111
	48,884	16,830	65,549	46,640	

Tally Marks for Partner 1

Tally Marks for Partner 2

A-Z
Glossary

Word List

- coordinate grid
- ordered pair
- origin
- *x*-axis
- *x*-coordinate
- *y*-axis
- *y*-coordinate

Understand Vocabulary

Choose the best term from the Word List. Write it on the blank.

1. The point where the axes of a coordinate grid intersect is the
   _____.

2. A(n) _____ names an exact location on a coordinate grid.

3. The first number of an ordered pair describes the distance from the origin along the _____.

4. The second number of an ordered pair is the
   _____.

5. A _____ is formed by two number lines that intersect at a right angle.

Draw a line from each lettered point in Column A to the ordered pair it represents.

	Column A	Column B
6.	A	(5, 2)
7.	B	(1, 7)
8.	C	(2, 3)
9.	D	(0, 7)
10.	E	(7, 1)
11.	F	(0, 6)

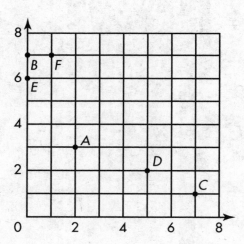

Use Vocabulary in Writing

12. Why is the order of the coordinates important in an ordered pair? Use terms from the Word List in your explanation.

© Pearson Education, Inc. 5

Reteaching

Set A pages 565–568

What ordered pair names Point *A*?

Start at the origin. The *x*-coordinate is the horizontal distance along the *x*-axis. The *y*-coordinate is the vertical distance along the *y*-axis.

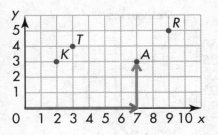

Point *A* is at (7, 3).

Remember to first find the *x*-coordinate. Then find the *y*-coordinate. Write the coordinates in (*x*, *y*) order.

Use the grid to answer the questions.

1. Which point is located at (9, 5)?

2. Which point is located at (2, 3)?

3. What ordered pair names Point *T*?

4. What is the ordered pair for the origin?

Set B pages 569–572, 573–576

In the table, the *x*-coordinate is in the left column and the *y*-coordinate is in the right column. Use the table to plot the ordered pairs. Then draw a line to connect the points.

x	y
1	1
2	4
3	7

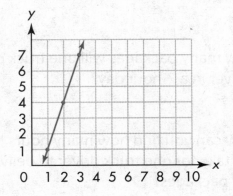

Remember that you can use a tool, such as a ruler, to draw a line to connect the points on the graph.

1. Use the table below to plot the ordered pairs. Then complete the graph by connecting the points.

x	y
2	1
4	2
6	3
8	4

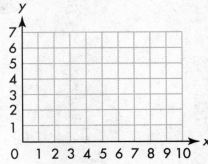

2. Write two ordered pairs with *x*-coordinates greater than 10 that are on the line.

Think about these questions to help you **use reasoning to solve problems**.

Thinking Habits

- What do the numbers and symbols in the problem mean?

- How are the numbers or quantities related?

- How can I represent a word problem using pictures, numbers, or equations?

Remember that you can use a graph or a table to reason about and solve word problems.

A company uses the graph to show how many packages each truck driver delivers. How many packages will one truck driver deliver in a 7-hour day?

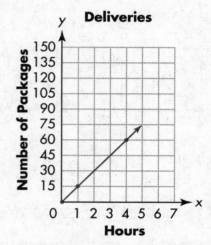

1. What information can help you solve the problem?

2. How can you find the number of packages a driver delivers in 3 hours?

3. How many packages will one truck driver deliver in a 7-hour day?

4. How can you find how many hours it will take for one truck driver to deliver 120 packages?

© Pearson Education, Inc. 5

Use the coordinate grid below to answer **1–4**.

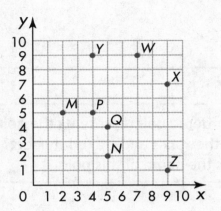

1. Which is the ordered pair for Point *Y*?

Ⓐ (4, 5)

Ⓑ (4, 9)

Ⓒ (7, 9)

Ⓓ (9, 4)

2. Which point is located at (5, 2) on the coordinate grid?

Ⓐ *M*

Ⓑ *N*

Ⓒ *Q*

Ⓓ *P*

3. What is the ordered pair for Point *Z*?

4. What is the ordered pair for Point *P*?

5. Each year, Ginny recorded the height of a tree growing in her front yard. The graph below shows her data.

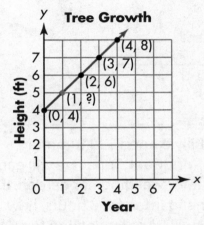

What does the point (1, ?) represent?

6. Explain how to graph the point (6, 4) on a coordinate plane.

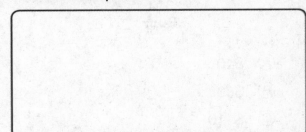

7. Varsha draws a map of her neighborhood on a coordinate plane. Her map shows the park at *P* (3, 1), her house at *H* (5, 6), and the soccer field at *S* (2, 4). Graph and label each location below.

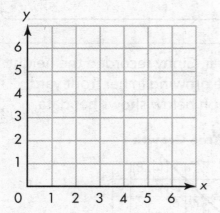

8. Yesterday Billy earned $30 trimming hedges for Mrs. Gant. Today he will earn $10 an hour for weeding her garden. If he weeds her garden for 8 hours, how much in all will he earn working for Mrs. Gant?

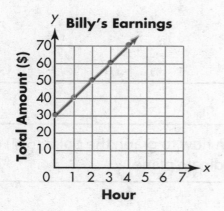

Ⓐ $40

Ⓑ $80

Ⓒ $110

Ⓓ $120

9. How is graphing (0, 12) different from graphing (12, 0)?

10. What ordered pair represents the point where the *x*-axis and *y*-axis intersect? What is the name of this point?

11. Three vertices of a rectangle are located at (1, 4), (1, 2), and (5, 2).

A. Graph and label each of the three vertices below.

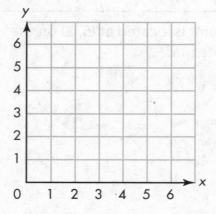

B. What are the coordinates of the fourth vertex of the rectangle?

© Pearson Education, Inc. 5

Digging for Dinosaur Bones

Omar's mother is a paleontologist. She digs up and studies dinosaur bones. Omar is helping at the dig site.

1. The **Dinosaur Bone Dig 1** grid shows the location of the tent and the triceratops skull Omar's mother found.

Part A 5.G.1.1

What ordered pair names the location of the triceratops skull? Explain how you know.

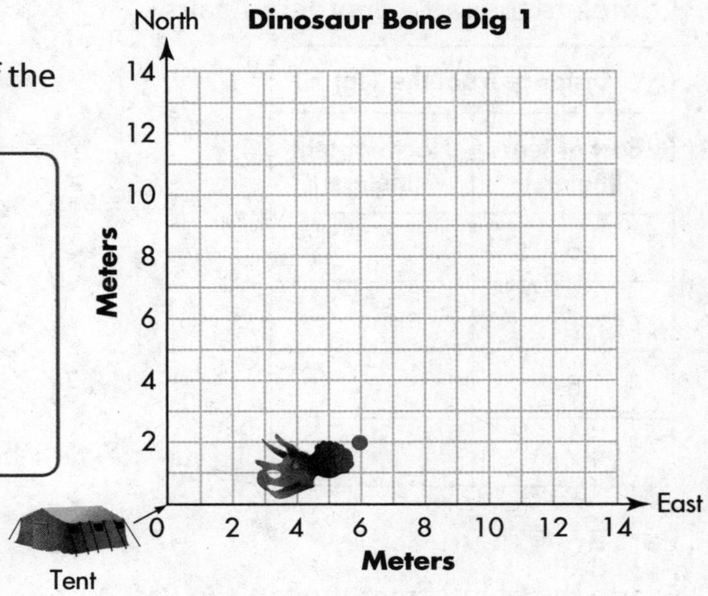

North   **Dinosaur Bone Dig 1**

Tent

Part B 5.G.1.2

Omar found a leg bone at (4, 12). Graph this point on the coordinate grid and label it *L*. Explain how you located the point using the terms origin, *x*-coordinate, *x*-axis, *y*-coordinate, and *y*-axis.

Part C 5.G.1.1

Next, Omar dug 3 meters east and 1 meter south from the leg bone. Graph a point where Omar dug and label it *A*. What ordered pair names the point?

2. Omar's mother started at the triceratops skull. She kept moving east 1 meter and north 2 meters to dig for more dinosaur bones. Complete the table and the graph to find how far north she was when she was 11 meters east of the tent.

Part A 5.G.1.1

Complete the table of ordered pairs.

Distance from the Tent	
East of tent (meters)	North of tent (meters)
6	
7	
8	
9	

Part B 5.G.1.2

Graph the points from the table in Part A on the coordinate grid in the **Dinosaur Bone Dig 2** grid. Draw a line through the points. Extend the line past 11 meters east.

Part C 5.G.1.1

How far north was Omar's mother when she was 11 meters east of the tent? Explain how to use the graph to solve and why your answer makes sense.

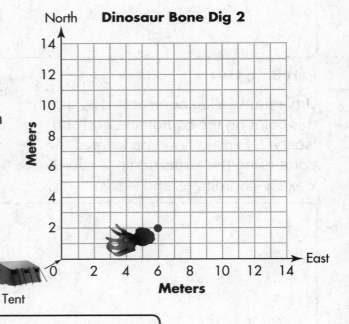

North **Dinosaur Bone Dig 2**

Tent

Algebra: Analyze Patterns and Relationships

Essential Questions: How can number patterns be analyzed and graphed? How can number patterns and graphs be used to solve problems?

Digital Resources

Interactive Student Edition Activity Visual Learning Video Practice

Assessment Games Tools Glossary

Buildings can be many different shapes and can have as many as 100 floors.

Many buildings have a pattern of glass and concrete for every floor.

Patterns occur in different places and things. Here is a project about finding patterns.

MAFS.5.OA.2.3, 5.G.1.2
MAFS.K12.MP.1.1, MP.2.1, MP.3.1, MP.5.1, MP.7.1, MP.8.1

enVision STEM Project: Analyze Patterns

Do Research Use the Internet or other sources to find patterns in cities and buildings in other parts of the world.

Journal: Write a Report Include what you found. Also in your report:

- Describe types of patterns found in nature.

- Describe types of patterns found in cities.

- Make a graph to show relationships between some of the patterns you found.

Review What You Know

Vocabulary

Choose the best term from the Word List.
Write it on the blank.

| • equation • expression • variable |
| • evaluate • ordered pair |

1. A numerical _____ is a mathematical phrase that has numbers and at least one operation.

2. A(n) _____ can be used to show the location of a point on the coordinate plane.

3. The letter n in $\$10 \times n$ is called a(n) _____ and is a quantity that can change.

Expressions

Write a numerical expression for each calculation.

4. Add 230 and 54, and then divide by 7.

5. Subtract 37 from the product of 126 and 4.

Solve Equations

Solve each equation.

6. $7,200 + x = 13,000$

7. $6,000 = 20 \times g$

8. $105 + 45 = w \times 3$

9. $38 + 42 = 480 \div b$

10. Janine has 85 hockey cards in one book and 105 hockey cards in another book. The hockey cards come in packages of 5 cards. If Janine bought all of her hockey cards in packages, how many packages did she buy?

Ⓐ 21 packages   Ⓑ 38 packages   Ⓒ 190 packages   Ⓓ 195 packages

Evaluate Expressions

11. Explain how to evaluate the expression $9 + (45 \times 2) \div 10$.

© Pearson Education, Inc. 5

Name _____

PROJECT 15A

How are piano keys arranged on a keyboard?

Project: Learn More About Keyboards

PROJECT 15B

Why is it important to protect gopher tortoises?

Project: Use Information to Write Problems

PROJECT 15C

How can you use patterns to make art?

Project: Create a Work of String Art

Math Modeling
Speed Stacks

Video

Before watching the video, think:

Stacking cups is a lot less messy when they're empty.

MAFS.K12.MP.4.1 Model with math. **Also MAFS.K12.MP.1.1, MAFS.K12.MP.2.1**
MAFS.5.OA.2.3 Generate two numerical patterns using two given rules. Identify apparent relationships between corresponding terms. Form ordered pairs consisting of corresponding terms from the two patterns, and graph the ordered pairs on a coordinate plane.... **Also MAFS.5.G.1.2**

Name _____

☆ ☆
Solve & Share

Emma has $100 in her savings account. Jorge has $50 in his savings account. They each put $10 in their accounts at the end of each week. Complete the tables to see how much each of them has saved after 5 weeks. What patterns do you notice?

I can ...

analyze numerical patterns.

MAFS.5.OA.2.3 Generate two numerical patterns using two given rules. Identify apparent relationships between corresponding terms. Form ordered pairs consisting of corresponding terms from the two patterns, and graph the ordered pairs on a coordinate plane....
MAFS.K12.MP.2.1, MP.3.1, MP.7.1

Week	Emma
Start	$100
1	
2	
3	
4	
5	

Week	Jorge
Start	$50
1	
2	
3	
4	
5	

Look for Relationships to see what is alike and what is different in the two tables.

Look Back! If the savings patterns continue, will Jorge ever have as much saved as Emma? Explain.

How Can You Solve Problems Involving Numerical Patterns?

A

Lindsey has a sage plant that is 3.5 inches tall. She also has a rosemary plant that is 5.2 inches tall. Both plants grow 1.5 inches taller each week. How tall will the plants be after 5 weeks? What is the relationship between the heights of the plants?

You can create tables to help identify relationships between corresponding terms in the number sequences.

B You can use the rule "add 1.5" to complete the tables.

Sage Plant	
Week	**Height (in inches)**
Start	3.5
1	5
2	6.5
3	8
4	9.5
5	11

Rosemary Plant	
Week	**Height (in inches)**
Start	5.2
1	6.7
2	8.2
3	9.7
4	11.2
5	12.7

The rosemary plant is always 1.7 inches taller than the sage plant!

Convince Me! Reasoning If the patterns continue, how can you tell that the rosemary plant will always be taller than the sage plant?

© Pearson Education, Inc. 5

Name _____

☆ Guided Practice *

Do You Understand?

1. Anthony says, "The pattern is that the sage plant is always 1.7 inches shorter than the rosemary plant." Do you agree? Explain.

2. How does making tables help you identify relationships between terms in patterns?

Do You Know How?

3. If the plants continue to grow 1.5 inches each week, how tall will each plant be after 10 weeks?

4. If the plants continue to grow 1.5 inches each week, how tall will each plant be after 15 weeks?

Independent Practice ☆

In **5–7**, use the rule "add $0.50" to help you.

5. Tim and Jill each have a piggy bank. Tim starts with $1.25 in his bank and puts in $0.50 each week. Jill starts with $2.75 in her bank and also puts in $0.50 each week. Complete the table to show how much money each has saved after five weeks.

Piggy Bank Savings		
Week	Tim	Jill
Start	$1.25	$2.75
1		
2		
3		
4		
5		

6. What relationship do you notice between the amount Tim has saved and the amount Jill has saved each week?

7. If Tim and Jill continue saving in this way, how much will each have saved after 10 weeks? Explain how you decided.

*For another example, see Set A on page 611.

Topic 15 | Lesson 15-1   **595**

Problem Solving

For **8–10**, use the table.

8. **enVision® STEM** Bur oak and hickory trees are *deciduous*, which means that they lose their leaves seasonally. A bur oak is $25\frac{1}{2}$ feet tall and grows $1\frac{1}{2}$ feet each year. A hickory is 30 feet tall and grows $1\frac{1}{2}$ feet each year. Complete the chart to show the heights of the two trees each year for five years.

Tree Heights (in feet)		
Year	Bur Oak	Hickory
Start	$25\frac{1}{2}$	30
1		
2		
3		
4		
5		

9. If each tree continues to grow $1\frac{1}{2}$ feet each year, how tall will each tree be after 15 years?

10. **Higher Order Thinking** What relationship do you notice between the height of the bur oak and the height of the hickory each year? Explain.

11. **Reasoning** Each small square on the chessboard is the same size. The length of a side of a small square is 2 inches. What is the area of the chessboard? Explain.

Assessment Practice

12. Jessica has saved $50. She will add $25 to her savings each week. Ron has saved $40 and will add $25 to his savings each week. How much will each person have saved after 5 weeks? 🔁 5.OA.2.3

   Ⓐ Jessica: $275; Ron: $225

   Ⓑ Jessica: $250; Ron: $240

   Ⓒ Jessica: $175; Ron: $165

   Ⓓ Jessica: $165; Ron: $175

13. Which of the following statements are true? 🔁 5.OA.2.3

   ☐ Jessica has always saved $25 more than Ron.

   ☐ Jessica has always saved $10 more than Ron.

   ☐ Ron has always saved $25 less than Jessica.

   ☐ Ron has always saved $10 less than Jessica.

© Pearson Education, Inc. 5

Name _____

Activity

Solve & Share

During summer vacation, Julie read 45 pages each day. Her brother Bret read 15 pages each day. Complete the tables to show how many pages each of them read after 5 days. What relationship do you notice between the terms in each pattern?

I can ...
use tables to identify relationships between patterns.

MAFS.5.OA.2.3 Generate two numerical patterns using two given rules. Identify apparent relationships between corresponding terms. Form ordered pairs consisting of corresponding terms from the two patterns, and graph the ordered pairs on a coordinate plane.... MAFS.K12.MP.2.1, MP.7.1, MP.8.1

Total Pages Read	
Day	Julie
1	45
2	
3	
4	
5	

Total Pages Read	
Day	Bret
1	15
2	
3	
4	
5	

Find a rule to help you complete each table.

Look Back! **Reasoning** Explain why this relationship exists between the terms.

Essential Question **How Can You Identify Relationships Between Patterns?**

A

Jack is training for a race. Each week, he runs 30 miles and bikes 120 miles. He created a table to record his progress. How many total miles will he run and bike after 5 weeks? Can you identify any relationship between the miles run and the miles biked?

You can use the rules "add 30" and "add 120" to help you complete the table.

B Since Jack runs 30 miles each week, add 30 to find the next term for the total miles run. Add 120 to find each term in the pattern for the total number of miles biked.

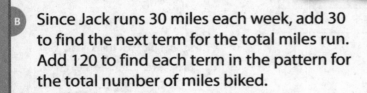

Week	Total Miles Run	Total Miles Biked
1	30	120
2	60	240
3	90	360
4	120	480
5	150	600

C Compare the corresponding terms in the patterns:

$$30 \times 4 = 120$$
$$60 \times 4 = 240$$
$$90 \times 4 = 360$$
$$120 \times 4 = 480$$
$$150 \times 4 = 600$$

So, the total number of miles biked is always 4 times the total number of miles run.

Convince Me! **Generalize** Do you think the relationship between the corresponding terms in the table Jack created will always be true? Explain.

© Pearson Education, Inc. 5

Name _____

☆ Guided Practice ☆

Do You Understand?

In **1–3**, use the table on page 598.

1. Neko says that the relationship between the terms is that the number of miles run is $\frac{1}{4}$ the number of miles biked. Do you agree? Explain.

Do You Know How?

2. How many total miles will Jack have run and biked after 10 weeks? 15 weeks?

3. Miguel says that he can use multiplication to find the terms in the patterns. Do you agree? Explain.

☆ Independent Practice ☆

In **4–6**, use the rules "add 250" and "add 125" to help you.

4. Maria and Henry are each starting a savings account. Maria puts $250 into her account each month. Henry puts $125 into his account each month. How much money will each of them have saved after 6 months? Complete the table to solve.

Total Amount Saved ($)		
Month	**Maria**	**Henry**
1		
2		
3		
4		
5		
6		

5. What relationship do you notice between the total amount Maria has saved after each month and the total amount Henry has saved after each month?

6. If Maria and Henry continue saving this way for a full year, how much more will Maria have saved than Henry?

Problem Solving

7. Sheila and Patrick are making a table to compare gallons, quarts, and pints. Use the rule "add 4" to complete the column for the number of quarts. Then use the rule "add 8" to complete the column for the number of pints.

Gallons	Quarts	Pints
1		
2		
3		
4		
5		
6		

8. Patrick has a 12-gallon fish tank at home. How many quarts of water will fill his fish tank? How many pints?

9. **Look for Relationships** What relationship do you notice between the number of quarts and the number of pints?

10. **Higher Order Thinking** At their family's pizzeria, Dan makes 8 pizzas in the first hour they are open and 6 pizzas each hour after that. Susan makes 12 pizzas in the first hour and 6 pizzas each hour after that. If the pizzeria is open for 6 hours, how many pizzas will they make in all? Complete the table using the rule "add 6" to help you.

Number of Pizzas Made		
Hour	Dan	Susan
1		
2		
3		
4		
5		
6		

11. **Look for Relationships** Compare the total number of pizzas made by each person after each hour. What relationship do you notice?

12. Mike and Sarah are packing boxes at a factory. Mike packs 30 boxes each hour. Sarah packs 15 boxes each hour.

    How many boxes will each person have packed after an 8-hour shift? 🔷 5.0A.2.3

    Ⓐ Mike: 38 boxes; Sarah: 23 boxes

    Ⓑ Mike: 86 boxes; Sarah: 71 boxes

    Ⓒ Mike: 120 boxes; Sarah: 240 boxes

    Ⓓ Mike: 240 boxes; Sarah: 120 boxes

13. Which of the following are true statements about the number of boxes Mike and Sarah have packed after each hour?

    🔷 5.0A.2.3

    ☐ Mike has always packed a total of 15 more boxes than Sarah.

    ☐ Mike has always packed twice as many boxes as Sarah.

    ☐ Sarah has always packed twice as many boxes as Mike.

    ☐ Sarah has always packed half as many boxes as Mike.

© Pearson Education, Inc. 5

Solve & Share

A bakery can fit either 6 regular muffins or 4 jumbo muffins in each box. Each box will contain either regular or jumbo muffins. Complete the table to show how many of each muffin will fit in 2, 3, or 4 boxes. Then generate ordered pairs and graph them.

	1 Box	2 Boxes	3 Boxes	4 Boxes
Regular Muffins	6	12	18	24
Jumbo Muffins	4	8	12	16

I can ...
analyze patterns and graph ordered pairs generated from number sequences.

MAFS.5.OA.2.3 Generate two numerical patterns using two given rules. Identify apparent relationships between corresponding terms. Form ordered pairs consisting of corresponding terms from the two patterns, and graph the ordered pairs on a coordinate plane.... **Also 5.G.1.2 MAFS.K12.MP.1.1, MP.7.1**

Find rules that describe the relationships between the number of boxes and the number of muffins.

Look Back! **Look for Relationships** The bakery can fit 12 mini-muffins in a box. How many mini-muffins will fit in 4 boxes? Without extending the table, what relationship do you notice between the number of mini-muffins and the number of boxes?

How Can You Generate and Graph Numerical Patterns?

A

Jill earns $5 per hour babysitting. Robin earns $15 per hour teaching ice skating lessons. The girls made a table using the rule "Add 5" to show Jill's earnings and the rule "Add 15" to show Robin's earnings. Complete the table, compare their earnings, and graph the ordered pairs of the corresponding terms.

You can look for a relationship between the corresponding terms in the patterns.

Hours	0	1	2	3	4
Jill's Earnings	$0	$5	$10	$15	20
Robin's Earnings	$0	$15	$30	$45	60

B Compare the numbers in Jill's and Robin's sequences.

Each sequence begins with zero. Then each term in Robin's pattern is 3 times as great as the corresponding term in Jill's pattern.

Generate ordered pairs from the total amount Jill and Robin have earned after each hour.

(0, 0), (5, 15), (10, 30), (15, 45), (20, 60)

C Graph the ordered pairs.

Jill's Earnings (x)	Robin's Earnings (y)
0	0
5	15
10	30
15	45
20	60

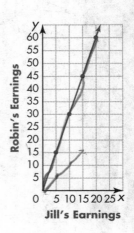

Convince Me! **Make Sense and Persevere** What does the point (0, 0) represent?

© Pearson Education, Inc. 5

Name _____

☆ Guided Practice ☆

Do You Understand?

1. In the example on page 602, what ordered pair would you write for how much Jill and Robin have each earned after 5 hours?

2. Ben says that the relationship is that Jill earns $\frac{1}{3}$ as much as Robin. Do you agree? Explain.

Do You Know How?

Sam and Eric record the total number of miles they walk in one week. Sam walks 2 miles each day. Eric walks 4 miles each day.

3. What ordered pair represents the number of miles each has walked in all after 7 days?

4. What relationship do you notice between the total number of miles Sam and Eric have each walked?

☆ Independent Practice ☆

In **5–8**, use the rule "add 4" to help you.

5. Megan and Scott go fishing while at camp. Megan catches 3 fish in the first hour and 4 fish each hour after that. Scott catches 5 fish in the first hour and 4 fish each hour after that. Complete the table to show the total number of fish each has caught after each hour.

Total Fish Caught		
Hours	Megan	Scott
1	3	5
2		
3		
4		

6. What ordered pair represents the total number of fish they each caught after 4 hours?

7. What relationship do you notice between the total number of fish each has caught after each hour?

8. Graph the ordered pairs of the total number of fish each has caught after each hour.

9. The pattern continues until Scott's total is 29 fish. What ordered pair represents the total number of fish they each caught when Scott's total is 29 fish?

Problem Solving

In **10–12**, use the rules "add 15" and "add 10" to help you.

10. The Snack Shack made a table to track the amount of money from sales of frozen yogurt and fruit cups for four hours. What are the missing values in the table?

	9 A.M.	10 A.M.	11 A.M.	12 P.M.
Money from Yogurt Sales	$0	$15	30	$45
Money from Fruit Cup Sales	$0	10	$20	$30

11. Use Structure If sales continue in the same manner, what ordered pair would represent the money from sales of yogurt and fruit cups at 1 P.M.? Explain how you know.

12. Graph the ordered pairs for the money from sales of yogurt and fruit cups from 9 A.M. to 1 P.M.

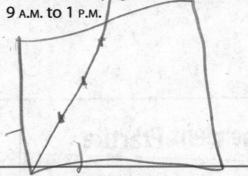

13. 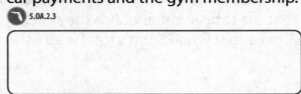 **Vocabulary** Write two **number sequences**. Then, circle **corresponding terms** in the two sequences.

14. Higher Order Thinking Pedro runs $2\frac{1}{2}$ miles each day for 5 days. Melissa runs 4 miles each day for 5 days. How many more miles will Melissa run in 5 days than Pedro? Make a table to help you.

Assessment Practice

15. Every month, Leonard pays $240 for a car payment. He spends $60 each month for a gym membership.

Write an ordered pair to represent how much Leonard spends in 12 months for car payments and the gym membership. 5.OA.2.3

16. What relationship do you notice between how much Leonard spends in 12 months on car payments and the gym membership? 5.OA.2.3

Name _____

☆ ☆
Solve & Share

Val is planning a bowling-and-pizza party. Including herself, there will be no more than 10 guests. Val wonders which bowling alley offers the less expensive party plan.

Complete the tables for Leonard's Lanes and Southside Bowl. On the same grid, graph the ordered pairs in each table. Use a different color for the values in each table. Which bowling alley would be less expensive? Explain how you know.

I can ...
make sense of problems and keep working if I get stuck.

MAFS.K12.MP.1.1 Make sense and persevere. **Also MP.2.1, MP.5.1**
MAFS.5.OA.2.3 Generate two numerical patterns using two given rules. Identify apparent relationships between corresponding terms. Form ordered pairs consisting of corresponding terms from the two patterns, and graph the ordered pairs on a coordinate plane....

Leonard's Lanes
Bowling and Pizza: $25 plus $10 per person

Guests	1	2	3	4	5	6	7	8	9	10
Cost ($)	35	45								

Southside Bowl
Bowling and Pizza: $15 per person

Guests	1	2	3	4	5	6	7	8	9	10
Cost ($)	15	30								

Thinking Habits
*Think about these questions to help you **make sense and persevere**.*

- What do I need to find?
- What do I know?
- What else can I try if I get stuck?
- How can I check that my solution makes sense?

Look Back! **Make Sense and Persevere** How did the graph help you answer the question?

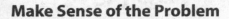

Essential Question

How Can You Make Sense of a Problem and Persevere in Solving It?

A

Make Sense of the Problem

On Aiden's farm, there are 12 acres of soybeans and 8 acres of corn. Aiden plans to replace his other crops with more acres of soybeans and corn. Will his farm ever have the same number of acres of soybeans and corn? Explain.

Plan for New Crops

Plant 3 more acres of soybeans every year.

Plant 4 more acres of corn every year.

You can make sense of the problem by answering these questions. What do you know? What are you asked to find?

Here's my thinking...

B **How can I make sense of and solve this problem?**

I can

- choose and implement an appropriate strategy.

- use ordered pairs to make graphs.

- identify and analyze patterns.

- check that my work and answer make sense.

C For each crop, I can write a rule, make a table, and plot the ordered pairs. Then I can see if the number of acres is ever the same.

Soybeans
Rule: Start at 12 and add 3.

Years	Start	1	2	3	4	5
Acres	12	15	18	21	24	27

Corn
Rule: Start at 8 and add 4.

Years	Start	1	2	3	4	5
Acres	8	12	16	20	24	28

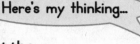

• Soybeans
• Corn

Where the lines intersect, at 4 years, Aiden's farm has 24 acres of each crop.

Convince Me! **Make Sense and Persevere** How can you check your work? Does your answer make sense? Explain.

© Pearson Education, Inc. 5

Name _____

☆ Guided Practice*

Mindy has already saved $20 and plans to save $8 each month. Georgette has no money saved yet but plans to save $5 each month. Will the girls ever have saved the same amount? Explain.

Month	Start	1	2	3		
$ Saved	20	28	36	44		

Month	Start	1	2	3	4
$ Saved					

1. Write a rule and complete each table.

   Rule: _____

   Rule: _____

2. On the same grid, graph the ordered pairs in each table.

3. Explain whether the girls will ever have the same amount of money saved.

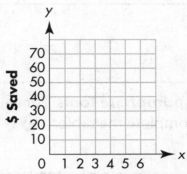

$ Saved / Number of Months

☆ Independent Practice ☆

Make Sense and Persevere

O'Brien's Landscaping pays employees $15 plus $12 per lawn. Carter's Landscaping pays $25 plus $10 per lawn. Which company pays more? Explain.

Lawns	Start					
Pay ($)	15					

Lawns	Start					
Pay ($)	25					

4. Write a rule and complete each table.

   Rule: _____

   Rule: _____

5. On the grid, graph the ordered pairs in each table. Explain which company pays more.

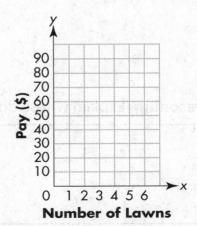

Pay ($) / Number of Lawns

*For another example, see Set D on page 612.

Problem Solving

Track-a-Thon

Jordan is running in a track-a-thon to raise money for charity. Who will make a larger donation, Aunt Meg or Grandma Diane? Explain.

Track-a-Thon Pledges	
Aunt Meg	$8 plus $2 per lap
Grandma Diane	$15 + $1 per lap

6. **Make Sense and Persevere** How can you use tables and a graph to solve the problem? 🌴 5.0A.2.3, MP.1.1

7. **Use Appropriate Tools** For each pledge, write a rule and complete the table. 🌴 5.0A.2.3, MP.5.1

Rule: _____

Laps	Start								
Donation ($)	8								

Rule: _____

Laps	Start								
Donation ($)	15								

8. **Use Appropriate Tools** On the grid, graph the ordered pairs in each table. 🌴 5.0A.2.3, MP.5.1

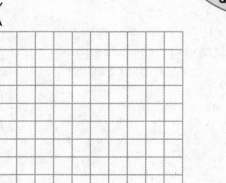

When you make sense and persevere, you choose and implement an appropriate strategy.

9. **Reasoning** Explain whose donation will be greater. 🌴 5.0A.2.3, MP.2.1

© Pearson Education, Inc. 5

Name _____

Solve each problem. Follow problems with an answer of 72,072 to shade a path from **START** to **FINISH**. You can only move up, down, right, or left.

I can ...
multiply multi-digit whole numbers.

 MAFS.5.NBT.2.5

Start				
5,544 × 13	819 × 88	1,144 × 63	1,716 × 42	792 × 91
2,012 × 36	4,059 × 18	2,007 × 36	6,562 × 11	1,287 × 56
728 × 99	1,092 × 66	3,432 × 21	2,772 × 26	936 × 77
2,574 × 28	4,504 × 16	1,002 × 71	6,311 × 12	4,039 × 18
1,386 × 52	924 × 78	1,638 × 44	1,848 × 39	1,001 × 72

Finish

A-Z
Glossary

Word List

- coordinate grid
- corresponding terms
- number sequence
- ordered pair
- origin
- *x*-axis
- *x*-coordinate
- *y*-axis
- *y*-coordinate

Understand Vocabulary

Write *always, sometimes,* or *never* on each blank.

1. Corresponding terms are _____ in the same position in a pair of number sequences.

2. An ordered pair can _____ be plotted on the origin of a coordinate grid.

3. The origin is _____ any other location on a coordinate grid besides (0, 0).

4. Two number lines that form a coordinate grid _____ intersect at a right angle.

5. The second number of an ordered pair _____ describes the distance to the right or left of the origin.

In **6–8**, use the lists of numbers below.

0 4 9 12 15	0 5 10 15 20	0 10 20 30 40
1 4 7 10 10	7 11 15 19 23	

	Example	**Non-example**
6. Number sequence	_____	_____
7. Another number sequence	_____	_____
8. Identify one pair of corresponding terms in your examples in Exercises 6 and 7.	_____	_____

Use Vocabulary in Writing

9. Explain how to identify corresponding terms in two number sequences. Use terms from the Word List in your explanation.

© Pearson Education, Inc. 5

Reteaching

Set A | pages 593–596

Maria has $4. She will save $10 each week. Stephen has $9 and will also save $10 each week.

Maria uses the rule "add 10" to create tables to see how much each will have saved after each week. What relationship do you notice between the **corresponding terms**?

Week	Maria
Start	$4
1	$14
2	$24
3	$34
4	$44

Week	Stephen
Start	$9
1	$19
2	$29
3	$39
4	$49

After each week, Stephen has $5 more saved than Maria. Or, Maria's savings are always $5 less than Stephen's savings.

Remember to compare corresponding terms to see if there is a relationship.

1. Two groups of students went hiking. After 1 hour, Group A hiked $1\frac{1}{2}$ miles and Group B hiked $2\frac{1}{2}$ miles. After that, each group hiked 2 miles each hour. Complete the tables to show how far each group had hiked after 3 hours.

Hour	Group A (mi)
1	$1\frac{1}{2}$
2	
3	

Hour	Group B (mi)
1	$2\frac{1}{2}$
2	
3	

2. What relationship do you notice between the corresponding terms?

Set B | pages 597–600

Each week, Andre lifts weights twice and runs 4 times. Andre uses the rules "add 2" and "add 4" to complete the table. What relationship do you notice between the corresponding terms?

Week	Lift Weights	Run
1	2	4
2	4	8
3	6	12
4	8	16

The number of times Andre went running is always 2 times the number of times he lifted weights.

Remember to use the rules to help you complete the tables.

1. A garden center sells 15 trees and 45 shrubs each day for one week. Complete the table to show how many trees and shrubs in all were sold in 4 days. Use the rules "add 15" and "add "45" to help you.

Days	Trees	Shrubs
1	15	45
2		
3		
4		

2. What is the relationship between the corresponding terms of the sequences?

Kelly uses 3 pounds of nuts and 2 pounds of cereal to make each batch of trail mix. The chart shows how many total pounds of each she will need for 4 batches. Graph ordered pairs of the corresponding terms. What does the point (12, 8) represent?

Batch	Nuts (lb)	Cereal (lb)
1	3	2
2	6	4
3	9	6
4	12	8

The chart and graph both represent the problem. The point (12, 8) shows that when Kelly uses 12 pounds of nuts, she will use 8 pounds of cereal.

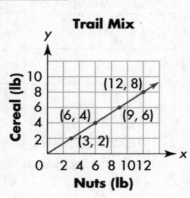

Trail Mix

Remember to make ordered pairs from corresponding terms.

1. Lauren has $6 and saves $5 each week. Derrick has $3 and saves $5 each week. How much will each have saved after 4 weeks? Use the rule "add 5" to complete the table.

Week	Lauren	Derrick
Start	$6	$3
1		
2		
3		
4		

2. What does the point (26, 23) represent?

3. What is the relationship between the corresponding terms?

Think about these questions to help you **make sense and persevere** in solving problems.

Thinking Habits

- What do I need to find?
- What do I know?
- What else can I try if I get stuck?
- How can I check that my solution makes sense?

Remember that you can use patterns, tables, and graphs to represent and solve problems.

1. Sam starts with 5 stamps and buys 10 more each month. Pat starts with 9 stamps and buys 9 more each month. Complete the table using the rules "add 10" and "add 9".

Month	Sam		Month	Pat
Start	5		Start	9
1			1	
2			2	
3			3	
4			4	

2. Make a graph from the data in the tables. Will Sam ever have more stamps than Pat?

© Pearson Education, Inc. 5

Name _____

1. Liz and Fareed each start a new savings account. Liz starts her account with $75. Fareed starts his account with $100. Each month, both save another $50.

A. Complete the table to show the total amount each has saved after each month. Use the rule "add 50".

Month	Liz	Fareed
Start	$75	$100
1		
2		
3		
4		

B. Select all the ordered pairs that represent amounts Liz and Fareed have each saved.

☐ (50, 75)

☐ (75, 100)

☐ (125, 150)

☐ (150, 200)

☐ (275, 300)

C. Describe the relationship between the amount each person has saved after each month.

2. There are 16 pawns and 2 kings in each chess set.

A. Complete the table to show how many pawns and kings in all are in different numbers of chess sets. Use the rules "add 16" and "add 2".

Sets	Pawns	Kings
1		
2		
3		
4		
5		

B. Use the total number of pawns and kings to form ordered pairs. Graph the ordered pairs below.

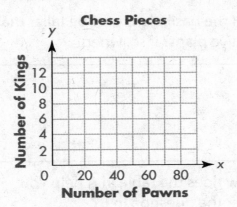

Chess Pieces

C. What would the ordered pair (96, 12) represent?

3. Luis kept track of the heights of his basil and chive plants. His basil plant was $15\frac{1}{2}$ cm tall and grew $1\frac{1}{2}$ cm each week. His chive plant was $18\frac{1}{2}$ cm tall and grew $\frac{1}{2}$ cm each week.

A. Complete the table to show the heights of each plant after each week. Use the rules "add $1\frac{1}{2}$" and "add $\frac{1}{2}$".

Plant Heights (cm)		
Week	Basil	Chive
Start	$15\frac{1}{2}$	$18\frac{1}{2}$
1		
2		
3		
4		

B. Will the basil plant ever be taller than the chive plant? If so, when?

C. How does the table in **A** help you answer the question in **B**?

4. Bonnie's Bakery makes 12 cakes and 36 muffins each hour.

A. Complete the table to show how many cakes and muffins in all the bakery has made after each hour. Use the rules "add 12" and "add 36".

Hour	Cakes	Muffins
1		
2		
3		
4		
5		

B. Miles says "the total number of muffins made is always 24 more than the total number of cakes made." Do you agree? Explain your reasoning.

C. Bonnie wants to graph this information. What ordered pair represents the total number of each item made after 6 hours?

Ⓐ (36, 12)

Ⓑ (18, 42)

Ⓒ (60, 180)

Ⓓ (72, 216)

© Pearson Education, Inc. 5

Butterfly Patterns

Use the **Butterflies** picture to explore patterns.

Butterflies

Butterflies have
4 wings and 6 legs.

1. Jessie and Jason use their cell phones to take pictures of butterflies. Jessie had 3 pictures of butterflies stored in her cell phone and Jason had 1 picture in his. On Saturday, they each took a picture of 1 butterfly every hour.

Part A

How many butterfly wings are in each photo collection after 3 hours? Complete the table. 5.OA.2.3

Part B

What is the relationship between the corresponding terms of the two patterns in Part A?  5.OA.2.3

Butterfly Wings		
Hour	Jessie's Pictures	Jason's Pictures
0		
1		
2		
3		

Part C

Write rules for the number of butterfly wings in Jessie's pictures and in Jason's pictures.  5.OA.2.3

2. Compare the number of wings to the number of legs in different numbers of butterflies.

Part A

Complete the table. 5.OA.2.3

Number of Butterflies	Wings	Legs
0	0	0
1		
2		
3		

Part B

What is the relationship between the number of wings and the number of legs you found in Part A? 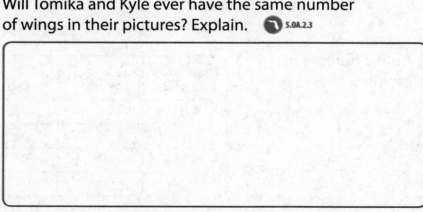 5.OA.2.3

3. Tomika has no pictures of butterflies in her cell phone, but Kyle has 3 pictures in his. On Saturday, Tomika takes 2 pictures of butterflies every hour and Kyle takes 1 picture every hour. Answer the following to find whether or not their collections of butterfly pictures will ever have the same number of wings.

Tomika's Pictures	
Hours	Wings
0	
1	
2	
3	

Part A

Write a rule and complete the **Tomika's Pictures** table. 5.OA.2.3

Part B

Write a rule and complete the **Kyle's Pictures** table. 5.OA.2.3

Kyle's Pictures	
Hours	Wings
0	
1	
2	
3	

Part C

Graph the ordered pairs from Part A and Part B on the same coordinate grid and draw lines through each set. 5.OA.2.3

Part D

Will Tomika and Kyle ever have the same number of wings in their pictures? Explain. 5.OA.2.3

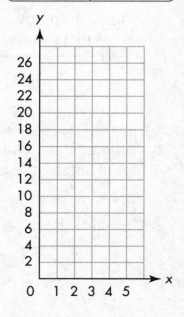

© Pearson Education, Inc. 5

Geometric Measurement: Classify Two-Dimensional Figures

Essential Question: How can triangles and quadrilaterals be described, classified, and named?

Digital Resources

Interactive Student Edition   Activity   Visual Learning   Video   Practice

Assessment   Games   Tools   Glossary

Prickly pears, coyotes, scorpions, sand, and rocks are all part of the desert ecosystem of the Guadalupe Mountains.

An *ecosystem* is an interaction of all living organisms in a particular environment.

MAFS.5.G.2.3, 5.G.2.4
MAFS.K12.MP.1.1, MP.2.1, MP.3.1, MP.6.1, MP.8.1

Hey, did you ever think of school as a kind of ecosystem? Here's a project about ecosystems.

enVision STEM Project: Ecosystems

Do Research Use the Internet or other sources to learn more about ecosystems. Look for examples of changes that living organisms might cause. List three different ecosystems and describe any changes that humans might have made to each one.

Journal: Write a Report Include what you found. Also in your report:

- Compare two ecosystems. List 10 living things and 5 non-living things you might find in each one.

- Think about changes that can occur in an ecosystem. Are the changes positive or negative? Why?

- Use two-dimensional shapes to make a map or diagram of an ecosystem.

Review What You Know

Vocabulary

Choose the best term from the box.
Write it on the blank.

> • degree
> • line segment
> • parallel
> • perimeter
> • polygon
> • quadrilateral
> • vertex

1. A _____ is a polygon with four sides.

2. The point where two sides of a polygon intersect is a _____.

3. The distance between _____ sides of a polygon is always the same.

4. The _____ is a unit of measure for angles.

Decimals

Find each answer.

5. $2.75 + 9.08$

6. $17.6 - 3.08$

7. 83.2×0.1

8. 24.27×10^3

Fractions

Find each answer.

9. $3\frac{2}{3} + 6\frac{9}{10}$

10. $8\frac{1}{2} - 4\frac{4}{5}$

11. $8 \div \frac{1}{2}$

12. $\frac{1}{3} \div 6$

Write an Equation

13. Louisa drew a polygon with six sides of equal length. If the perimeter of Louisa's polygon is 95.4 centimeters, how long is each side? Use an equation to solve.

14. The area of a rectangle is 112 square inches. If the length of the rectangle is 16 inches, what is the width of the rectangle? Use an equation to solve.

© Pearson Education, Inc. 5

Name _____

PROJECT 16A

Where can you find a pyramid?

Project: Build a Pyramid

PROJECT 16B

How do blueprints use different shapes?

Project: Draw a Blueprint

PROJECT 16C

What shapes make up a map?

Project: Hunt for Shapes in a Map

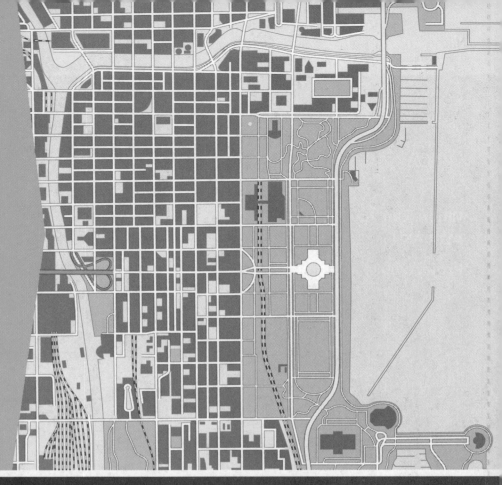

PROJECT 16D

What does the Florida flag look like?

Project: Design a Flag

© Pearson Education, Inc. 5

Name _____

Solve & Share

One triangle is shown below. Draw five more triangles with different properties. Next to each triangle, list its properties such as 2 equal sides, 1 right angle, 3 acute angles, and so on. *Work with a partner to solve this problem.*

I can …
classify triangles by their angles and sides.

MAFS.5.G.2.3 Understand that attributes belonging to a category of two-dimensional figures also belong to all subcategories of that category….
MAFS.K12.MP.1.1, MP.2.1, MP.3.1

In a triangle, angles will be either acute, right, or obtuse.

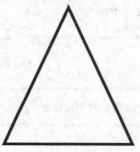

Look Back! **Reasoning** What are some different ways you can put triangles into categories? Explain.

Essential Question **How Can You Classify Triangles?**

A

Triangles can be classified by the lengths of their sides.

Equilateral triangle
All sides are the
same length.

Isosceles triangle
At least two sides are
the same length.

Scalene triangle
No sides are the
same length.

Can you tell if the sides
of a triangle are the same length
without measuring them?

The total measure of all
the angles in a triangle is 180°.

B

Triangles can also be classified by the measures of their angles.

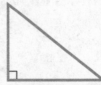

Right triangle
One angle is a right angle.

Acute triangle
All three angles are
acute angles.

Obtuse triangle
One angle is an
obtuse angle.

Convince Me! **Construct Arguments**
Can you draw an equilateral right triangle?
Explain using precise mathematical language.

To justify a
mathematical argument,
you must use precise
mathematical language
and ideas to explain
your thinking.

© Pearson Education, Inc. 5

Name _____

☆ Guided Practice *

Do You Understand?

1. Can a right triangle have an obtuse angle? Why or why not?

2. Can an equilateral triangle have only two sides of equal length? Why or why not?

Do You Know How?

In **3** and **4**, classify each triangle by its sides and then by its angles.

3.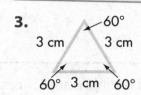
3 cm 3 cm 60° 60° 3 cm 60°

4.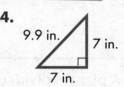
9.9 in. 7 in. 7 in.

☆ Independent Practice ☆

In **5–10**, classify each triangle by its sides and then by its angles.

5.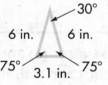
30° 6 in. 6 in. 75° 3.1 in. 75°

6.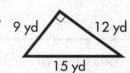
9 yd 12 yd 15 yd

> Think about what you need to compare to classify the triangle correctly.

7.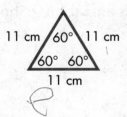
11 cm 60° 11 cm 60° 60° 11 cm

8.
15.1 m 9.2 m 110° 9.2 m

9.
6 m 10 m 8 m

10.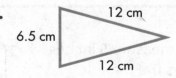
12 cm 6.5 cm 12 cm

*For another example, see Set A on page 639.   **Topic 16** | Lesson 16-1   **623**

Problem Solving

11. The Louvre Pyramid serves as an entrance to the Louvre Museum in Paris. The base of the pyramid is 35 meters long and the sides are 32 meters long. Classify the triangle on the front of the Louvre Pyramid by the lengths of its sides and the measures of its angles.

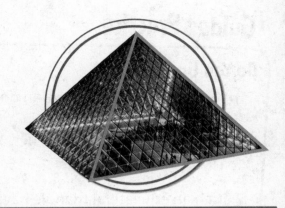

12. A pizza is divided into twelve equal slices. Glenn and Ben each ate $\frac{1}{6}$ of the pizza on Monday. The next day Ben ate $\frac{1}{2}$ of the pizza that was left over. How many slices of the original pizza remain? Explain your reasoning.

13. During a sale at the bookstore, books sold for $3 and magazines sold for $2.50. Jan spent $16 and bought a total of 6 books and magazines. How many of each did she buy?

14. **Higher Order Thinking** The measures of two angles of a triangle are 23° and 67°. Is the triangle acute, right, or obtuse? Use geometric terms in your explanation.

15. **Make Sense and Persevere** An animal shelter houses dogs, cats, and rabbits. There are 126 animals at the shelter. Of the animals, $\frac{1}{3}$ are cats. Three fourths of the remaining animals are dogs. How many of the animals are rabbits? Show your work.

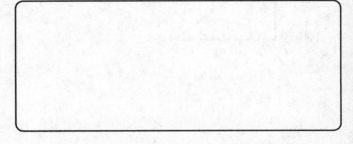

Assessment Practice

16. Two sides of a triangle measure 5 inches and 6 inches. Jason says the triangle must be scalene. Is Jason correct? Explain. 🔶 5.6.2.3

© Pearson Education, Inc. 5

Name _____

Solve & Share

Draw any length line segment that will fit in the space below. The line segment can go in any direction, but it must be straight. Draw another line segment of any length that is parallel to the first one. Connect the ends of each line segment with line segments to make a closed four-sided figure. What does your shape look like? Can you classify it? *Discuss your ideas with a partner.*

I can ...
classify quadrilaterals by their properties.

MAFS.5.G.2.4 Classify and organize two-dimensional figures into Venn diagrams based on the attributes of the figures. **Also 5.G.2.3** MAFS.K12.MP.2.1, MP.6.1, MP.8.1

You can use reasoning to find the differences and similarities between shapes when classifying quadrilaterals. *Show your work!*

Look Back! **Reasoning** How can you draw a quadrilateral different from the one above? Describe what you can change and why it changes the quadrilateral.

What Are Some Properties of Quadrilaterals?

Essential Question

A

Categories of quadrilaterals are classified by their properties.

Think about the questions below when you are classifying quadrilaterals.

- How many pairs of opposite sides are parallel?

- Which sides have equal lengths?

- How many right angles are there?

B

A trapezoid has one pair of parallel sides.

A parallelogram has two pairs of opposite sides parallel and equal in length.

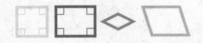

C

A rectangle has four right angles.

A rhombus has all sides the same length.

D

A square has all sides the same length.

A square has four right angles.

Convince Me! Generalize How is a parallelogram different from a rhombus? How are they similar?

© Pearson Education, Inc. 5

Name _____

☆ Guided Practice*

Do You Understand?

1. **Vocabulary** How are a square and a rhombus alike?

2. **A-Z** **Vocabulary** How is a trapezoid different from a parallelogram?

Use the questions at the top of page 626 to help you classify the quadrilaterals.

Do You Know How?

In **3–6**, use as many names as possible to identify each polygon. Tell which name is most specific.

3.

4.

5.

6.

☆ Independent Practice ☆

7. Identify the polygon using as many names as possible.

8. Identify the polygon using as many names as possible.

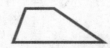

9. Why is a square also a rectangle?

10. Which special quadrilateral is both a rectangle and a rhombus? Explain how you know.

*For another example, see Set B on page 639.

Topic 16 | Lesson 16-2

627

Problem Solving

11. Each time Sophie makes a cut to a polygon, she can make a new type of polygon. What kind of polygon is left if Sophie cuts off the top of the isosceles triangle shown?

---

12. **Number Sense** Donald's car gets about 30 miles per gallon. About how many miles can Donald drive on 9.2 gallons of gas? At $3.15 a gallon, about how much would that amount of gas cost?

13. Is it possible to draw a quadrilateral that is not a rectangle but has at least one right angle? Explain.

---

14. The area of a quadrilateral is 8.4 square feet. Find two decimals that give a product close to 8.4.

15. **Be Precise** Suppose you cut a square into two identical triangles. What type of triangles will you make?

---

16. **Higher Order Thinking** A parallelogram has four sides that are the same length. Is it a square? Explain how you know.

What do you know about the sides of a parallelogram?

17. Which quadrilateral could have side lengths 1 m, 5 m, 1 m, 5 m? 5.G.2.4

   (A) square

   (B) rectangle

   (C) trapezoid

   (D) rhombus

18. Which of the following statements is **NOT** true? 5.G.2.4

   (A) A rectangle is also a parallelogram.

   (B) A trapezoid is also a quadrilateral.

   (C) A rhombus is also a rectangle.

   (D) A square is also a rectangle.

© Pearson Education, Inc. 5

Activity

Lesson 16-3
Continue to Classify Quadrilaterals

Solve & Share

Look at the quadrilaterals below. In the table, write the letters for all the figures that are trapezoids. Then do the same with each of the other quadrilaterals. *Work with a partner to solve this problem.*

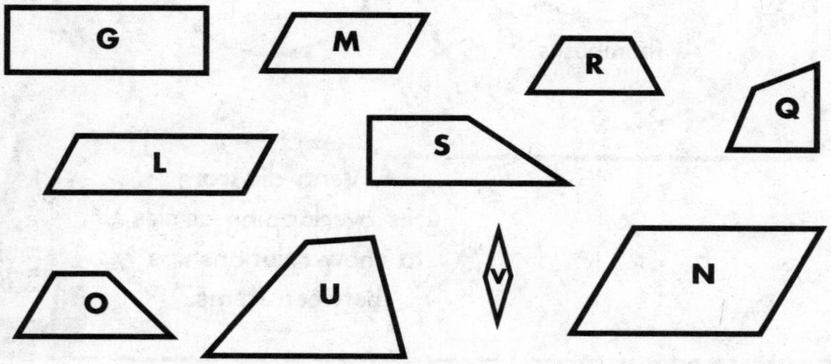

I can ...
classify quadrilaterals using a hierarchy.

MAFS.5.G.2.4 Classify and organize two-dimensional figures into Venn diagrams based on the attributes of the figures. Also 5.G.2.3 MAFS.K12.MP.3.1

G   M   R   Q

L   S

O   U   V   N

List the letter of each figure in each group.

Trapezoids	
Parallelograms	
Rectangles	
Squares	
Rhombuses	

You can classify quadrilaterals that have more than one property. *Show your work!*

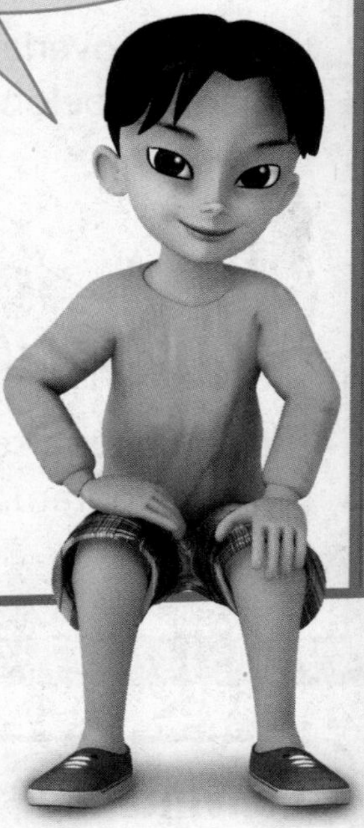

Look Back! **Construct Arguments** Which quadrilateral had the most figures listed? Explain why this group had the most.

Essential Question

How Are Special Quadrilaterals Related to Each Other?

A

This Venn diagram shows how special quadrilaterals are related to each other.

How can you use the Venn diagram to describe other ways to classify a square? What does the diagram show about how a trapezoid relates to other special quadrilaterals?

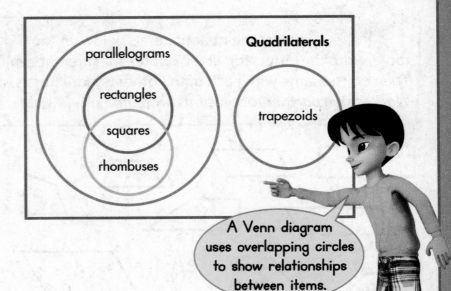

A Venn diagram uses overlapping circles to show relationships between items.

B Each circle in the Venn diagram shows a category of quadrilateral.

Items in overlapping sections of the Venn diagram belong to more than one group.

"Square" is in more than one circle in the Venn diagram.

A square is also a rectangle, rhombus, parallelogram, and quadrilateral.

C In the diagram, the circle for trapezoids does not intersect with any other circles. This shows that a trapezoid is also a quadrilateral, but never a parallelogram, rectangle, rhombus, or square.

Convince Me! **Construct Arguments** When can a rectangle be a rhombus? Can a rhombus be a rectangle? Explain using examples.

© Pearson Education, Inc. 5

Name _____

 # ☆Guided Practice☆

Do You Understand?

1. Explain how the Venn diagram on page 630 shows that every rectangle is a parallelogram.

2. How are a rectangle and a rhombus alike?

Do You Know How?

In **3–6**, tell whether each statement is true or false. If false, explain.

3. All rectangles are squares.

4. Every rhombus is a parallelogram.

5. Parallelograms are special rectangles.

6. A trapezoid can be a square.

 # Independent Practice ☆

In **7–10**, write whether each statement is true or false. If false, explain why.

7. All rhombuses are rectangles.

8. Every trapezoid is a quadrilateral.

9. Rhombuses are special parallelograms.

10. All rectangles are quadrilaterals.

11. What properties does the shape have? Why is it not a parallelogram?

12. Why is a square also a rhombus?

Problem Solving

13. Construct Arguments Draw a quadrilateral with one pair of parallel sides and two right angles. Explain why this figure is a trapezoid.

14. A reflecting pool is shaped like a rhombus with a side length of 6 meters. What is the perimeter of the pool? Explain how you found your answer.

Think about the properties of a rhombus to help you solve.

15. A bakery sold 31 bagels in the first hour of business and 42 bagels in the second hour. If the bakery had 246 bagels to start with, how many bagels were left after the second hour?

246 bagels		
31	42	?

16. Higher Order Thinking Ann says the figure below is a square. Pablo says that it is a parallelogram. Felix says that it is a rectangle. Can they all be right? Explain.

Assessment Practice

17. Below is the Venn diagram of quadrilaterals.

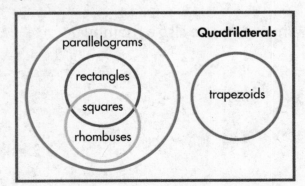

Part A

Are rhombuses also rectangles? Explain.

🏴 5.G.2.4

Part B

What are all of the names that describe a rhombus? 🏴 5.G.2.4

© Pearson Education, Inc. 5

Name _____

☆ **Solve & Share**

Alfie thinks that if he cuts a parallelogram along a diagonal, he will get two triangles that have the same shape and size. Is he correct? *Solve this problem any way you choose.* Construct a math argument to justify your answer.

● Activity

I can ...
construct arguments about geometric figures.

MAFS.K12.MP.3.1 Construct arguments. **Also MP.1.1, MP.2.1**
MAFS.5.G.2.3 Understand that attributes belonging to a category of two-dimensional figures also belong to all subcategories of that category.... **Also, 5.G.2.4**

Thinking Habits
Be a good thinker!
These questions can help you.

• How can I use numbers, objects, drawings, or actions to justify my argument?

• Am I using numbers and symbols correctly?

• Is my explanation clear and complete?

• Can I use a counterexample in my argument?

Look Back! **Construct Arguments** Suppose you cut along a diagonal of a rhombus, a rectangle, or a square. Would you get two triangles that have the same shape and size? Construct an argument to justify your answer.

A

Anika says, "If I draw a diagonal in a parallelogram, I will always form two right triangles." Is she correct? Construct a math argument to justify your answer.

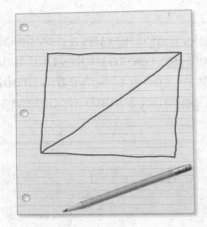

You can construct an argument using what you know about triangles and quadrilaterals.

What do I need to do to solve the problem?

I need to examine several cases, including special parallelograms. Then I need to state my conclusion and write a good argument to justify it.

Here's my thinking...

B

How can I construct an argument?

I can

- use math to explain my reasoning.
- use the correct words and symbols.
- give a complete explanation.
- use a counterexample in my argument.

C

Anika is incorrect. The triangles are right triangles only when the parallelogram is a rectangle or square.

Rectangles and squares have four right angles. So, each triangle formed by drawing a diagonal will have a right angle and be a right triangle. But if the parallelogram does not have right angles, each triangle will not have a right angle.

Convince Me! **Construct Arguments** How can counterexamples be helpful in constructing an argument?

Name _____

☆ Guided Practice*

Jamal says, "Two equilateral triangles that are the same size can be joined to make a rhombus."

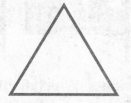

1. What is the definition of an equilateral triangle? What is the definition of a rhombus?

2. How could knowing these definitions help in constructing your argument?

3. Is Jamal correct? Construct an argument to justify your answer.

Independent Practice ☆

Construct Arguments

Lauren says, "If I draw a diagonal in a trapezoid, neither of the triangles formed will have a right angle."

4. What is the definition of a trapezoid?

5. Draw examples of a diagonal in a trapezoid.

6. How can you use a drawing to construct an argument?

7. Is Lauren correct? Construct a math argument to justify your answer.

Stuck? Answering this question might help. *Have I interpreted all word meanings correctly?*

A diagram can help you construct arguments.

For another example, see Set D on page 640.   **Topic 16** | Lesson 16-4   **635**

Problem Solving

Flag Making

Mr. Herrera's class is studying quadrilaterals. The class worked in groups, and each group made a "quadrilateral flag."

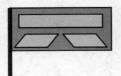 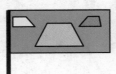 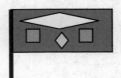 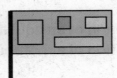

8. **Construct Arguments** Which flags show parallelograms? Construct a math argument to justify your answer. 🐢 5.G.2.3, MP.3.1

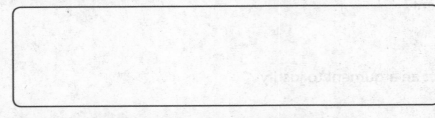

> The definitions of the different quadrilaterals will help you construct arguments.

9. **Reasoning** Explain how you would classify the quadrilaterals on the green flag and the blue flag. 🐢 5.G.2.3, MP.2.1

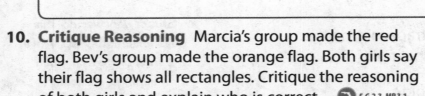

10. **Critique Reasoning** Marcia's group made the red flag. Bev's group made the orange flag. Both girls say their flag shows all rectangles. Critique the reasoning of both girls and explain who is correct. 🐢 5.G.2.3, MP.3.1

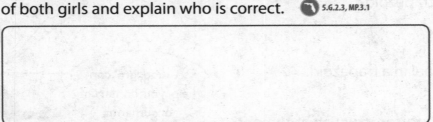

11. **Make Sense and Persevere** Does it make sense for this quadrilateral to be on any of the flags? 🐢 5.G.2.3, MP.1.1

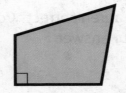

© Pearson Education, Inc. 5

Find a partner. Get paper and a pencil. Each partner chooses light blue or dark blue.

At the same time, Partner 1 and Partner 2 each point to one of their black numbers. Both partners find the product of the two numbers.

The partner who chose the color where the product appears gets a tally mark. Work until one partner has seven tally marks.

I can ...
multiply multi-digit whole numbers.

MAFS.5.NBT.2.5

Partner 1					Partner 2
29	12,264	77,532	204,204	70,499	**17**
76	612,339	64,752	195,141	14,600	**146**
84	4,234	672,900	13,286	11,096	**852**
91	85,200	1,292	71,568	243,100	**2,431**
100	184,756	565,236	493	221,221	**6,729**
	1,547	24,708	511,404	1,428	

Tally Marks for Partner 1

Tally Marks for Partner 2

Word List

- acute triangle
- equilateral triangle
- isosceles triangle
- obtuse triangle
- parallelogram
- rectangle
- rhombus
- right triangle
- scalene triangle
- square
- trapezoid

Understand Vocabulary

Choose the best term from the Word List. Write it on the blank.

1. A 3-sided polygon with at least two sides the same length is a(n) _____.

2. A polygon with one pair of parallel sides is a(n) _____.

3. A(n) _____ has four right angles and all four sides the same length.

4. All three sides of a(n) _____ are different lengths.

5. The measure of each of the three angles in a(n) _____ is less than 90°.

6. A rectangle is a special type of _____.

For each of these terms, draw an example and a non-example.

	Example	**Non-example**
7. Obtuse triangle	_____	_____
8. Rhombus with no right angle	_____	_____
9. Isosceles right triangle	_____	_____

Use Vocabulary in Writing

10. Alana claims that not all 4-sided polygons with 2 pairs of equal sides are parallelograms. Is Alana correct? Use terms from the Word List in your answer.

© Pearson Education, Inc. 5

Set A pages 621–624

Classify the triangle by the measures of its angles and the lengths of its sides.

Since one of the angles is right, this is a right triangle. Since two of the sides are the same length, this is an isosceles triangle.

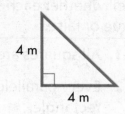

4 m

4 m

It is a right, isosceles triangle.

Remember that right, obtuse, and acute describe the angles of a triangle. Equilateral, scalene, and isosceles describe the sides of a triangle.

Reteaching

Classify each triangle by the measures of its angles and the lengths of its sides.

1.
60°
60° 60°

2.
5 in.
3 in.
4 in.

3.
8 cm 105° 8 cm

4.
16.4 cm
70°
10 cm 75° 16 cm

Set B pages 625–628

Quadrilaterals are classified by their properties.

A **trapezoid** has one pair of parallel sides.

A **parallelogram** has two pairs of equal parallel sides.

A **rectangle** is a parallelogram with 4 right angles.

A **rhombus** is a parallelogram with 4 equal sides.

A **square** is a parallelogram with 4 right angles and 4 equal sides.

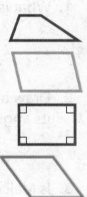

Remember that some quadrilaterals can be identified by more than one name.

Identify each quadrilateral. Describe each quadrilateral by as many names as possible.

1.

2.

3.

4.

This Venn diagram shows how special quadrilaterals are related to each other.

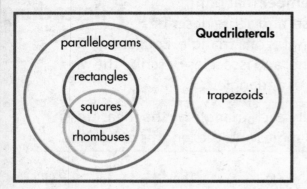

Remember that each circle of the Venn diagram shows a subgroup of quadrilaterals.

Tell whether each statement is true or false.

1. All squares are rectangles.

2. Every parallelogram is a rectangle.

3. Rhombuses are special parallelograms.

4. All trapezoids are quadrilaterals.

Think about these questions to help you **construct arguments**.

Thinking Habits

• How can I use numbers, objects, drawings, or actions to justify my argument?

• Am I using numbers and symbols correctly?

• Is my explanation clear and complete?

• Can I use a counterexample in my argument?

Remember that using definitions of geometric figures can help you construct arguments.

Malcolm says, "The sum of the angle measures in any rectangle is 180°."

1. What is the definition of a rectangle?

2. Draw a picture of a rectangle and label its angles.

3. Is Malcolm correct? Construct a math argument to justify your answer.

© Pearson Education, Inc. 5

1. Which of the following correctly describes the triangles? Select all that apply.

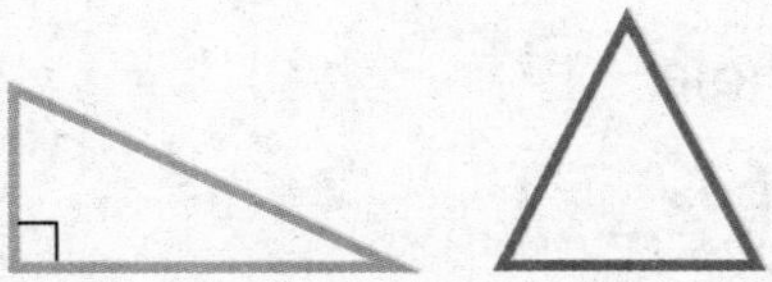

☐ Both triangles have a right angle.

☐ Only one triangle is a right triangle.

☐ Only one triangle has an acute angle.

☐ Both triangles have an obtuse angle.

☐ Both triangles have at least two acute angles.

2. Which statement is true?

Ⓐ Trapezoids are parallelograms.

Ⓑ A square is always a rectangle.

Ⓒ A rectangle is always a square.

Ⓓ A rhombus is a trapezoid.

3. Select all the shapes that are parallelograms.

☐

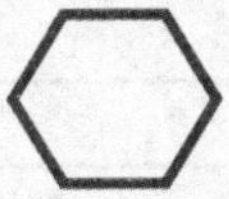

☐

☐

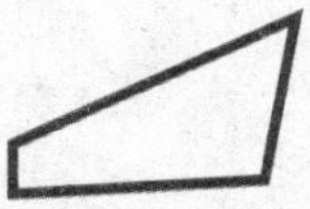

☐

☐

4. The necklace charm shown has one pair of parallel sides. What type of quadrilateral is the charm? Explain.

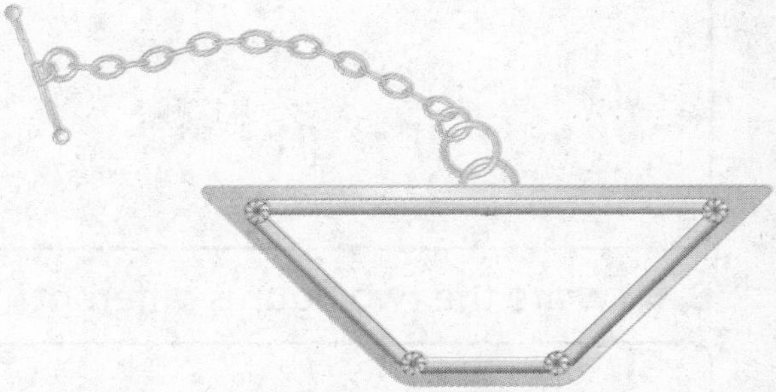

5. Identify the figure below using as many names as possible.

6. Claim 1: A square is a rectangle because it has 4 right angles.
Claim 2: A square is a rhombus because it has 4 equal sides.
Which claim is correct? Explain.

7. Look at the rhombus and square below.

A. How are the two figures the same?

B. How are the two figures different?

8. Identify the figure below using as many names as possible.

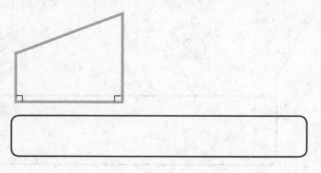

9. Identify the figure below using as many names as possible.

10. What shape has two pairs of opposite sides that are parallel and has all sides of equal length but does **NOT** have four right angles?

Ⓐ Square

Ⓑ Rectangle

Ⓒ Rhombus

Ⓓ Trapezoid

11. Use the Venn diagram. Are rhombuses always, sometimes, or never also parallelograms? Explain.

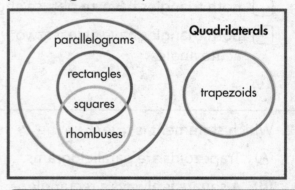

12. Describe triangle *HJK* in terms of its sides and angles.

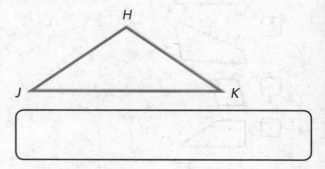

© Pearson Education, Inc. 5

Geometry in Art

Artists often use triangles and quadrilaterals in their pictures.

1. Use the **Poster** to answer the following questions.

Part A

Classify Triangle 1 in the **Poster** by its angles and by its sides. 🌀 5.G.2.3

Part B

What are all of the names you can use to describe Shape 2 in the **Poster**? 🌀 5.G.2.3

Part C

Triangles 3 and 4 are identical. They are joined in the **Poster** to form a square. Construct a math argument to show why Triangles 3 and 4 are isosceles right triangles. 🌀 5.G.2.3

Part D

If Triangle 3 is joined with another triangle that is the same size and shape, do the two triangles always form a square? Construct a math argument to explain your reasoning. 🌀 5.G.2.3

Part E

What are the measures of the angles of Triangle 3? Note that two angles in an isosceles triangle always have the same measure. Explain. 🏫 5.G.2.3

2. Classify the triangles and quadrilaterals in the **Houses** drawing to answer the following questions.

Part A

Are all the triangles shown in the design isosceles? Are they all equilateral? Construct a math argument, using properties, to explain why or why not. 🏫 5.G.2.3

Part B

All of the quadrilaterals in the **Houses** drawing are rectangles. Does that mean all of the quadrilaterals are parallelograms? Does that mean all are squares? Construct a math argument, using properties, to explain your reasoning. 🏫 5.G.2.3

© Pearson Education, Inc. 5

enVision® Florida
MATHEMATICS

Photographs

Every effort has been made to secure permission and provide appropriate credit for photographic material. The publisher deeply regrets any omission and pledges to correct errors called to its attention in subsequent editions.

Unless otherwise acknowledged, all photographs are the property of Pearson Education, Inc.

Photo locators denoted as follows: Top (T), Center (C), Bottom (B), Left (L), Right (R), Background (Bkgd)

1 James Laurie/Shutterstock; 3 (T) Wayne Johnson/Shutterstock, (C) Foto-bee/Alamy Stock Photo, (B) Macrovector/Shutterstock; 4 (T) Underworld/Shutterstock; (B) Danny E Hooks/Shutterstock, 6 Risteski goce/Shutterstock; 12 John Foxx/Getty Images; 18 Vladislav Gajic/Fotolia; 22 (L) James Steidl/Fotolia, (C) Hemera Technologies/Getty Images; (R) Ivelin Radkov/Fotolia. 41 Inacio pires/Shutterstock; 43 (T) Rudy Umans/Shutterstock; 43 (B) Findlay/Alamy Stock Photo; 44 (T) Elenadesign/Shutterstock; (B) Georgejmclittle/123RF; 62 (L) Getty Images; (R) Fuse/Getty Images. 77 Samuel Liverio/Shutterstock; 79 (T) Porco_photograph/iStock/Getty Images, (C) Iofoto/Shutterstock, (B) M. Shcherbyna/Shutterstock; 80 (T) China Images/Liu Xiaoyang/Alamy Stock Photo; (B) Val lawless/Shutterstock, (L) EcoView/Fotolia, 92 (CL) Andreanita/Fotolia; (CR) Algre/Fotolia, (R) Eduardo Rivero/Fotolia, 96 Rikke/Fotolia; 102 Cphoto/Fotolia; 109 Tatiana Popova/Shutterstock. 125 Smileus/Shutterstock; 127 (T) FatCamera/E+/Getty Images, (B) Mario Houben/CSM/REX/Shutterstock; 128 (T) AF archive/Alamy Stock Photo, (B) Kali9/E+/Getty Images; 141 Viacheslav Krylov/Fotolia; 149 Alisonhancock/Fotolia. 177 Tom Wang/Shutterstock; 179 (T) Andre Jenny/Alamy Stock Photo, (C) Chronicle/Alamy Stock Photo, (B) David Grossman/Alamy Stock Photo; 180 (T) Kuvona/Shutterstock;(B) Sailou/Shutterstock. 225 Lisastrachan/Fotolia; 227 (T) Steve Debenport/E+/Getty Images, (B) Monkey Business Images/Shutterstock; 228 (T) Accept photo/Shutterstock, (B) Ton Koene/Picture Alliance/Newscom. 265 Marcio Jose Bastos Silva/Shutterstock; 267 (T) Arsenik/E+/Getty Images, (C) Des Westmore/Alamy Stock Photo, (B) Roman Diachkin/Shutterstock; 268 Prostock-studio/Shutterstock; Jarabee123/Shutterstock, Nattika/Shutterstock, Boonchuay1970/Shutterstock, 298 Esanbanhao/Fotolia. 306 Image Source/Jupiter Images; 313 (B) by-studio/Fotolia; (T) Paul Orr/Shutterstock, 329 Simone van den Berg/Fotolia; 331 (T) Philip Images/Shutterstock, (B) Bubbers BB/Shutterstock; 332 (T) Ian Allenden/123RF, (B) ImageBROKER/REX/Shutterstock. 381 Zest_Marina/Fotolia; 383 (T) Stacey Newman/Shutterstock, (C) Arve Bettum/Shutterstock, (B) Fluid work shop/Shutterstock; 384 Cathy Yeulet/123RF; Jarabee123/Shutterstock, 406 Bev/Fotolia. 425 Jon Beard/Shutterstock; 427 (T) Wk1003mike/Shutterstock, (B) W. Scott McGill/Shutterstock; 428 (T) Neale Clark/Robertharding/Alamy Stock Photo, (B) Emmanuel Lattes/Alamy Stock Photo. 453 Morgan Lane Photography/Shutterstock; 455 (T) 146914/Shutterstock, (C) Africa Studio/Shutterstock, (B) Tomasz Szymanski/Shutterstock; 456 Showcake/Shutterstock; Chutima Chaochaiya/Shutterstock. 485 Iktomi/Fotolia; 487 (T) Stefano Paterna/Alamy Stock Photo, (B) NASA; 488 (T) Elena Veselova/Shutterstock, (B) MaZiKab/Shutterstock; 498 Getty Images; 510 (L) Marianne de Jong/Shutterstock, (R) Brocreative/Fotolia, 531 (T) Evgeny Karandaev/Shutterstock, (B) Volff/Fotolia. 533 Natalia Pavlova/Fotolia; 535 (T) M.R. Brennan/Shutterstock, (C) Viktoria White/Shutterstock, (B) JPL-Caltech/MSSS/NASA; 536 LWA/Dann Tardif/Blend Images/Alamy Stock Photo. 561 Solarseven/Shutterstock; 563 (T) Sean Pavone/Alamy Stock Photo, (B) Kai Chiang/123RF; 564 (T) Oleksii Chumachenko/Shutterstock, (B) Alice McBroom/Pearson Education Australia Pty Ltd. 589 Pisaphotography/Shutterstock; 591 (T) Eugene Lu/Shutterstock, (C) Timothy Holle/Shutterstock, (B) Chameleons Eye/Shutterstock; 592 123RF; 615 Leekris/Fotolia. 617 Michael J Thompson/ShutterStock; 619 (T) Pius Lee/Shutterstock, (B) Solis Images/Shutterstock; 620 (T) Rainer Lesniewski/Alamy Stock Photo, (B) Railway fx/Shutterstock; 624 2010/Photos to Go/Photolibrary.

$$\frac{2}{75} \times \frac{45}{9}$$